EDUCATION MANAGEMENT SERIES

Series Editor: John Sayer

POWER AND POLITICS AT THE DEPARTMENT OF EDUCATION AND SCIENCE

TITLES IN THE EDUCATION MANAGEMENT SERIES

M. Bottery:
The Ethics of Educational Management: Personal, Social and Political Perspectives on School Organization

M. Hattersley (ed.):
The Appraisal of Headteachers

I. Lawrence:
Power and Politics at the Department of Education and Science

P. Leighton:
Schools and Employment Law

J. Sayer:
The Future Governance of Education

POWER AND POLITICS AT THE DEPARTMENT OF EDUCATION AND SCIENCE

Ian Lawrence

CASSELL

Cassell
Villiers House
41/47 Strand
London WC2N 5JE

387 Park Avenue South
New York
NY 10016-8810

First published 1992

British Library Cataloguing-in-Publication Data
A catalogue record for this book is available from the British Library.

Library of Congress Cataloging-in-Publication Data
Lawrence, Ian, 1933-
Power and politics at the Department of Education and Science / Ian Lawrence.
p. cm. — (Education management series)
Includes bibliographical references (p.) and index.
ISBN 0-304-32624-0 — ISBN 0-304-32607-0 (pbk.)
1. Great Britain. Dept. of Education and Science—History—20th century. 2. Politics and education—Great Britain—History—20th century. 3. Education and state—Great Britain—History—20th century.
I. Title. II. Series.
LC93.G7L36 1992
379.41—dc20 91-44403
CIP

ISBN 0-304-32624-0 (hardback)
ISBN 0-304-32607-0 (paperback)

Typeset by Colset Private Limited, Singapore
Printed and bound in Great Britain by
Dotesios Ltd, Trowbridge, Wilts

Contents

List of abbreviations

AEC	Association of Education Committees
APU	Assessment of Performance Unit
CACE	Central Advisory Council for Education
CATE	Council for the Accreditation of Teacher Education
CNAA	Council for National Academic Awards
CSE	Certificate of Secondary Education
CTC	City Technology College
DES	Department of Education and Science
DHSS	Department of Health and Social Security
DPO	Department Planning Organization
DSS	Department of Social Security
DTI	Department of Trade and Industry
ERM	Exchange Rate Mechanism
ESAC	Education, Science and Arts Committee
GCE	General Certificate of Education
GCSE	General Certificate of Secondary Education
GTC	General Teaching Council
HMI	Her Majesty's Inspector/Inspectorate
ILEA	Inner London Education Authority
LEA	local education authority
MEP	Member of the European Parliament
MP	Member of Parliament
NHS	National Health Service
NUT	National Union of Teachers
OECD	Organization for Economic Co-operation and Development
PPS	Parliamentary Private Secretary
SEN	special educational needs
SCI	Senior Chief Inspector
SPER	System for Policy Evolution and Review
TES	*Times Educational Supplement*
TVEI	Training and Vocational Education Initiative
UNESCO	United Nations Educational, Scientific and Cultural Organisation

Foreword by the series editor

This is a highly topical, well-researched, well-conceived and readable book, and the Introduction sets the tone with its reference to the rise and fall of the DES as a tragicomedy.

This is a study of shifts of both policy and the location of power. Although at the start of the book the distinction can be made between policy information and policy management, we are left post-1988 with a DES involved in direct interventionist management and control. The book has therefore a special place in the context of the Education Management series, and is an excellent backdrop for it.

Not nearly enough of substance has been written on this topic; what has been is now dated by a couple of decades. This particular study is unique among recent writings on education in England and Wales. It will attract the attention of readers right across the spectrum of those under study, and of students of policy and management.

The timing is excellent, assuming that regardless of party fortunes, the DES is about to suffer the fate of La Fontaine's *grenouille qui veut se faire aussi grosse qu'un bœuf*, and that better ways have now to be found for the future governance of education in the next session of Parliament. This book will both meet a need of the moment and last as a study and exposé of half-a-century of government.

For the years 1945-92, Ian Lawrence takes us through the six periods of party government, and studies in each case the party manifestos, the contribution of DES politicians, the roles of the leading DES civil servants and HMI, and the nature and extent of policy change carried out. That in itself is a disciplined *tour de force*. He brings the chief actors alive again as real persons with their own agenda and interests.

Some of the reminders are compelling to present-day readers; Churchill against a prescribed curriculum, Maud on teacher freedom, Smieton on control and freedom, Percy Wilson opposed to legislating on pettifogging detail, Hunt on the regional dimension, Boyle as guardian rather than administrative head of the education system. If only more recent actors had read back as we now can!

The concluding chapter pulls together the stream of acute perceptions which accompany this account and looks closely at the relationships between the DES and Parliament, within the DES between politicians and administrators, between central and local government, and finally between the teaching profession and its employers. There are plenty of leads into, rather than prescriptions for, a better future.

John Sayer

Acknowledgements

It is a pleasure to acknowledge the generous help I have received from all those many persons who have discussed this topic with me over many years. They are, regrettably, too numerous to name individually. To Bryan Rhodes, however, I owe a special debt for his good advice and warm encouragement, and also to my wife Margaret for her patience and support during the writing of this book and for her skilful proof-reading at the end.

Introduction

The Department of Education and Science (DES) was established in April 1964, and since that time no fewer than fourteen politicians have held the office of Secretary of State. It superseded the Ministry of Education, which had seen eight different Ministers in charge in its twenty years of endeavour.[1] More than once the incumbents have given the distinct impression that they found themselves in profound agreement with Archbishop Thomas Cranmer when he said, 'I protest before you all, there was never man [or woman] came more unwillingly to [office] than I did to that: insomuch that when [the Prime Minister] did send for me . . . I prolonged my journey by seven weeks at the least, thinking that he [or she] would be forgetful of me in the meantime.' At least their stay was relatively short: an average of two years in the DES compared with two and a half in the ministry. For some, appointment to the DES has signified preferment, a staging-post to political glory; while for others it marked the end of their governmental careers. Perhaps only two or three have found it genuinely fulfilling.

The tenure of junior Ministers has been even shorter, their comings and goings marked only in the margins of the media. It is therefore not altogether surprising that the relative permanence of the Permanent Secretaries has provided a degree of stability, or at least, as one of their number has so elegantly put it, has demonstrated 'a concern for the continuity of things'.[2] There have been only five such civil servants since 1964. During their reigns, the department has grown in size and power, seeking further and further control of an education system that was always on the verge of disintegration. Unfortunately the DES itself created not the solution to, but the main source of, the problem. The rise and fall of the DES is therefore a tragicomedy of unfulfilled ambitions, humiliating miscalculations and abandoned promises.

For those who are interested in the way we are governed in general in the UK, the particular scrutiny of the DES does offer the possibility of broader political understandings. The self-stated purpose of the DES is intentionally coded: 'The DES promotes education in England: it is responsible for the Government's relations with universities in England, Wales and Scotland and it fosters the progress of civil science both in Britain and in collaboration with other nations.' What is meant by *promoting, having responsibility for* and *fostering* is, of course, a theme which runs throughout what follows. So also is the whole muddle over geographical limitations. But the creation of the DES can be comprehended only if the twenty-year history of the ministry is at least placed in a proper context.[3] I start therefore with two chapters covering the Labour and Conservative administrations between 1945 and 1964. And as Maurice Kogan has so ably put it, 'If . . . education responds to both social demands and individual aspirations, an examination of the main educational issues since 1945 will also entail an inquiry into some of the most important arguments about politics and society during that period' (Kogan, 1978, p. 16). Since I am concerned with the study of educational policy (and not civil science) at the DES, these arguments are mostly set in *England*, but they have *British* implications. Unlike most other departments of state, the DES chiefly concerns itself with 47.3 million English people, although it does exercise a number of controls over higher education throughout the UK.[4] It has very close links with the educational system for the 2.8 million inhabitants of Wales through the Welsh Office, and for some time now most documents from the DES are issued by the Joint Secretaries of State. Although Scotland (5.1 million) and Northern Ireland (1.6 million) have separate systems, the educational administration of all four countries is closely related, especially in their dependency upon Treasury policies and in their representation at Westminster. Since most Scots believe that what happens in Scottish education today will reach other parts of the UK tomorrow, the recent publication of a very wide-ranging and searching study of education policy in Scotland must be welcomed, not only for its intrinsic value, but also because it allows the present study to pursue its main objectives in the knowledge that the Scottish context has already been comprehensively analysed with imagination and insight (McPherson and Raab, 1988).

In the broadest terms Chapters 1 and 2 investigate the so-called period of political consensus when the preoccupation of both the Labour and Conservative governments was postwar recovery; Chapters 3, 4, 5 and 6 analyse the development of the DES from 1964 to the present day; and Chapter 7 attempts to explain the nature of the systems failure that has overtaken contemporary British education, and suggests alternative strategies.

The structure of Chapters 1 to 6 employs a chronological sequencing of events based on six alternating periods of party government:

Labour 1945-51	Conservative 1951-64
Labour 1964-70	Conservative 1970-74
Labour 1974-79	Conservative 1979-92

For each period four constant elements are described and analysed:

1. the educational proposals in party manifestos and pre-election conferences;
2. the contribution of the politicians at the DES who were most closely involved at the time;
3. the roles of the Permanent and Deputy Secretaries at the DES, and of the Senior Chief Inspector (HMI);
4. the extent and nature of actual policy implementation.

The principal justification for such accounting of political events in education is simply that without it our understanding of what has happened, and what may be about to happen, is severely impaired. Brian Simon has rightly said that 'the historical record clearly shows that there is nothing inevitable about educational advance. Far from progress being linear, advances are more often met by setbacks, by new crises, by ideological and political struggles of all kinds. Our present age is no exception' (Simon, 1985, p. 52). Setbacks, crises and struggles are so familiar in the development of British educational policy since 1945 that many have come to regard them as inevitable. A familiar axiom suggests that in the analysis of an administration, one should always allow for what would have happened anyway. In the case of educational administration, one should always allow for what has never happened, however often it has been promised.

We can also attempt to investigate the extent to which the setbacks and crises are actually created by the machinery of government rather than by external events or the individual acts of will of misguided ministers. In pursuing the progress (or lack of it) of an educational policy innovation from party conference to manifesto, to a White Paper, to a Bill, and then to an Act, readers can trace for themselves just where the setbacks and crises originated, and then what actions were taken by the *dramatis personae* in furthering or mitigating the consequences of such exigencies. In the British system, of course, the operational consequences of an Act next pass to the local authorities and governing bodies in the case of primary, secondary and further education, and to the colleges, polytechnics and universities in the case of higher education. But the social and economic consequences of an Education Act have a much wider impact on the whole landscape of human activity. Thus, the dissemination of a policy in turn re-creates the need for, and process of, modification again, and another round of committee resolutions may reach conferences, manifestos, White Papers and so on.

The justification for the examination of conference resolutions and manifesto promises rests in the notion of the continuity of intention and practice. It is possible to dismiss such phenomena as containing no more than empty rhetoric, particularly if the rhetoric comes from a party that has been out of office for some time. But rhetoric is one of the key weapons in winning elections, and the winners who form a government are imprisoned by their own rhetoric, at least for the first few months in office. It follows that the grounds for looking more closely at the individual roles of both politicians and civil servants are threefold: that policies are not simply abstractions, but carry some traits of the personalities of their producers; that the exchanges between politicians and civil servants depend as much on the processes of human interaction as one would expect in any other walk of life;[5] and that the career structures within which politicians and civil servants separately operate contribute to the nature of the environment in which they develop and disseminate policies. As Ball has so aptly put it, there is a need in these matters to 'capture the messy realities of influence, pressure, dogma, expediency, conflict, compromise, intransigence, resistance, error, opposition and pragmatism in the policy process' (Ball, 1990, p. 9). It is, of course, not possible in a book of this size to do more than sketch in the background of most of the 50 or more politicians and 30 or so top civil servants since 1945 who have been responsible for the development of education. But it is important that the reader does begin to form a picture of *who* was influencing *what* in order to understand the *how* and the *why*.

These circumstances in the UK have obvious parallels with the recent situation in the USA. As one recent American writer has concluded,

> professional educators and school policy-makers have come to fully appreciate the essentially political character of public education. We now recognize that both the content and form of schooling are determined through the conflicts and coalitions found at the core of local, state and national political systems. With that knowledge has come an awareness that public support and organizational effectiveness depend on identifying and resolving fundamental questions regarding the goals of education and the strategies to be utilized in pursuing those goals.
>
> (Mitchell and Goertz, 1990, p. 166)

Policy implementation - the translation of good intentions into effective practice - is the key element of purposeful government, and its critical observation and analysis need no justification. But such processes occupy very uncertain territory. On the one hand we have research being carried out on almost every aspect of educational theory and practice in the universities, polytechnics and colleges; on the other hand we have politicians, civil servants, HMI and funded research organizations developing policies notionally informed by investigation. What is the relationship between these two areas? There is a temptation to answer that there is no relation: that politicians and their advisers do not read research papers for they are too busy reading opinion polls, and that, in so far as educational researchers write only for each other and in coded languages, their attitude towards politicians is non-communicative. And yet research findings can, according to Torsten Husen, 'become ammunition for the side that finds certain research conclusions congenial with its standpoint' (Husen and Kogan, 1984, p. 16), and research projects or committees of inquiry can be used as a way of distracting attention from a sensitive matter until such time as the (delayed) report is available, by which time the chances are the topic will have become of less than pressing importance.

There is also the problem of the relation between policy formation and policy management. The reader may wish to keep in mind a guiding principle which has influenced many observers, and which has been so lucidly expressed by David Marquand:

> It is true that the issues which politicians have to decide nowadays often seem too complex for the ordinary public to grasp. One reason . . . is that politics are increasingly equated with management, and the role of the politician with that of the technocrat . . . Politicians sometimes manage and managers sometimes engage in politics, but politics is not management and management is not politics. *Politics has to do with questions of value, not with questions of technique; with appraising, debating and deciding between different ends, not with discovering the most efficient means to achieve ends which have already been agreed.*
>
> (Marquand, 1988, p. 235)

It is the political processes that attend the passage of an idea, from the point at which it surfaces in public debate to the point at which it is accepted or abandoned, that concern us here. Of course the *management* of the parliamentary process is itself intrinsically a political skill, and the covert political influence of the 'non-politicized' administrators, both in Whitehall and in the town halls, is a factor which must not be overlooked. But this book is concerned essentially with the role of the DES in the politics of education, and not directly with its management of education. This must involve, therefore, an attempt to differentiate between the role of civil servants in the development and articulation of policy and their subsequent roles in managing the policy once it has been agreed. Of course the *interpretation* of educational policy as it appears in DES circulars will also involve 'appraising, debating and deciding between different ends', and in so far as these procedures throw light on the main political strategies under discussion they may form part of the analysis. To devote too much space, however, to the details of 'discovering the most efficient means to achieve ends' would only distract the reader from the principal themes of the book.

The DES has at various times carried out responsibilities for the arts and sport (with specialist ministers), for libraries and museums, and for aspects of science such as the funding of scientific research and international scientific relations. It is not my intention to deal with these matters in this book, although it must be remembered that their existence at the DES has inevitably affected the overall responsibilities of ministers and some civil servants. Nor is it part of my argument that these other aspects of DES activity have in any marked way contributed to the problems which have arisen over its conduct in respect of the promotion of education in schools and in further and higher education.

If we wish to understand a government's actions, then we need to take account of the circumstances and traditions within which it operates; and in the UK these circumstances and these traditions include not only the relationship between government and Parliament, but also the relationship between ministers and civil servants; between the machinery of government and the machinery of administration; between Westminster and Whitehall. To understand the development and application of education policy, we also need to pay particular attention to the nature of the relationship between ministers and civil servants at the DES, and between the DES on the one hand and the Cabinet and the whole civil service on the other.

NOTES

1 There were actually nine, if R. K. Law's stay of 35 days in Churchill's caretaker government of 1945 is counted. Sir David Eccles also had two separate spells in office, from October 1954 to December 1956, and from October 1959 to July 1962.

2 Sir William Pile (1979, p. 228). Throughout the book I have used the term 'Permanent Secretary' to define the chief civil servant in the department, even though variants were used in the early days of the DES.

3 Much recent work has drawn attention both to the setting up of the Ministry of Education and to its operation in the period 1944–64. Of particular interest are Addison (1975); Gosden (1974 and 1983); Lowe (1988); Simon (1985); Simon (1986).

4 Until 1983 the DES had at various times *responsibility for* the government's concern with

the arts, with sport, and with libraries, museums and art galleries. While the exercise of these responsibilities is not analysed in this study, their impact on the Secretary of State is a factor to be considered in the evaluation of that office.

5 As Sir Edward Boyle freely admitted, 'It's unreal to suppose that in any dialogue between Ministers and civil servants, the civil servants' value-judgements won't play some part as well . . . they also have their own preferences which will out in discussion' (1971, p. 75).

Chapter 1

'Not by instruction or order but by suggestion': the Labour governments 1945-51

Although 1944 has come to be synonymous with the Butler[1] Education Act for many of us, it was also the year in which, apart from the major issue of the reversal of Hitler's ambitions in Europe, two much more significant social innovations were introduced - the dissemination of the Beveridge Report on the social services, and the publication of the *White Paper on Employment*, with its commitment to 'a high and stable level of employment' after the war. It was undoubtedly the radical Beveridge and Keynes proposals that had an immensely powerful impact on the pattern of postwar educational provision; rather more, perhaps, than could have been recognized at the time. But, as Marwick has pointed out, what would be the point in having 'national insurance benefits, free medical care, proper housing, and wise schooling, if there were no jobs? It was a fundamental assumption of the war and postwar period that all of the different pieces of welfare state legislation would be backed up by an economic policy deliberately designed to create jobs and *avoid unemployment*' (1982, p. 49). Indeed, this was stated in all the 1945 election manifestos, perhaps in its clearest form by the Conservatives: 'The Government accepts as one of its primary aims and responsibilities the maintenance of a high and stable level of employment.'[2]

The proposals contained in the 1944 Education Act had not sprung up overnight. Indeed, the Board of Education (the predecessor of first the Ministry of Education and later the Department of Education and Science) had given lengthy consideration to the Hadow Report (1926) and the Spens Report (1938), as well as the consequences of its own 1936 Education Act, before publishing its *White Paper on Educational Reconstruction* in 1943.[3] Recent studies have shown that it was the civil service which 'had determined the scope of that legislation by May 1941, and fought off Butler's efforts to modify it. The policy which emerged triumphant in 1944 was that of the Board.'[4]

Despite the war, education policy had continued to receive party attention. At the 1942 Labour Party Conference, for example, Harold Clay brought a resolution which outlined the party's aspirations in all levels of state education. As part of the social service programme, schools should provide free milk, subsidized meals, and medical and dental screening; nursery, infant and junior provision should be upgraded; free secondary education to 15 (and subsequently 16) should be provided and the 'common school principle' introduced for new schools, with multilateral curricula; and from the age of 15 (or later 16) to 18 free, part-time further education for those who had left school should be provided. At the 1945 conferences, the Conservatives had emphasized 'the importance of developing the academic and cultural side of education' and the 'need for a considerable expansion in technical and vocational training', while Labour had looked for the 'development of the standards of human culture and dignity and the encouragement of individual character'.

It was natural that for the 1945 general election the Conservative, Labour and Liberal parties should all give due weight in their manifestos to the implementation of the 1944 Act. The Conservatives assured the electorate that 'educational facilities will be developed as fast as the necessary teaching staff and buildings can be made available', while Labour was convinced that 'the nation wants an educational system that will give every boy and girl a chance to develop the best that is in them', and the Liberals emphasized that 'our place in the world will depend on the character of our people and on minds trained to understand and operate the complex technical achievements of the modern world. We cannot afford to neglect talent which lies unused because of the poverty of parents.'

The Conservatives had no trouble in searching for a title for their manifesto: *Mr Churchill's Declaration of Policy* said everything. Moreover, although R.A. Butler had a hand in drafting the education policy section, the resonant Churchillian rhetoric can clearly be heard throughout:

> Our object is to provide education which will not produce a standardised or utility child, useful only as a cog in a nationalised and bureaucratic machine, but will enable the child to develop his or her responsible place, first in the world of school, and then as a citizen. Many parents will be able to choose the school they like and to play their part with the educational authorities in the physical and spiritual well being of their children. Our aim must be to produce the good citizen of tomorrow. Our primary schools call for much encouragement and improvement. Secondary Education for all will have no meaning unless variety, practical training and, above all, quality of standards convince parents that the extra schooling for their children is worth while. Technical education, at all levels, must be greatly extended and improved. No system of education can be complete unless it heightens what is splendid and glorious in life and art. Art, science and learning are the means by which the life of the whole people can be beautified and enriched.

Labour responded with *Let Us Face the Future*, a document which reinforced the 1942 conference resolutions and reached its climax with its own brand of rhetoric: 'Above all, let us remember that the great purpose of education is to give us individual citizens capable of thinking for themselves.'

As a result of the general election on 26 July 1945, Clement Attlee, with an overall majority of 146 seats, formed a Labour administration in which the key figures were Hugh Dalton as Chancellor of the Exchequer, Ernest Bevin as Foreign Secretary and Herbert Morrison as Lord President of the Council. James Chuter Ede, who, as Butler's Parliamentary Secretary, might have been given the Ministry of Education, was instead promoted to Home Secretary (in which office he served successfully until 1951), and Ellen Wilkinson (1891-1947) was the person chosen to move into the Education Ministry.

THE POLITICIANS

Some characteristics of the 394 Labour MPs need to be emphasized: 244 of them were taking up their seat at Westminster for the first time; almost a third of them were graduates of universities; nearly a third had been to an independent school; and of course many had scarcely got out of uniform before being plunged into conflicts of an entirely different order. These factors meant that not only was the nature of the Parliamentary party very different from that of the 1930s, but also that the discontinuity of the war had led to an element of unpredictability in adherence to policy.

Wilkinson, however, was a very well-established figure. She had entered Parliament in 1924 as the member for Middlesbrough East with a majority of only 927. She increased her majority in the 1929 election, but was defeated in 1931. She returned to Westminster in 1935 as the member for Jarrow, which she represented until her death in 1947. She entered the wartime coalition government as Parliamentary Secretary, first in the Ministry of Pensions and then in the Home Office. She was made a Privy Councillor in January 1945.

She had gained a little experience of teaching while she was attending the Manchester Day Training College, before entering Manchester University in 1910. But in all other respects she brought to the Ministry of Education only those valuable educational experiences which were the result of her struggle to enter university as a woman from a Northern working-class background. She had, for example, taken little part in the Labour Party's development of education policy in the 1920s and 1930s through groups such as the Fabians or the National Association of Labour Teachers. Her political career, however, had given her a reputation as a fighter for women's rights and for the welfare of the poor.

Her position, both as the only woman member of cabinet and as the first state-educated Minister of Education, may have aroused prejudice, both in Parliament and in Whitehall. She headed a ministry that was dominated at every level by men whose background had been the major public schools and Oxbridge. Sir John Maud was her Permanent Secretary (from November 1945); the Deputy Secretaries were Sir Robert Wood and Sir William Cleary; her Personal Private Secretary was A.A. (later Sir Antony) Part; the Permanent Secretary of the Welsh Education Department was Sir Ben Thomas; two of her Under-Secretaries were G.N. (later Sir Gilbert) Flemming and G.G. (later Sir Griffith) Williams; and Neville Heaton, P.R. Odgers and T.R. (later Sir Toby) Weaver, already in positions of influence within the ministry, were later to become Deputy Secretaries. Even the Senior Chief Inspector, Martin Roseveare, was knighted in 1947. Only two out of 22 Assistant Secretaries were women, and only eight out of 51 Principals were women. Her political career had, of course, accustomed her to male-dominated groups, but whether that experience equipped her to deal with such a formidable array of subtle establishment figures and Whitehall knights is open to question.

Together with other members of her staff, John Maud regarded her with a certain affection, and had this to say of her approach to the work:

> About the details of her own business as Education Minister she (like her new Permanent Secretary) had everything to learn; but from the start she was passionately determined that all children should have a far better chance of secondary education than she and her generation had had . . . Nor was it only about children that she passionately cared. She wanted people of all ages to have the opportunity of growing to their full stature as individuals; and that was what she meant when she later declared to the consternation of those who already thought elitism a dirty word, that she wanted Britain to become a 'Third Programme' nation.[5]

She entered into the spirit of Attlee's reconstruction politics with immense enthusiasm. The circumstances in which she found herself were extremely challenging. The implementation of the 1944 Act required considerable financial investment. The war in Europe had ended only in May, and Japan did not surrender until 15 August. By the end of August the United States had announced the end of lend-lease, the financial life-jacket on which the government had pinned many of its aspirations. Coal and electricity nationalization, National Insurance, housing, introduction of the National Health Service and food shortages all took precedence over educational legislation. At the same time she was subjected to a considerable amount of back-bench pressure from her own party to deliver the programmes that the party had already endorsed. Not the least of her problems was her own continuing ill-health. She died in office on 6 February 1947.[6]

George Tomlinson (1890-1952) had been Minister of Works since 1945. He was happy, however, to respond to Attlee's request to move to the Ministry of Education to replace Ellen Wilkinson. Many commentators have seen his role as very similar not only to that of his predecessor, but, more surprisingly, to that of his Conservative successors in the 1950s. 'In the 1940s and 1950s,' writes Kogan, 'in spite of underlying tensions and conflicts, the appearance was of tranquil progress and consensus. No politician worth his salt could contemplate office in the Ministry of Education for long because it lacked . . . newsworthiness' (Kogan, 1978, p. 29). Worth his salt or not, Tomlinson undoubtedly regarded his appointment as the climax of his political career; this appointment was, by any standards, a major achievement for a man who had left school at the age of 12.

He had developed his political skills first at the local level in Farnworth (where he became Chairman of the Education Committee) and then as a county councillor for Lancashire. His election to Westminster in January 1938 gave him the safe seat of Farnworth with a majority of nearly 7500. His continued interest in education led to his appointment as Chairman of the Association of Education Committees (AEC), a base from which he was able to bring first-hand administrative knowledge to the back benches. During the war he served as Parliamentary Secretary to Ernest Bevin at the Ministry of Labour. At the 1945 election he was returned with a majority of nearly 14,000, and became Attlee's Minister of Works, a post which had already brought him into close contact with the work of the Ministry of Education in the massive school-rebuilding programme and the rapid growth in teacher training which Ellen Wilkinson was encouraging.

His arrival at the Ministry of Education as a replacement Minister meant that he had to join a programme that was already in full swing. 'What legislation there was during his term of office,' wrote his biographer, 'was of minor character but the task presented by the implementation of the 1944 Act was immense' (Blackburn, 1954, p. 170). While he was in office the ministry produced just over one hundred circulars dealing with such implementations. Tomlinson recognized, as would be expected of an ex-chairman of the Association of Education Committees, that the development of the Act's strategies depended upon the wholehearted support of the local education authorities (LEAs). It was his grasp of this principle that made him popular with the education system as a whole, a popularity that allowed him to say to those assembled at Liverpool University to see him receive an honorary degree, 'Perhaps you thought I was not qualified for my present job and are trying to make me respectable' (Blackburn, 1954, p. 170). 'So far as policy goes,' as one of his civil servants was later to write, 'he was not a Labour theorist. He represented himself as a man with a strong sympathy for the underdog, anxious to get on with a practical job in very difficult circumstances, and he did this to great effect' (Part, 1990, p. 58). In the 1950 election he was again returned with a huge majority, but had to resume his ministerial responsibilities in a government with an overall majority of only five. Tomlinson was one of many Labour MPs who became ill at this time, and when Attlee called another general election in October 1951 he was already in hospital. He died in September 1952.

David Hardman (1901-89) was a politician with a unique record. As Parliamentary Secretary from July 1945 to October 1951, he held a continuous ministerial position longer (by far) than any other politician in the Ministry or Department of Education at any level between 1945 and the present day. And yet he is perhaps the least known of all those who have held such office. Ellen Wilkinson's biographer claimed that they did not get on with each other too well, and George Tomlinson's biographer offers no more than that he helped out when Tomlinson was ill. What accounts for this obscurity? He graduated from Christ's College, Cambridge, in 1925 in English and went on to study law. Between 1937 and 1946 he served as a borough and county councillor in Cambridge. He was elected the new MP for Darlington in 1945 and was immediately given a post in government. Perhaps his frequent absences from Westminster as the UK's delegate to UNESCO between 1946 and 1951 provide a clue, as also does his role as an Attlee protégé. At the 1951 election he lost his seat by 813 votes and never returned to Westminster. In the 1960s he became a visiting professor of English literature in American universities, publishing a book on Shakespeare and a collection of poems.

THE CIVIL SERVANTS

> A good civil servant is meant to do a minister's bidding, but part of that job is to remind a minister of things that he might prefer not to know. In opposition, a minister could ignore obstacles; in

> office to do this would be to court disaster. Civil servants tend to be the institutional spokesmen for the obstacles.
>
> (Rose, 1984, p. 150)

Sir John Maud (1910-83; later Lord Redcliffe-Maud) replaced Sir Maurice Holmes as Permanent Secretary in November 1945. Holmes had been in post since 1937 and had not only steered the Board of Education successfully through the war, but had overseen the 1944 Act and the establishment of the ministry. Maud was an outsider. Like so many other wartime civil servants, he had been drafted into Whitehall in 1939 in response to the emergency, first to the Ministry of Food (where he became secretary to a War Cabinet committee), and then to the Office of the Minister of Reconstruction. When he was offered the Ministry of Education he had no hesitation in opting for Permanent Secretary rather than returning to university life.

He was the son of a bishop and had been educated at Eton (where he was a King's Scholar) and Oxford, where he read Greats. After a year at Harvard he returned to Oxford as a research fellow in politics at University College. He taught in Oxford between 1929 and 1939 and was Dean of University College for several years. Writing later of this latter experience, he compared the close relationship between the Dean and the College butler as having a lot in common with the relationship between a Permanent Secretary and a Minister. He refrained, however, from defining who led and who followed. He believed that 'Ellen [Wilkinson] trusted her civil servants, recognized they offered her a fund of goodwill and was angelic in assuming that they would help rather than obstruct. She therefore accepted rather than resisted advice' (Vernon, 1982, p. 205). It says much for Ellen Wilkinson that she was able to gain the confidence of her Permanent Secretary (Eton and Oxford) and her Private Secretary (Harrow and Cambridge), but the challenge should not be underestimated.

Wilkinson was almost entirely inexperienced in the politics of education, and Maud was new to the administration of public education. Maud believed that it was Antony Part (her experienced Private Secretary) and Robert Wood (his own Deputy) who provided the necessary continuity with the wartime Board of Education and from whom it was possible to learn the established procedures. When Tomlinson took over the ministry, he brought with him a close working knowledge of local authority education systems which complemented Maud's own theoretical (he had published *English Local Government* in 1932) and practical (he had been an independent City of Oxford councillor before the war) knowledge of local government.

Maud's career was unlike that of any of his successors. To become a Permanent Secretary at the age of 35 is unusual enough, but he was also to be promoted to the Ministry of Power in the 1950s (where 'for the first time since the war' he was 'near the margin of great political events'[7]), and then appointed to be the last High Commissioner and first Ambassador to South Africa. He returned to Oxford in 1963 where he was Master of University College until 1976, during which time he chaired the Schools' Council from 1964 to 1966 and the Royal Commission on English Local Government. If his name is more readily associated with this latter activity (and the resultant vandalism it caused to English county boundaries that had remained largely intact for nine centuries), it is still also remembered in the context of the Attlee administration. He was undoubtedly the most influential educational figure of the immediate post-war period, his power base as Permanent Secretary of a new ministry being enhanced by the relative weakness in political terms of his ministers. What, then, did he regard as the achievements of his office?

Maud saw schooling as a means of creating an 'artificial community', by which he meant the 'deliberately contrived community of the school' (1951, p. 80). Within such an artificial community the young citizen could be nurtured in controlled conditions by freethinking teachers. 'Freedom is what the teacher needs more than anything' and 'perhaps the most essential freedom of the teacher is to decide for himself what to teach and how to teach it', supported by a Ministry which 'has relied on HMI to stimulate and inspire teachers' (1952, pp. 239-41).

From the perspective of his 1981 memoirs, Maud saw his time at the ministry as being concerned with three principal and two important, though peripheral, activities. The three major initiatives were the postwar school-building programme, the proposed development of technical and modern schools as viable alternatives to grammar schools, and the opening up of access to higher education for grant-supported students. Since the ministry controlled the funding of new school-building projects, and since, in the aftermath of the war, the provision of new schools was a high-profile educational activity, it is understandable why a Permanent Secretary and his or her staff would be so heavily involved. What was doubtful at the time, and has remained a matter of discussion ever since, is whether it would not have been better to leave LEAs to look after their own building programmes without interference from government. What was gained by centralization? Maud's answer was that 'British schools built in this period, for all their imperfections, have proved to be *better* schools from an educational point of view than most of those built before the war. Our school building is as good as any school building abroad and compares well with other types of British building' (1981, pp. 53-4). While many readers will find these assertions unsupported by the evidence, they will nevertheless recognize in them a contemporary statement of the nature of the 1940s priorities.

If the role of the ministry as an arm of management in a major reconstruction programme seemed reasonably straightforward to Maud, so also was its role in the second initiative, the development of secondary schools. The 1944 Act had suggested a tripartite system, and that was what the ministry felt obliged to oversee. It was not required to *provide* such a system, for that was the responsibility of the LEAs, nor was it required to develop curriculum strategies for such different types of schooling, for again that was the job of schools, and particularly of headteachers. For Maud and his colleagues, it would have been unthinkable to interfere with the only successful working models of state secondary education, the grammar schools, and such a view prevailed among his political bosses. 'It would have been mad,' he later wrote, 'as well as impractical to scrap [the grammar school] in favour of any one alternative. It was right to expand it on a grand scale and make it available to *all* children who had the ability and aptitude to profit from it . . . There was no sensible alternative to variety' (1981, pp. 56-7).

The tripartite system depended for its credibility on the quality of education provided by the technical and modern schools. Wilkinson, Tomlinson and Hardman always appeared confident that it was only a matter of variable aptitudes rather than abilities; that the state could exercise an even-handed treatment of all secondary children more effectively by providing genuine alternative schemes of schooling. Maud reflected this point of view when he defined the situation in the following terms:

> The Minister and all of us were committed to securing equality of *status* for all kinds of secondary school. We did everything possible to ensure that local authorities treated their secondary modern and their grammar schools with equal consideration in terms of staffing, buildings and equipment. But 'status' depended inevitably on past history and the subjective judgment of the parents. Until new kinds of school had had time to establish themselves and prove their quality, parents were bound to think them inferior to the grammar school, if only because grammar schools had hitherto been the one form of secondary education.
>
> (1981, p. 56)

This paragraph demonstrates only too well the dilemmas and illusions that were characteristic of the immediate postwar scene. Of course some parents wanted more grammar school places to be opened up for their children, but others remained deeply sceptical of secondary schooling of any sort and resented the raising of the school-leaving age to 15. Wilkinson had to fight against a strong body of opinion which took the line that it was against the national interest to deprive British industry of a whole cohort of trainees at the very time it was facing an acute shortage of manpower. It is also misguided to suggest that parents were entirely unfamiliar with post-11-year-old schools, even if they were not called secondary. The central (and other similarly titled) schools which provided separate courses for the 11-14 age band had flourished in many urban areas for some time. The notion that parents should be patient and wait for improvements in secondary modern and secondary technical schools was also fundamentally unrealistic. For parents, schooling is always *now*, not at some unspecified time in the future. Finally, it must be said that the ministry was demonstrably unsuccessful in persuading the LEAs to enter wholeheartedly into the creation of the third element of the tripartite system, the technical schools. But this is an issue that we shall take up later in this book.

The third matter which Maud singled out for attention was the university sector. He apparently remained content that his ministry should not exercise the responsibilities for this sector which were later taken up by the DES, although he was glad to join the University Grants Committee as an assessor. What he felt was of great significance, however, was the legislation that led to LEAs paying the fees of all qualified entrants to universities. While he was Permanent Secretary the steps were taken which would lead to the massive expansion of higher education in the 1960s.

The two minor matters which Maud recalled (with obvious pleasure) were the ministry's (and his personal) involvement in the work of the Arts Council and in UNESCO. 'Some of my colleagues in the Ministry,' he observed, 'disapproved of my engagement in this extraneous work. But I still think they were wrong' (1981, p. 61).

Sir Robert Wood (1886-1963) had joined the Board of Education in 1911 and, as Deputy Secretary during the war, was widely backed to succeed Sir Maurice Holmes. But Ellen Wilkinson objected to Wood's promotion, apparently on the grounds of social background. As we have seen, John Maud was brought in from the Ministry of Reconstruction to be Permanent Secretary: whether or not his background (Eton and Oxford) was any more appropriate than Wood's (City of London and Cambridge) remains a matter for conjecture. The processing of the 1944 Act was Wood's major responsibility, especially as technical education (of which he had been in charge in 1936-40) was a significant feature of the legislation. He left the ministry in 1946 to become the Principal of University College, Southampton, and when it became a full university, its first Vice-Chancellor. Sir William Cleary (1886-1971) was educated at Bedford School and Trinity College, Cambridge. He joined the Board of Education in 1910 and was a Deputy Secretary from 1945 to 1950. Butler called upon 'his great reservoir of experience' (1971, p. 93) in elementary school organization in the drafting of the 1944 Act, and during the immediate postwar period he was influential in the development of the primary schools, and in the implementation of raising of the school-leaving age to 15.[8] Sir Griffith Williams (1890-1974) was briefly a teacher at Wellington and Lancing before joining the Board in 1919. His conventional background (Westminster School and Christ Church, Oxford) and sustained endeavour led to the post of Deputy Secretary from 1946 to 1953. As a traditionalist and head of the secondary schools branch, he was 'possibly the least convinced of the need for change and the most reluctant of the most senior officials . . . who in the event served the useful function within the office of raising the questions which those opposed to change would raise elsewhere'.[9]

The role of the Minister's Principal Private Secretary, though crucial to the relationship between Westminster and Whitehall, is one that, by its very nature, rarely attracts public attention. It is also, in civil service terms, a relatively junior position, and therefore not associated with a particular aspect of policy. In the case of (Sir) Antony Part (1916-90), however, there are particular reasons for introducing his name at this stage. He had held the same position with Butler and Richard Law (the caretaker Minister in June 1945) and remained Ellen Wilkinson's Principal Private Secretary during her period as Minister. He was promoted to Under-Secretary at the Ministry of Education in 1954, and became a Deputy Secretary in 1960. He was to leave the ministry some months before it became the Department of Education and Science in 1964, and later served as Permanent Secretary in no fewer than four departments.

Thus Wilkinson found herself relying on the experience and skills of someone who not only was very aware of the thrust of the 1944 Act (having worked at the Board of Education since 1937) but also was clearly a high-flyer. Harrow and Trinity College, Cambridge (with a first in languages), a career as a very young lieutenant colonel in the Intelligence Corps during the war, and a family background in the business world all combined to provide him with considerable self-confidence. Much later he described his Minister's arrival as one in which the permanent officers were apprehensive of her lack of background in educational policy and of her reputation for combative political style. The apprehensiveness was apparently short-lived and replaced with affection (Vernon, 1982, p. 204).

We have already seen that Wilkinson, Tomlinson and Maud all regarded their school-building programme as the foremost activity of the ministry. Part not only took a significant role in this initiative (he became head of Buildings and Priority Branch in 1947) but also later displayed a fervour that can only be described as a high level of missionary zeal: 'This apparently pedestrian post led to one of the most exciting and stimulating jobs that any civil servant could have ... School building was a good example of one of the most characteristic functions of civil servants. In a very great deal of their work it is their task to be realistic but imaginative scene-setters so as to enable the prime-movers ... to do their job to the best advantage' (Part, 1990, pp. 56, 59). The programme which he devised with military precision (and which employed as Regional Priority Officers a considerable number of former wartime senior officers) depended on prefabricated (but permanent) buildings which could be quickly assembled on site. However, 'this resulted in flat roofs (which were anathema to some people) and, in the early stages, a rather utilitarian appearance' (p. 63). Unfortunately, this anathema was proved in the long run to be entirely justified, especially in the 1980s and 1990s when the flat-roof problem was to become 'a time bomb waiting to explode' (see Chapters 6 and 7).

Maud (1981, pp. 51-2) described Part as a 'regular civil servant of quite exceptional ability' who was able to help Wilkinson and him 'to get on valid terms with each other'. But later, when Part was Permanent Secretary at the Department of Industry in the 1970s, Tony Benn, the Secretary of State, said of him: 'I have serious differences with Part but as I see very little of him, it doesn't bother me very much. I see him once a week or once a fortnight, and the rest of the time I don't know what he does' (Benn, 1989, 7.1.75). Such open conflicts with ministers were not, however, characteristic either of Maud's ministry or of the behaviour of a junior civil servant, and Wilkinson seems to have got on with him very well. What remains uncertain is the extent to which Part, Maud, Wood, Cleary and Williams were able to influence Wilkinson towards policies which the ministry approved rather than those which many party activists would have preferred.

Sir Martin Roseveare (1898-1985) was the senior HMI from 1944 to 1957, making him easily the longest-serving Senior Chief Inspector since the war. He had been educated at Marlborough and St John's College, Cambridge, where he achieved a first in mathematics. After teaching at Repton and Haileybury, he joined HMI in 1927. Between 1939 and 1944 he was seconded to the ministries of Information and Food (where he was chiefly responsible for the food-rationing system, an achievement for which he was knighted). Maud's view (1981, p. 54) was that 'the enthusiasm of Martin and his senior colleagues gave the Ministry a corps of fresh-minded educationists, and this was what we needed at a time when we were faced not only with administrative problems but with fundamental questions of education.' He also believed that HMI was strongly in favour of the tripartite system, and that it was this opinion, based on the Spens Report of 1938 and firmly articulated by Roseveare, that persuaded Wilkinson and Tomlinson to resist Labour back-bench attempts to introduce wholesale comprehensive secondary schooling forthwith. Roseveare also led the argument which asserted that comprehensives would have to take over 2000 pupils to provide viable options at the sixth-form level, a fallacy which remained in circulation for another 25 years (Maud, 1981, pp. 55-6). The title of Roseveare's famous speech, 'Age, ability and aptitude', might suggest a concern with selection; in fact, closer reading reveals that he was more concerned that all children needed appropriate *individual* attention. 'Let us admit quite frankly what we know to be true, that no group of 30 or more children can readily be justifiably at the same point and moving at the same pace in a wide variety of subjects' (Roseveare, 1950, p. 619).

POLICY IMPLEMENTATION

The raising of the school-leaving age to 15 was eventually set for April 1947, although final cabinet approval for this date was not given until 16 January 1947. Opposition within the cabinet had arisen mostly on the grounds of practicalities. Another year in school not only meant the need for more teachers and more classrooms to cope with some 400,000 extra pupils when there was already an acute shortage of both, but it also meant that industry would be denied the same number of school-leavers at a time when the postwar shortage of labour was at its most acute. On the other hand, the principle of commitment to the 1944 Act was powerful. Raising the leaving age to 15 had been called for in the Hadow Report of 1926 (itself written in the shadow of Tawney's emphatic 1922 document) and had been set for 1939 by the Education Act of 1936. Its implementation can be regarded as an achievement, therefore, but the delay of 21 years from government report to government action cannot be regarded as one of the great successes of British educational legislation, however much the politicians of the period may have wished it to be seen as such.

The government attached great importance to its emergency training scheme for teachers, which was largely administered by Gilbert Flemming, later to become Maud's successor as Permanent Secretary. From 1946 until 1951 it provided a one-year training for unqualified ex-service men and women, producing over 35,000 teachers. The advantages were that it helped to solve the immediate chronic shortage of teachers and brought into the teaching profession people with experience, often profound experience, of life outside schooling and higher education. But it did have disadvantages: it caused acute administrative problems as a result of the very high level of demand, as well as shortages of buildings and resources, and it gave a professional status for life to people whose own experience of formal education was minimal, thereby creating long-term problems for schools, which, in some cases, were still employing one-year-trained teachers in the late 1970s. It can also be argued that the plentiful supply of mature entrants to teaching helped to depress the relative salary levels of teachers, who saw their incomes rise by only 20 to 25 per cent compared with the national average of 34 per cent during the period of the Attlee governments.

Much Labour Party thinking on secondary education had focused on the concept of the common school which would in effect provide a wide range of appropriate courses, academic, technical or 'modern': what was later to become known as the multilateral comprehensive school. But to most Labour MPs in the 1945-50 Parliament the first priority was to provide free secondary education to 15 (and preferably 16) irrespective of curriculum variants, in schools that were clearly differentiated from the old elementary schools with classes for the 11-14-year-olds. The resource implications of restructuring secondary education before it had even been proved that teachers and classrooms were available seemed overwhelming.

Both Wilkinson and Tomlinson came under regular attack from MPs such as W.G. Cove, who was a former teacher, president of the National Association of Labour Teachers, and a former president of the National Union of Teachers (NUT). In 1946 he had asserted in Parliament that Wilkinson was a source of 'great disappointment . . . She has undoubtedly given the impression that she has not got to grips with her Department, and that she does not understand . . . the direction and drift of the educational policy she is pursuing . . . [she] is a danger to the whole Labour movement so far as education policy is concerned' (Hansard, 1 July 1946). It is not the purpose of this chapter to rehearse the political arguments about comprehensive schooling.[10] What we need to confront, however, is the significance of the political and administrative process that was taking place. Since the Hadow Report in 1926 a series of agreements, deferments and ambiguities had led to the passing of the 1944 Act. The Labour Party manifesto of 1945 had promised the implementation of the Act, and the government's view was that a cautious approach to secondary schooling would be entirely appropriate. As Kenneth Morgan summed the situation up in his brilliant account of the period, 'It is easy to see that, in the perspective of 1945, the comprehensive idea might have appeared risky and unfamiliar, especially given Labour's old commitment to the grammar schools as the avenue for self-improvement for working-class boys and girls.'[11] The ministry (in succession to the board) was by nature cautious about everything. It was staffed by administrators for whom lack of caution, prudence or circumspection was the most deadly of sins. It was hardly to be expected, therefore, that the ministry would pursue a course of uninhibited restructuring of a system which, immediately after the European war, was in need of very careful nurturing. And, as Lowe (1988, p. 9) has so neatly expressed it, 'The demographic imperative chimed precisely with the political will.' That is, the postwar surge in the birth rate required the ministry to give priority to resources for primary children, who would need the extra classrooms and extra teachers by 1950, and who would not reach their secondary schools until 1956 at the earliest. For many administrators, therefore, the reorganization of secondary education on a large scale was perceived as a problem that could safely be shelved until the 'demographic imperative' created new priorities in the 1960s.

THE 1950 GENERAL ELECTION

Between 1945 and 1950 the party conferences tackled education in very contrasting ways. The Conservatives produced only one, strangely muted resolution during the entire period: 'That the contentment of the teaching profession should have the earliest attention of the Minister of Education on our Party's return to power.' Labour, on the other hand, not only generated annual education debates, but its resolutions usually contained so many contentious clauses that some were either withdrawn, defeated or remitted for further discussion on the grounds that the agreed parts could not be separated from the disputed elements.

When the manifestos were published, all three parties maintained the view that implementing the 1944 Act was still the priority. Labour claimed that its record in creating more schools and more teachers in very difficult circumstances should be acknowledged by the electorate, but it also recognized that 'The community needs more and more people of individuality who can think for themselves as co-operative members of our democratic community.' The Liberals came out against standardization and for differentiation and urged that raising of the school-leaving age to 16 should await the production of appropriate school accommodation and an increased supply of teachers. In the event, Attlee's government was returned to power, but with an overall majority of only five.[12] Tomlinson and Hardman continued as Ministers, and were supported by the enduring self-reliance of Maud, Williams and Roseveare. The 1950-51 administration, however, was not without turbulence.

The extent to which Ministers of Education occupied themselves with operational breakdowns in the system is one of their more disappointing characteristics. It is almost certainly a product of their perception of themselves as carrying out managerial roles. Tomlinson was drawn into a dispute with Durham County Council which inevitably wasted time that should have been devoted to strategic planning. The circumstances were these. Durham County Council resolved that all its employees, including teachers, should be members of a trade union. The teachers, supported by the NUT, were determined to defend the rights of the individual. Tomlinson, despite being a life-long trade unionist and local authority man, did not hesitate to support this right and found himself eventually in the position of having to issue a directive (under Section 68 of the 1944 Act) restraining the County Council. The intervention was justified on the grounds that the Minister had a duty to ensure that the LEA discharged its statutory obligations, which it would not have been able to do if all its teachers had resigned *en bloc*, as they threatened to do.

Some would argue that ministers (of all government departments) properly involve themselves in resolving disputes in so far as theirs is the final responsibility. But this is to agree with the management concept. If we are being asked to see the minister as the managing director of an extremely large company (and in reality a nationalized industry) employing many thousands of teachers and owning property all over the country, then his or her alarmingly short-lived tenure of office must be regarded as a built-in destructive mechanism.

There are two major issues on which Attlee's second government kept a watchful eye but nothing more: the public schools and comprehensive secondary schools. Tomlinson was essentially a pragmatist on both issues. On public schools he took the romantic view that in the long run no one would want to pay for their children to go to schools markedly inferior to those that the LEAs could provide free, and the realistic view (Blackburn, 1954, p. 192) that 'at present our hands are full enough with coping with the increase in the birth-rate and the movement of population to new housing estates'. On comprehensive schools, he, like most ministers between 1945 and 1965, took the view that they were *experimental*, and that the ministry should leave the conduct of such experiments to the LEAs.

* * *

It would not be unfair to say that during the six years of the Labour government no fundamental policy matters were introduced in the field of education. Why, then, did Attlee's cabinet so strongly support the 1944 Act, and what can we learn from the ministry's conduct of affairs during this period that may help us to understand more readily the course of subsequent events?

In the first place, we need to recognize that education policy, just as much in the 1940s as in the 1980s, was driven by political forces and personalities from outside the ministry or department itself. James Chuter Ede, as Butler's wartime deputy, had been a major designer of the 1944 Act (even if the Act itself will always be known as the Butler Act). As Home Secretary throughout the Attlee administration, he exercised a general stabilizing influence on policy. The implementation of the wartime act was therefore *the* educational priority of the cabinet, and Wilkinson, Hardman and Tomlinson were obviously fully committed to it. Similarly, in the 1980s Margaret Thatcher, as Prime Minister, but a former DES Secretary of State, controlled education policy in cabinet, even if Carlisle, Joseph, Baker, MacGregor and Clarke undertook the day-to-day business.

In the second place, the ministry, led by Sir John Maud, believed that the 1944 reforms were sufficiently far-reaching to satisfy the need for restructuring for many years to come. The idea of peaks and troughs of activity reappeared in the 1960s, when comprehensive secondary education was the main agenda, and in the 1980s, when the National Curriculum dominated DES thinking.

Thirdly, education policy in the immediate postwar period was subjected to the restraints and disappointments caused by economic and international events in much the same way as education policies from the 1960s to the 1980s have been curtailed, diminished or even wholly abandoned. Aspirations such as equality among the elements of the secondary tripartite system, or financial support of 15-18-year-olds, or substantial improvement of technical education failed to achieve the implementation that across-party support seemed to promise 40 years ago.

Finally, Labour government policy allowed the private sector of education to flourish in parallel with the state system, just as it did in 1966-70 and 1974-79. The long-term relationship between policy implementation and manifesto pledges is still the subject of debate in both the Labour and Conservative parties.

NOTES

1 When Churchill offered R. A. Butler the post of president of the Board of Education in 1941, he said, 'I think that you can leave your mark there. You will be independent . . . I am too old now to think you can improve people's natures. Everyone has to learn to defend himself. I should not object if you could introduce a note of patriotism into the schools . . . [*and in respect of influencing what is taught*] not by instruction or order but by suggestion' (Butler, 1971, p. 90).

2 Conservative Party Manifesto, June 1945: see F. W. S. Craig (1970).

3 Sir William Hadow: the report of the Consultative Committee of the Board of Education (given its terms of reference in 1924), entitled *The Education of the Adolescent*. Sir Will Spens: the report of the Consultative Committee of the Board of Education (given its terms of reference in 1933) on Secondary Education with Special Reference to Grammar and Technical High Schools.

4 Lowe (1988), p. 7; see also Cleary (1941); Wallace (1981), Addison (1975); Barker (1972); Gosden (1974; 1989); Jeffreys (1984); Simon (1974).

5 Maud (1981), p. 51. Readers who are confused by this reference should know that the BBC Third Programme was the predecessor of Radio 3 and broadcast drama, poetry, discussions and lectures, as well as music.

6 Readers who may wish to extend their enquiries into the Wilkinson legacy should read Wann (1971), Rubinstein (1979), Hughes (1979), C. Benn (1980), Vernon (1982) and Dean (1986).

7 Maud (1981), p. 2. An alternative account of this event was provided by Antony Part, who believed Maud had been removed from Education by Churchill in response to a complaint from Horsburgh: see Part (1990), p. 90.

8 See also Cleary (1941).

9 Gosden (1989), p. 183. See also Williams (1955).

10 See Barker (1972), Fenwick (1976), Gosden (1974), Parkinson (1970), and Simon (1974).

11 Morgan (1984), p. 177. See also Attlee (1954), G. Tomlinson (1949), Tomlinson and Maud (1951).

12 Labour received 46 per cent of the votes, the Conservatives 43.5 per cent and the Liberals only 9 per cent.

Chapter 2

The creation of the DES: the Conservative governments 1951-64

At a cabinet meeting on 19 September 1951, Attlee informed his colleagues that the government could no longer survive the complications created by such a small majority in Parliament and the growing vulnerability of his MPs to illness and fatigue. The general election which took place on 25 October was won by the Conservatives with an overall majority of 17, even though Labour had gained 48.8 per cent of the votes to the Conservatives' 48.0 per cent. The new government went on to win the elections of 1955 and 1959 and thus sustain a period of thirteen years, under the leadership of Churchill, Eden, Macmillan and Douglas-Home, in which to establish and develop its own view of educational provision throughout the UK.

PARTY CONFERENCES AND MANIFESTOS

The party manifestos for October 1951 were minimalist. All Labour could say was that 'we shall extend our policy of giving all young people equal opportunities in education', a real sign, as Morgan (1984, p. 462) has observed, that 'its parliamentary supporters were pulverized by late-night sittings and filibustered debates, its ministers exhausted by intractable problems at home and abroad. It had no legislative initiatives to offer.' The Conservatives looked back to 1944 again, saying that 'some of the most crying needs are not being met. For the money now being spent we will provide better services and so fulfil the high hopes we all held when we planned the improvements during the war.' Since it had universally come to be known as the Butler Act, there seemed to be plenty of political mileage in claiming it as sovereign Conservative territory, in spite of the fact that, as we have seen in Chapter 1, the Act was more the intellectual property of the board's civil servants and James Chuter Ede. The Liberal Party, after its dismal performance in the previous election, now found nothing at all to say about education.

The Conservatives found themselves in an ambiguous position as far as policy was concerned. If the 1944 Act really was their own, and if the Labour government had done little else than carry out the implementation of these very same policies (as its critics asserted), then the new Minister could not complain about much other than lack of efficiency. The position has been aptly described thus:

> While in opposition following their crushing defeat in 1945, the Conservatives, after a brief period of confusion and incoherence, had rapidly adjusted their policies to a major acceptance of the Welfare State and Managed Economy, including the principal

> reforms that the Labour Government had introduced ... Such adaptation may seem not only rational, but also typical. In a democratic two-party system ... competition for votes will force the policies of the two parties towards one another.
>
> (Beer, 1982, p. 218)

It is just as much in the nature of Conservative conferences to lean towards the self-congratulatory resolution as it is for Labour conferences to criticize. Between 1952 and 1963 the Conservatives passed nine short resolutions, containing four references to the desire to keep grammar schools intact and four stressing the need to improve technical education. The Labour conferences, after an angry outburst in 1952, ignored education entirely until 1958 when Labour chose to applaud its own policy document, *Learning to Live*, and to defeat a motion calling for the total abolition of the private sector. After yet another reversal in the 1959 election the party concentrated on educational expansion, realistically sensing that the ever-increasing birth rate was creating a demographic time bomb which the British education system was ill-equipped to deal with. The expansion should also include industrial training and apprenticeships, technical and scientific education, and a substantial growth in funding. Throughout the period there was continued reference to the (approved) growth of comprehensive schools and in 1958 to the need for intermediate schools (later called middle schools), which 'could provide more homogeneous age groups, abolish once and for all the myth of the validity of 11 + selection, and sensibly restrict the numbers in High Schools of a comprehensive character'.

The manifestos of 1955 and 1959 still make interesting reading, not only for what they tell us about the political cross-currents of the period, but also for the shadows they throw across our contemporary educational landscape. Of course they must be treated with caution:

> What parties say is not what parties do; hence, to understand the role of parties in government we must distinguish clearly between rhetoric and reality. Rhetoric has its place in securing the support of activists within a party, and in swaying the opinions of voters. But rhetorical skills are of little avail in the face of the problems that confront politicians in government. The ability to face up to reality is crucial if politicians are to survive in office. Rhetorical skills then become a necessary means to convince voters that government policy is not what governors want to do, but what they have to do.
>
> (Rose, 1984, p. xiii)

But these manifestos do reveal certain trends in educational thinking that characterize DES planning in later years. The 1955 Conservative document, *United for Peace and Progress*, presented the bald truth that 'the most urgent problem in education since the war has been to provide for the high rise in the school roll'. This headache was to go on intensifying during 1960s and appeared so to concentrate the mind of ministry and DES officials that vital long-term strategies to deal with other concerns such as scientific and technical education and the take-up of courses for 15-19-year-olds never took root. The manifesto actually itemized the need for 'a system of increased maintenance allowances to be introduced for senior pupils who might otherwise leave school before finishing an advanced course', only to be ignored by a succession of ministers.

The 1955 Labour manifesto, *Forward with Labour*, claimed that the party was 'determined on a radical reform of our education service' by substantially increasing the number of teachers in the system, by improving the standards of the buildings, and by 'removing from the primary schools the strain of the 11 + examination. This cramps the free and happy life which should stimulate the children's early years. It penalizes the children who develop late and gives an inferior place in our education to the practical skills increasingly essential to our industrial efficiency.' The Liberals again had nothing to offer the voters on education policy.

Both major parties, then, were emphasizing the need to develop technical and scientific education, but, as David Marquand (in Hennessy and Seldon, 1987, p. 318) has indicated, the postwar inheritance of 'Britain's industrial structure was already obsolescent . . . so [was] . . . every level of its skimpy system of public education.' This 'skimpy system' could be defended by governments and attacked by oppositions simply by demonstrating quantifiable measurements of new roofs over new heads. It was not, however, that the ministry could not claim limited progress, but that the fundamentally skimpy, meagre, beggarly and negligible inheritance could never be publicly admitted because the widespread antipathy towards public expenditure on the intellectual and the academic was ingrained in the fabric of British life. At the heart of the predicament lay the nationally held view that British schools and British universities were the best in the world. Even when the Russian Yuri Gagarin achieved the first orbital space flight in April 1961, few Britons were prepared to acknowledge that there might be something wrong in their classrooms. Sadly, another 30 years was to pass before the UK woke up to the idea of its being the worst-educated nation among the modern industrial states.

For the 1959 elections the Liberals re-entered the education arena in their manifesto, *People Count*. It seized upon the notion that 'Russia spends seven times as much per head on education as we do and America spends twice as much', which meant that the UK should try to catch up by spending more on teachers, schools and universities. Labour agreed, urging more to be spent on technical education within a secondary comprehensive framework and for maintenance grants to be paid to pupils staying on at school after the age of 15. They were still anxious to do away with eleven-plus selection, but offered more subtle arguments than in the previous electoral disaster:

> The Tories say this means abolishing the grammar schools. On the contrary, it means that grammar-school education will be open to all who can benefit by it. In our system of comprehensive education we do not intend to impose one uniform pattern of school. LEAs will have the right to decide how best to apply the comprehensive principle.

The voter now had to differentiate between grammar schools and grammar-school education, and between comprehensive schools and the comprehensive principle. The Conservatives had four main programmes of expansion: more teachers (with three-year training), more universities, new technical colleges and more funding to improve the quality of school buildings. They also remained ready to '*defend* the grammar schools against doctrinaire socialist attack', even though it was becoming obvious that the Labour position was more pragmatic than ideological. Paradoxically, at the following general election in 1964, it was Harold Wilson who claimed that grammar schools would be abolished 'only over my dead body'.

THE POLITICIANS

Ministerial power depends not only upon an individual's capacity for leadership, personal magnetism and potential for harnessing the support of the administration, but also upon his or her standing and influence within the party of government. Churchill's new cabinet included Butler, as Chancellor of the Exchequer, and two future Prime Ministers (Eden and Macmillan). The new Minister of Education was Florence Horsburgh (1889-1969), who had been MP for Dundee since 1931 and during the war was a junior minister in Health (where she had a role in the wartime evacuation of children and in the framing of the National Health scheme). She lost her seat in the 1945 election but returned to Westminster in 1950 as MP for Moss Side. She was deprived of a seat in the cabinet until September 1953 and was, of course, not the first or last ex-minister to be given a grace-and-favour post in a returning government. Accused later of being 'a dreary and disliked minister who was brought only late into the Cabinet, who never fought for and never received an adequate educational budget' (Kogan, 1978, p. 34), she saw in Butler, the Chancellor, a far less generous educationist than the mythology suggests. She was widely opposed on the Teachers' Superannuation Bill in 1954, which attempted to increase the contribution from the teachers from 5 to 6 per cent. The National Union of Teachers mounted a strenuous campaign against her, supported by the Labour opposition and many back-bench Conservatives. Churchill replaced her with Sir David Eccles in October. The year she spent in the cabinet did, however, provide her with the consolation of being the first woman to hold a cabinet post in a Conservative government. She was made a life peeress in 1959.

Her successor was Sir David Eccles (b. 1904), who was educated at Winchester and New College, Oxford, and elected MP for Chippenham in 1943, a seat which he retained until receiving a peerage in 1963. He joined the government in 1951 at the Ministry of Works and came to Education for the first time in 1954. After a period as President of the Board of Trade from 1957 to 1959, he served a further period in Education from October 1959 until June 1962, when together with several other cabinet ministers he was sacked by Macmillan in the famous purge often referred to as 'the night of the long knives'. He was 'perhaps the minister who best typified the optimism and opportunism of the time' (Kogan, 1978, p. 34). Given the continuing prioritization of building schools, his experience at the Ministry of Works no doubt provided an invaluable asset at the time, although only 30 years later his work was seen in a very different light (see Chapters 6 and 7).

Eccles was the high priest of the remnants of nineteenth-century romanticism, bringing to the ministry the imagined values and style of the rural community he represented. His speeches and writings were constantly tinged with a nostalgia for a society in which all knew their place, and in which the new urban affluence which had exploded during the Macmillan era was regarded with the deepest suspicion. If the phrase had been in use at the time, he would certainly have been called a 'born-again Christian' as his two post-ministerial books (1966; 1967) indicate most strongly. For example, he could say, apparently in all innocence,

> Parliament, congratulating itself on recognising the source of the morality that kept our society together, inserted a provision in the Education Act of 1944 that religion must be taught in the schools and each day must start with an act of worship. This part of the Act has not been a success for ... teachers, whose duty it was to teach religion, were not themselves convinced believers ... and they found too little support from the children's parents and from the grown-up world in general.
>
> (Eccles, 1967, p. 10)

Kogan (1975, p. 27) has correctly pointed to the fact that 'his policies more than any others represent the consensual, expansionist and ameliorist era of British education.' This is surely borne out by the following examples:

> Having been for a number of years Minister of Education and now back in business, I am frequently aware that management do not take the trouble to go into the differences between the education which today's school-leavers have had and the education of twenty years ago. An employer ... should study the results of those changes in the schools ... and no longer be surprised at the way his employees react if all their thinking is done for them and they are not allowed to participate in decisions affecting their particular jobs. At the Ministry of Education I was very conscious that I had put my hand to a revolution the nature of which my friends who had been with me at the university, and especially those who were in industry, knew very little about.
>
> (Eccles, 1967, p. 100)

> How does the new entrant to industry feel about his job? Having been educated by the new teaching to express himself, and having in a modest way used his gifts in the practice of the arts, he is often conscious that he possesses creative power. He is shocked and rubbed on the raw if he finds himself subordinate to the machines, and in repetitive jobs treated as a stand-in until such time as a better machine can be invented to take over his work, to the evident pleasure of everyone in authority over him.
>
> (*ibid.*, p. 101)

> Looking back on my time at the Ministry of Education, my greatest mistake was to spend far too little of my budget on adult education.
>
> (*ibid.*, p. 108)

> The Education Act of 1944 proposed three types of maintained schools and assumed that if these were imaginatively built up to correspond to real differences in children's abilities and aptitudes, they would enjoy parity of esteem. Today it is fashionable to laugh at this hope ... This reveals more than a difference in politics, it marks a failure in our vision and in our character ... I agreed that the class divisions of thirty or forty years ago required a drastic change, but these divisions are now being closed ... Reforming the structure of the schools becomes a matter of timing.
>
> (*ibid.*, p. 115)

> British people now receive a much better education. The Primary Schools are able to do far more for the young children than before the war. All secondary-school children will soon be staying at school till they are sixteen, and the range of opportunity in further education is growing so quickly that it is almost a social revolution in itself.
>
> (*ibid.*, p. 136)

While it would obviously be only too easy to develop critical perspectives on all these assertions, the flavour of what is said gives a very clear impression of the attitudes and assumptions of a man whose influence on the ministry spanned some eight years in all.

Viscount Hailsham (b. 1907), a man in whom ambition was not wholly suppressed, replaced Eccles in January 1957 for the first of his brief associations with the ministry. As Quintin Hogg, he had been educated at Eton and Christ Church, Oxford, where he was president of the Union. In 1932 he had been both called to the Bar and elected MP for Oxford City, a seat which he held until 1950. At this point he succeeded to his father's title of Viscount Hailsham and continued his nomadic career in government in the House of Lords. He remained at Education for only nine months, giving way to Geoffrey Lloyd in order to take up the senior posts of Leader of the House of Lords, Lord Privy Seal, Lord President of the Council, and Minister of Science and Technology. When Science was merged with Education to form the DES in April 1964, he became its first Secretary of State, a post which he held for only six months because of the Conservatives' election defeat in October. As if this sequence of events were not complicated enough already, Hailsham had returned to being Hogg in October 1963 in order to become a candidate for the premiership, and became Hailsham for the second time in 1970 in order to become Lord Chancellor, a post which he held between 1970 and 1974 and 1979 and 1987. The point of the story for today's reader is this: if a department of state cannot depend upon the continuity of its political management structure, then it may feel itself obliged to compensate for the political discontinuity by providing its own administrative cohesion and coherence; and if such cohesion and coherence in turn creates a self-reliant but impenetrable bureaucracy, then government by consent becomes government by administrative convenience.

After Harrow and Trinity College, Cambridge, Geoffrey Lloyd (1902-84) had entered Parliament as a Birmingham MP in 1931. He was to go on representing Birmingham constituencies until 1974, although, like Florence Horsburgh, he was out of Westminster between 1945 and 1950. He had held various government positions between 1935 and 1945 and Churchill made him his Minister of Fuel and Power in 1951. Macmillan brought him into Education in 1957, presumably on the grounds of his ministerial experience rather than educational expertise. His tenure of this office lasted only until the next election. He was remembered in his obituary as 'the first man of a technological bent to occupy the post. Nevertheless he yielded his place in 1959 to give younger men a chance, having in that time done much to enhance the standing of technology' (*The Times*, 13 September 1984). This was incorrect on two counts: he was replaced by David Eccles (again) only two years his junior, and technology was still a long way from receiving academic approval in the schools.

The fifth incumbent was Sir Edward Boyle (1923-81), who, like Hailsham, was educated at Eton and Christ Church, Oxford, where he was also president of the Union. He entered Parliament as its youngest member in 1950 as MP for Handsworth (Birmingham), a seat which he retained until leaving politics in 1970. Within four years he had been appointed a junior minister in the Ministry of Supply and in less than a year he was promoted to the Treasury, where he served as Economic Secretary. In late 1956, however, the Suez crisis led to his resignation from the government. When Macmillan replaced Eden as Prime Minister in January 1957, Boyle took up his post as Parliamentary Secretary for Education (that is, as number two at the ministry to Hogg), where he remained until the general election of October 1959. He then moved to the key post of Financial Secretary to the Treasury and returned to take charge of Education in July 1962. When Education was merged with Science to form the DES in April 1964, he again became second in command to Hogg (but still with a seat in cabinet), until the general election of October 1964. His government role in education therefore spanned nearly eight years altogether, although he held the top job for only 21 months.

He brought to this post an astonishing array of talents and interests (including cricket, music and India) together with an apparently unquenchable appetite for writing and speaking on educational matters (see Bibliography for selection). His two spells at the Treasury gave him a firm grasp of economic affairs, and although he had spent only a short time as a back-bencher he possessed a flair for keeping in touch with other MPs. He took a strongly liberal stance on race relations (including opposition to South African apartheid policies), capital punishment, educational opportunities for the handicapped, wider access to higher education and the education of girls. On the matter of secondary comprehensive schools in the UK, he maintained a resolutely pragmatic, but closely argued case for their gradual introduction. His fundamental interest in, and enthusiasm for, all aspects of education continued during the remainder of the 1960s (when he served as opposition spokesman on education) and in the 1970s when he had left Westminster to take up the post of Vice-Chancellor of the University of Leeds.

Boyle had plenty of opportunities to analyse the role of a minister and his writings reveal a breadth of understanding on a whole range of issues which justifies repeated readings. On the crucial relationship between ministers and civil servants he believed

> One important difference is that the top-level administrative civil servant ... identifies key issues for Ministers, orders the relevant facts and figures and sets out possible courses of action. This is one of the most important jobs that civil servants perform for Ministers ... If they [Ministers] have creative imagination ... they may become chiefly committed to ... certain policies ... but it's not their first responsibility to identify the issues.
>
> (Boyle and Crosland, 1971, pp. 73-4)

In this simple observation lies a clue to the nature of policy formation and delivery. From the point of view of a political party the minister's task may be to carry out conference and manifesto obligations which were generally created in precise terms in order to satisfy an electorate clamouring for particularity. But from the point of view of a minister, what is important is the ability to make firm decisions, informed by a carefully prepared selection of available options and illuminated by his or her own political intelligence and grasp of principle. Boyle had no illusions about civil servants' prejudices, and used them in argument to clear his own mind:

> I think the interplay between Ministers and civil servants works most successfully when their views are instinctively neither too close nor too far apart. Often the partnership comes when the head of a Department holds broadly the same philosophy as the government, but has important reservations. Then he will be listened to.
>
> (Boyle and Crosland, 1971, p. 76)

Boyle's absence from the ministry between 1959 and 1962 allowed him to judge for himself how it was functioning. He believed that changes of personnel (Smieton for Flemming, and the promotion of Part and Weaver to Deputies) in turn created changes of emphasis within the department, while at the same time changes in the Cabinet influenced the subtle balance of relations between Education and other departments such as the Treasury. He also felt that the ministry was sufficiently sensitive to the trend of educational ideas (emerging both from the LEAs and from the academic world) to be responsive to what he liked to call the 'logic of the education service' (Boyle and Crosland, 1971, pp. 90-1).

Apart from Boyle himself, there were four other MPs who served as junior Ministers between 1951 and 1964. They were (Sir) Kenneth Pickthorn (1892-1975), Dennis Vosper (Lord Runcorn, 1916-68), (Sir) Kenneth Thompson (1909-84) and Christopher Chataway (b. 1931). When the enlarged DES was formed in

April 1964 and Boyle became a Minister of State, he was joined at that level by Lord Newton (b. 1915) the former MP for Petersfield (Hants), who had been in the Lords since his father's death in 1950. He no doubt felt at home in the company of Hogg and Boyle, for, like theirs, his background was Eton and Christ Church, Oxford, as also was that of Sir Alec Douglas-Home, the new Prime Minister. The Oxford mafia had struck again.

By contrast, Dr Pickthorn from Aldenhelm School and Trinity College, Cambridge, had been a History Fellow of Corpus Christi College, Cambridge, since 1914 and was a late entrant into politics. He became MP for the University in 1935 and for Carlton in Nottinghamshire between 1950 and 1966. His period at the ministry from 1951 until October 1954 was, if unspectacular, an interesting Churchillian experiment. He was replaced by Dennis Vosper (Marlborough and Pembroke College, Cambridge), the MP for Runcorn (1950-64), who had become a government Whip after only a year in Westminster and who was later to hold posts in the Ministry of Health and the Home Office. His span in Education ran from October 1954 until January 1957. Kenneth Thompson arrived at the Ministry in October 1959 after a two-year spell as Assistant Postmaster General. He was highly influential in the political life of Liverpool, representing the Walton constituency between 1950 and 1964 (see Thompson, 1966; 1967).

Christopher Chataway (b. 1931) became a Parliamentary Secretary at the ministry in 1962, only three years after entering Westminster. Having successfully survived the merger with Science, he went out of office after the 1964 election and then went on to lose his Lewisham seat in 1966. He pursued his enthusiasm for educational politics as leader of the Conservatives in ILEA between 1967 and 1969. After his return in 1969 as MP for Chichester, he joined Edward Heath's government as Minister for Posts and Telecommunications and later Minister at the Department of Trade and Industry. If, on the grounds of continuity, Heath had made him, rather than Margaret Thatcher, Secretary of State in 1970, the course of British politics might have been very different. Boyle (who, had he not left Westminster for better things, might have been Heath's first choice) expressed considerable confidence in Chataway: 'There was a certain amount of Parliamentary and lowish-level administrative work [that] Geoffrey Lloyd . . . let me do . . . I hope I did the same with Chris Chataway . . . and of course he was exceptionally good at it' (Boyle and Crosland, 1971, p. 87).

THE CIVIL SERVANTS

When Sir John Maud left the Ministry of Education to join the Ministry of Fuel and Power in 1952, he was replaced by his recently appointed Deputy, (Sir) Gilbert Flemming (1897-1981), who 'was just the man they needed . . . [He] made fewer speeches and was less often outside his office' (Maud, 1981, p. 66). After Rugby and Trinity College, Oxford, he had joined the Board of Education in 1921 and remained in education (except for a short time during the war) until his retirement in 1959. He was responsible for the administration of raising the school-leaving age in 1947, and especially for the emergency trained teachers, 'one of the most satisfying jobs I ever undertook' (Vernon, 1982, p. 207). On retirement he said that 'the controversies of secondary education are largely sterile ... [but] the calculations that led to the concept of the monster comprehensive schools were wrongly based and they would be short-lived' (*TES*, 9 October 1959).

Dame Mary Smieton (b. 1902) succeeded Flemming in October 1959. From Wimbledon High School and Lady Margaret Hall, Oxford, not only was she the first woman to hold this post,[1] but also her career so far had been *in another ministry* (Labour and National Service). This double shock to the senior men of the ministry was not seen in the same light as John Maud's earlier arrival from outside, for he was a *wartime* exception. The surprise that greeted her appointment was later echoed in the case of Sir Herbert Andrew. The educational press could not understand why an outsider was selected, but conceded that she had been appointed, 'not because she is a woman, but because she is a distinguished civil servant. All the same, education, with its great body of women teachers, will give her a special welcome' (*TES*, 17 July 1959). She was correctly described as 'genuinely averse to personal publicity' (*TES*, 14 August 1959), and during her five years in office she kept an extremely low profile. Nevertheless, in her evidence to the Robbins Committee she provided a tiny glimpse of a formidable personality:

> I am sure that the size and cost of higher education will result in greatly increased Parliamentary and public interest in the Parliamentary control of how this money is spent. It seems to us very important that, first, a limit should be set beyond which these controls cannot go if academic freedom is to be maintained, and secondly, that it should be made plain that certain measures could be taken to see that this proper public interest could be enforced without interfering with those freedoms.[2]

These academic freedoms, or 'essential liberties', were 'the freedom of an institution to appoint and dismiss its own staff, freedom to select its students and freedom in the curriculum and methods of teaching'.[3]

Her Deputies were Heaton and Part. Neville Heaton (b. 1912) was educated at Westminster School and Christ Church, Oxford. He had worked on the 1944 Act with Butler, who used him extensively as a committee secretary; in Butler's opinion he should have become a Permanent Secretary. Instead he spent seven years as Deputy to Flemming and (briefly) Smieton before moving to deputy posts in the larger ministries of Transport and Economic Affairs. We have already encountered the early career of Antony Part (1916-90) in Chapter 1. In 1954 he had been promoted to Under-Secretary and in 1960 to Deputy Secretary. The air of illusion that had surrounded the actual achievements of the school-building programme of the 1940s and 1950s was paralleled by Part's astonishing ignorance about technical education, for which he had responsibilities for some six or more years, as he revealed later:

> This was completely strange territory to me - and deplorably, to most of the Ministry's administrators: a highly specialised world full of initials such as HND and ONC and the titles of various craft qualifications supervised by the City and Guilds of London

> Institute. It had quite close links with management and unions and relationships which varied from the cordial to the caustic with the professional bodies such as the various Institutions in the engineering world.
>
> (Part, 1990, pp. 90-1)

Need we look further for an explanation of the UK's abysmal industrial performance in the second half of the twentieth century?

In HMI, Percy Wilson (1904-86) replaced Sir Martin Roseveare as Senior Chief Inspector from 1957 to 1965 and served under Hogg, Lloyd, Eccles, Boyle, Steward and Crosland, among the politicians, and Flemming, Smieton and Andrew as Permanent Secretaries. He had been educated at Market Rasen Grammar School and Jesus College, Cambridge. After teaching in schools from 1927 to 1935, he joined HMI as an English specialist.

In *Views and Prospects from Curzon Street* (the then location of the ministry), Wilson portrays the civilized and essentially gradualist traditions that he believed himself to have inherited from Thomas Arnold, and which were very much in tune with the Eccles perspective on educational matters. When we consider the nature of educational reform, Wilson told the Association of Headmistresses in June 1960, we must keep to four principles: historical perspective, structural clarity, detachment and selective prioritization. All Wilson's written speeches convey a very strong sense of history, and he captures that same sense of assumed *inevitability* about educational systems that characterizes so many writers from the Ministry, and later the Department, of Education. To give politicians advice that was not based on at least 100 years of evidence was for Wilson a major failure of responsibility.

The notion of structural clarity is seen at its best, according to Wilson, in the 1944 Act. 'Not to legislate in pettifogging detail' was his advice to all drafters of education acts. In the early 1960s, when the ministry was more than happy to act as no more than a guide and friend to the LEAs, this was undoubtedly the commonly held view. The third principle, freedom from political prejudice and what he calls 'educational obsession', reveals Wilson's essentially mixed feelings about the political process. He was quick to admit that 'you can't take education out of politics or you take it out of life altogether' (Wilson, 1961, p. 16). But this also led to 'passion and prejudice . . . excitement, emotion and perhaps frenzy. . . . These undoubtedly supply some of the steam or energy for change and development. But I think their importance is over-rated and, in any case, the reforming statesman and the enlightened administrator ought, so far as possible, to stand above them' (*ibid.*).

The final principle is not a principle at all, of course. Wilson believed that the successful politician and the successful administrator can select the important elements from the trivial. For him, in 1960 the agenda was too big, too fantastic. It is worth quoting in full:

> Raise the school-leaving age. Start county colleges. Double the capacity of the universities. Double or treble the capacity of the training colleges. Expand the university departments of education and make professional training compulsory. Expand further and

> very considerably all levels of technical education from the craftsman's to the degree level sandwich. Aim at a graduate teaching profession. Open up the Public Schools. Extend the direct grant list. Abolish the Eleven Plus examination. Build more comprehensive schools. Extend the Leicestershire Plan. Reduce all classes in primary and secondary schools to thirty. And even that is not all. Those are all proposals of reasonably responsible groups. If you add the special fads of the lunatic fringe, you could nearly double that list.
>
> (*ibid.*, p. 18)

What Wilson refused to recognize was that nearly all these proposals had been in circulation for many, many years, and but for the pronounced dragging of feet by senior civil servants and HMI would already have been in practice.

THE POLICIES

Throughout much of the 1950s, it has been observed, the Conservative administration 'applied in an open and single-minded fashion the policy which Tomlinson had pursued with a measure of confusion' during the last years of the Labour government (Barker, 1972, p. 95). This was especially true of David Eccles, whose previous experience of government undoubtedly secured for Education a more robust performance than at any time since the war. But this is not to suggest that it had gained anything remotely recognizable as a high profile. For Churchill, Eden, Macmillan and Douglas-Home, the education service was perhaps no more than a routine obligation. Indeed, as James Barnes (in Hennessy and Seldon, 1987, p. 108) so deftly put it, 'it would be hard to guess from Macmillan's memoirs that education formed any part of the government's responsibility.'

During the thirteen years of Conservative government there were no fewer than six changes of political leadership in Education (see Chronology). Even if we take account of Eccles and Hogg's each having two terms in office, and Boyle's gaining ample experience in both junior and senior roles, the instability is still very marked. To some extent the gradual delivery of government reports helped to provide some sort of developmental structure. In 1954 the Ashby Report on adult education drew attention to needs and circumstances which allowed the ministry to show an interest in a neglected area without an obligation to take much action. More difficult was the Central Advisory Council for Education (CACE) report, *Early Leaving* (also 1954), which indicated that little progress had been made in ten years since the 1944 Act towards the important objective of successfully encouraging pupils to stay on at school after 15. The recognition that in an era of high employment only a small proportion of the age group saw any point in further study, at least further school study, came as a disappointment to idealists who had thought that universal free secondary education would solve everything. Not for the first or the last time did the idea of the Treasury's providing maintenance allowances come to the surface, only to sink beneath the waves of political indifference.

Two years later CACE was again asked to look at the same problem. It took three years to produce the Crowther Report, *15 to 18* which urged the implementation of the 1944 Act's suggestion that raising the school-leaving age to 16 should follow the rise to 15. 'Our main case is not economic at all. It rests on the conviction that all boys and girls of 15 have much to learn, and that school (in the broadest sense) and not work is the best place for this' (par. 201). Still within the ambitions of the 1944 Act, the report stressed the need to provide part-time educational facilities for 16- and 17-year-olds not in full-time schooling. The Crowther Report went further by suggesting that such part-time attendance at county colleges should be compulsory. Needless to say, when these matters were brought before the House of Commons in March 1960, the Treasury and the ministry recommended no immediate action.

In complete contrast, the *Albermarle Report on the Youth Service* (1960) was more or less accepted on the spot, perhaps partly because it did not affect mainstream provision and partly because the committee included the former junior Minister Dennis Vosper, who knew at first hand what would be eligible for ministry support. The Newsom report, *Half Our Future* (1963), on the other hand, provoked more controversy. Addressing itself to the needs of secondary modern pupils, it felt that

> unsuitable programmes and teaching methods may aggravate their difficulties, and frustration express itself in apathy or rebelliousness. The country cannot afford this wastage, humanly or economically speaking. If it is to be avoided, several things will be necessary. The pupils will need to have a longer period of full-time education than most of them now receive. The schools will need to present that education in terms more acceptable to the pupils and their parents, by relating school more directly to adult life, and especially by taking a proper account of vocational interests (par. 3).

The Central Advisory Council took two and half years to produce this report. After another six months the ministry changed to the DES and Labour won the general election. Newsom disappeared from view. Its recommendation to raise the leaving age to 16 was not achieved until 1972. For most pupils the aim that the curriculum should be 'more acceptable to pupils' has still not been achieved.

Newsom was partly upstaged by the arrival in the same month of the Robbins Report, *Higher Education*, which had taken even longer to produce. However, the new Prime Minister (Douglas-Home) immediately announced the full acceptance of its programme for a substantial increase in higher education.[4] It was, of course, only after the establishment of the DES in April 1964 that the university and new polytechnic sectors came within the full responsibility of the department.

The main thrust of ministry innovation, however, lay in the area of technical education, which its annual report for 1958 placed number one on its list of priorities. In 1956 the White Paper, *Technical Education*, tried to come to terms with the realization that less than 4 per cent of the secondary age group were actually attending technical schools. So much for parity of esteem. Circulars abounded on the topic, leading eventually to another White Paper, *Better*

Opportunities in Technical Education (January 1961), and the White Paper, *Industrial Training*, appeared in 1962. Much of this activity was generated by Eccles, while Boyle was closely associated with the foundation of the Schools' Council (replacing the Curriculum Study Group[5]) and the Council for National Academic Awards (CNAA), which was to take a huge part in the development of the Polytechnics and the Colleges of Higher Education. The 1964 Education Act was also mainly a Boyle document, which specifically attempted to ease the transition to a comprehensive system by the authorization of middle schools.

The comprehensive secondary school was to become one of the bigger issues of the 1960s, over which politicians fell into dispute both between and within the parties. This is not the occasion to rehearse the arguments. But it was also a problem which caused later-to-be-revealed schisms within the ministry itself. Here, for example, is Boyle's relaxed approach:

> One thing I think a Minister should always do when dealing with a big issue like secondary school reorganization ... is to take a decision that leaves the maximum of options open for the future ... planning schools in such a way ... was a good thing. I remember in 1963 that no fewer than ninety LEAs had reorganization plans.
>
> (Boyle and Crosland, 1971, p. 78)

Compare Boyle's approach with that of his Under-Secretaries:

> The Ministry was not at this time, or at any time later, entirely opposed to multilateral or comprehensive schools. It was prepared to consider individual proposals for such schools in certain conditions. However, for most of the first two decades after 1944 it regarded this type of school as being in the experimental stage, to be authorized only in specified circumstances. Thus the White Paper of 1958, which inaugurated a major new drive to develop secondary education, said that comprehensive schools must not be established where this would involve the abolition of existing grammar schools, and warned about the dangers of very large schools.
>
> (Pile, 1979, p. 85)

Next compare Boyle's approach with that of his chief HMI (speaking of the same period):

> It is not intended to concede the social argument for comprehensive schools, which I personally would not accept, now, any more than fifteen years ago.[6]

* * *

Education had joined the major government departments - the Foreign Office, the Home Office, the Treasury, the Commonwealth Office, the Department of Industry and Trade, and (formed at the same time) the Defence Department. This had largely been achieved in the Eccles-Boyle period, which was expansionist at every level of educational provision.[7] At various moments after 1964 the new department was also to take responsibility for the arts and for sport, thus introducing the question as to whether it might become the Department of Culture, a development resisted not only by those who regarded all culture as foreign and subversive, but also by those who felt that government should keep its distance from the arts and from sport.

Amid the celebrations of reaching its new status, there was nevertheless some unease about certain questions which had reached the surface of the educational village pond, and which were to send out ripples throughout the later 1960s:

How would the new department stand in the partnership with the schools, with the LEAs and now with the universities?
How would a department work with five 'ministers', to only one of whom (the Secretary of State) the civil servants felt themselves to be answerable?
How long could the expansionist policies be sustained?
How would the teachers react to the 1963 Boyle initiative which made the DES part of the teachers' and lecturers' pay bargaining machinery?

In search of answers to these and other questions, we must now turn to the events of the Wilson governments from 1964 to 1970.

NOTES

1 And still the only one: nor has there yet been a woman appointed at Deputy level.
2 Robbins Report (1963), Written and Oral Evidence [Monday, 2 July 1962], p. 1934.
3 Ibid., p. 1935.
4 For a later perspective on Robbins, see Alexander (1984) and Scott (1988).
5 Eccles set up the Curriculum Study Group in 1962 with DES officials, HMI and academics as members, having introduced a Research and Intelligence Branch at the ministry in the previous year.
6 Wilson (1961), p. 108; see also Wilson (1964).
7 And it continued with Crosland. The end of growth can be precisely pinpointed to 16 January 1968 when Wilson brought to the cabinet his deflationary package.

Chapter 3

The DES explores its power base: the Labour governments 1964-70

> During an election campaign, a party first of all presents itself as an organization; it is a team of candidates seeking office ... To interpret an election as a choice between ideologies is to misunderstand the nature of both parties and ideologies. A political party is not a thinking organization ... parties do not make ideologies ... for the institutions that constitute a party are multiple and intellectually not coherent, nor are election organizers interested in philosophical matters ... A general election campaign is about choice between organizations, not ideas.
>
> (Rose, 1984, p. 44)

The Labour Party went into the 1964 election with a firm grasp of this principle, or what may be called *Rose's first law of electioneering.* Harold Wilson was cast as the bright young technocrat in charge of a new-look organization brimming with imaginative innovations, while Sir Alec Douglas-Home could only play the role of chairman of the board of Old Etonians in Westminster. The manifesto slogans illustrated this mood exactly: *Let's Go with Labour for the New Britain* was in strong contrast to the Conservatives' sober *Prosperity with a Purpose*, and the Liberals' *Think for Yourself.*

For the Conservatives, education was 'the most rapidly developing feature of our social outlay ... This reflects our view of education as at once a right of the child, a need of society, and a condition of economic efficiency.' All three parties agreed on the need to expand higher education, further education (with Labour urging compulsory day release), and teacher supply. They were also united on the necessity of improving school buildings, now giving special attention to the primary sector, and all three wanted a rise to 16 for the leaving age. Where they disagreed was on the matter of secondary school selection, although the disagreements were not as clear-cut as many have assumed. The Conservatives maintained Boyle's pragmatism while both Labour and the Liberals argued for change, but in terms that left the nature of such a reform wide open. Labour's statement was cleverly ambiguous: 'Within the new system, grammar school education will be extended: in future no child will be denied the opportunity of benefiting from it through arbitrary selection at 11.' As we have already seen in Chapter 2, this differentiation between *grammar schools* and *grammar-school education* was a tactic already encountered at party conferences. The Liberals concentrated on *selection* rather than schools: 'The 11 plus exam must go. It is socially divisive and unfair ... we will encourage forms of non-selective secondary education.' The only genuinely divergent views were contained in two other promises offered by Labour: the proposal to 'set up an educational trust to advise on the best way of integrating the public schools into the state system' and the idea that the burden of teachers' salaries should be transferred to the Exchequer, a strategy that was not to take centre stage again until the Poll Tax fiasco of 1991.

The result of the October election was that Labour (with 44.1 per cent of the votes) gained an overall majority of four over the Conservatives (43.4 per cent) and the Liberals (11.2 per cent). Eighteen months later, in March 1966, another election reinforced the government's position by giving Labour (48.1 per cent) an overall majority of 97 over the Conservatives (41.9 per cent), while the Liberals received 8.5 per cent of the vote. It is therefore appropriate to consider the period 1964-70 as a single entity as far as policy formation and delivery are concerned. But before we do so, let us spend a moment on the manifestos of 1966. Between the two elections there had been time for only one round of conferences, in which there was little room for education as a discussion point. Labour had restated its position on selection, and the Conservatives, while maintaining their principle of choice, nevertheless came much nearer a consensus view by 'acknowledging that comprehensive schools have an important part to play in the educational system'. In its manifestos Labour, being the party in government, was able to spell out in considerable detail its plans for the next five years, which, in addition to further secondary school moves, included the start of the Open University, the accelerated expansion of the universities, polytechnics and colleges of higher education, and the delivery of earlier promises about technical and industrial training. The Conservatives still wanted 'to judge proposals for reorganization [of secondary schools] on their merits' and to 'give independent schools of high standing the opportunity to become direct grant schools, *thus narrowing the gap between State schools and fee-paying schools*' [my italics]. The Liberals joined the near consensus by saying that 'Liberals regard the abolition of all selection at 11 + not as a dogmatic principle, but as a necessary and long overdue reform', and that they 'would oppose any plan to abolish individual fee-paying schools although the role of the direct grant, grammar and independent schools must be reexamined.'

The National Plan, which had been published by the government in 1965, may be compared with the manifestos of 1966. The Plan stated that

> Education is both an important social service and an investment for the future. It helps to satisfy the needs of the economy for skilled manpower of all kinds, the needs of any civilized society for educated citizens who have been able to develop to the utmost their individual abilities, and the demands by individuals for education as a means both to improve economic prospects and to a richer and more constructive life.

The emphasis on schooling with dual objectives - an important social service *and* an investment for the future, producing skilled manpower *and* educated citizens, responding to the demands of the economy *and* those of the individual - puts into much sharper focus the political aims of the 1960s. We can turn now to the people charged with achieving them.

THE POLITICIANS

If we compare the six years of the Attlee administration with the six years of the first two Wilson administrations, we can see that whereas between 1945 and 1951 only three politicians were involved in Education (Wilkinson, Tomlinson and Hardman), in the period 1964-70 no fewer than thirteen were working at the DES (excluding the new Parliamentary Secretaries with responsibilities for the Arts or Sport). There appear to be four main factors in the Wilson years for the proliferation of government changes: politics, promotion, pensioning-off and perseverance.

Internal party politics have usually led Prime Ministers to seek a balance within their governments of conflicting party interests. As Samuel Beer (1982, p. 234) has put it, 'A major political party will at least be a coalition of interest groups. Sometimes it will be united by nothing beyond these ties and some broad and perhaps confused tendencies in social outlook.' Wilson was particularly skilful in the balancing game. In career terms, Parliamentary Under-Secretaries who performed well were usually promoted to Minister-of-State level *in another department*. Successful ministers were also shifted elsewhere to become Secretaries of State. The concept of promotion also took into account a hierarchical notion of government posts: league one included the offices of state such as Lord Chancellor, Foreign Secretary, Home Secretary and Chancellor of the Exchequer. League two included Lord President of the Council, Lord Privy Seal, Chancellor of the Duchy of Lancaster, and all the economic departments. League three included all those other posts that were within cabinet. League four was the rest. In order to make room for such promotions, there was an assumption during Wilson's time that 60 was the natural retiring age from government. Perseverance is a more fragile principle, however familiar it may be in staffing procedures. It can be seen in operation in many governments, particularly when a party is restored to power after a period in opposition.

Wilson's decision to appoint Patrick Gordon-Walker as Foreign Secretary in October 1964, even though he had lost his seat at Smethwick, was made in the hope that he would return to Parliament at the first by-election. The need for a by-election was created by persuading the sitting MP for Leyton (Sorenson) to go to the House of Lords. When the Foreign Secretary also failed to win this seat, he was replaced by Michael Stewart (1906-90), who had spent only three months at the DES as Secretary of State for Education. However beneficial to the Foreign Office this move may subsequently have proved to be, it meant that Education was faced with a fourth change at the top in two and a half years. There are two contrasting perspectives on such rapid change: the first is that the department was not unduly worried by these events because ministers do not make much difference in any case; the second is that the failure to implement coherent policies in the 1960s (including the failure to act on the recommendations of the major reports) was a direct consequence of ministerial instability. Stewart was one of the 37 members of the NUT in this Parliament, and had been the chief opposition spokesman on education during the Douglas-Home government. Wilson's view of Stewart's brief time at the DES was summed up in the following glowing terms:

> He was a dedicated educationalist, and in three months . . . he had recharted the policy of the country and smoothly redirected it on comprehensive lines. In a debate on the day of the [by-election] the Conservatives had launched an all-out attack on our policy to end selectivity in secondary education, and Michael had enjoyed a triumph such as few enjoy in Parliament.
>
> (Wilson, 1974, p. 66)

Stewart was replaced by Anthony Crosland (1918-77), though not before the post had been offered to Roy Jenkins (whose preference was to become Home Secretary, which he duly achieved in December 1965). Wilson (1974, p. 66) hoped that 'whoever went to education . . . would stay for two or three years at least, and his heart must be in the job . . . [Crosland] had always taken a close interest in education . . . and his stay of nearly three years in the department was a great success.' Crosland's background was Highgate School and Trinity College, Oxford, where he gained a first in PPE (philosophy, politics and economics) and became president of the Union. He returned to Oxford after the war as a lecturer in economics. He became an MP in 1950, but lost his seat between 1955 and 1959. Wilson appointed him Minister of State for Economic Affairs in 1964 and, after his spell in Education, president of the Board of Trade. In the 1970s Labour government he was to became Foreign Minister.

In 1956 he had laid out his views on education in *The Future of Socialism* with a clarity and breadth unrivalled by any of the postwar ministers. Even Edward Boyle's most lucid writing did not precede his taking office, as was the case with Crosland. Indeed, just before he arrived at the DES his publishers had helpfully produced an abridged and revised edition, thus ensuring that those who were not already familiar with his views should experience no difficulties in catching up with them. 'The schools system in Britain,' argued Crosland, 'remains the most divisive, unjust and wasteful of all the aspects of social inequality.' He identified two major and neglected controls in the system: the *social influence*, 'less educated parents, the more crowded (and noisy) homes, the smaller opportunities for extracurricular learning, of working-class children', and the *financial influences*, that is, the family's need to increase the weekly income through the earning capacity of adolescents (1964, p. 188).

On the question of secondary school reorganization, his position (1964, p. 191) was more complex than those of many of his contemporaries. 'I have never been able to understand why socialists have been so obsessed with the question of grammar schools, and so indifferent to the much more glaring injustice of the independent schools' (*ibid.*, p. 191). He suggested that there were three options facing such institutions: the first was their total proscription which he ruled out on the grounds that such action would both be an infringement of liberty and be politically impractical. The second was to encourage their gradual decline (which he thought unlikely) by the imposition of increased taxation on their sources of income. The third, which he recommended, was the gradual integration of the independent and public sectors, starting with regulations requiring independent schools to take 25 per cent of their pupils on government grants, and for fixed targets in reaching 50 per cent, 75 per cent and so on. This would mean that the financial basis of the independent sector would be brought into line with the direct-grant schools. His proposals attracted a lot of attention and some sympathy, although it must be said that they did appear to overlook two prominent features of the larger independent schools: that they were mostly boarding schools based on religious foundations, characteristics not necessarily attractive to the majority of parents or pupils.

Crosland was in favour of comprehensive schools because they made it possible 'to avoid the extreme social division caused by physical segregation into schools of widely divergent status', but he was strongly in favour of selection *within* a school, without which 'both common sense and American experience suggest this would lead to a really serious levelling-down of standards, and a quite excessive handicap to the clever child. Division into streams, according to ability, remains essential' (1964, p. 202). He was frequently accused of making education a political issue, as if it had not been one at least since the Forster Act of 1870. His view was quite clear, however: since only elected politicians can decide on expenditure for public resources, education cannot avoid being a political issue. As we have seen, the DES was still inclined to regard the comprehensive school as an *experiment* which should await research evidence before producing any long-term policy shifts. But Crosland was convinced that 'no previous educational change - including the 1944 Act - ever waited on the results of research . . . [which] can give new facts, illuminate the range of choice, show how better to achieve a given objective, but cannot say what the objective ought to be. For this must depend ... on judgments which have a value-component and a social dimension.'[1] Crosland's stay at the DES lasted until August 1967.

We have already seen that Michael Stewart's short period at the DES was a direct result of Gordon-Walker's unfortunate electoral experiences at Smethwick and Leyton. When he returned as an MP after the 1966 election, he entered the cabinet as Minister without portfolio (the Duchy of Lancaster), where his seniority in the party could be usefully employed. But when Crosland was 'promoted' from the DES to be President of the Board of Trade, Gordon-Walker (1907-81, Wellington and Christ Church College, Oxford) became Secretary of State for Education. It was a post he was to hold for less than nine months. After some bad by-election results, Wilson shuffled his government again, and Gordon-Walker was replaced by Edward Short (who had been Postmaster-General). In Wilson's view (1974, p. 523), Gordon-Walker 'had had a rough ride at Education, almost entirely for reasons outside his control - such as an important case ... in which the Department was involved within days of his taking over, and also the school-leaving age decision'.

The 'important case' was the Enfield affair, in which both the LEA and the DES were held to be in the wrong by the Court of Appeal. The court ruling was made on 23 August 1967, and Gordon-Walker was appointed Secretary of State on 28 August. Further litigation in September not only failed to ensure the introduction of the Council's comprehensive scheme, but also brought the DES in general, and Gordon-Walker in particular, some unfavourable publicity. The deferment of the plans to raise the school-leaving age to 16 was announced by Wilson with the expenditure cuts of January 1968. This was something that cut deep wounds into Labour educationists, and although Gordon-Walker was caught up in a general cabinet decision, he was held personally responsible for not fighting for an objective that had been part of the party's philosophy for half a century. Wilson had persevered with Gordon-Walker as a trusted colleague from the Attlee days. It was a gamble that did not pay off.

His replacement was Edward Short (Lord Glenamara, b. 1912), the Newcastle MP from 1951 to 1976 and a former secondary headteacher who had topped up his early training at Bede College, Durham, with a London law degree. He had been a junior Minister at the Treasury from 1964 to 1966 and Postmaster-General from 1966 to 1968. His appointment as Secretary of State bestowed on the DES a much-needed period of stability, for his 'administrative and parliamentary success at the Post Office had become a by-word . . . and he knew the local education authority side as a former leader of the Newcastle City Council' (Wilson, 1974, p. 523). As a long-standing member of the National Union of Teachers, he shared with Michael Stewart the status of being a professional schoolteacher who was given the opportunity to take on the overall responsibilities of the service. Unfortunately, we shall never know the merits of such a solution, for, like Stewart, he soon went on to higher things. In just over two years his party was out of office, and when Labour was returned in 1974 his conspicuous talents were employed as Leader of the House of Commons. Nevertheless, Short gave notice of his intentions for education by announcing soon after his arrival his aim to establish a Teachers' General Council, and in a book completed soon after his departure from the DES he set out very clearly his own personal agenda for the 1970s:

> extension of statutory school life (to be from 3 to 18);
> reduction of class size in order to promote individualized learning;
> improved teacher supply;
> expansion of the school-building programme;
> end of all selection procedures in state schools, including streaming;
> development of programmed learning with the help of technological advance;
> stronger links between social services and schools;
> tertiary education for all.

Short's agenda was based on the educational aims of 'nurturing the uniqueness of each child with a wider curriculum which respects the oneness of knowledge and is dictated more by the child's self-assessed needs than by adult assessment of them, and the development of reason and objectivity tempered by compassion' (1971, pp. 146-8).

The four Secretaries of State had averaged fewer than seventeen months in office, and the situation among the junior Ministers was at least as precarious. It must be conceded, however, that Harold Wilson at least started with an interesting experiment when he appointed Lord Bowden (b. 1910) as one of the two Ministers of State. Dr Bowden was a Cambridge physicist and Principal of the University of Manchester Institute of Science and Technology. He was given a year's leave of absence to lead the development of higher education and science at the DES. Later, in his 1974 administration, Wilson was to repeat the experiment with Lord Crowther-Hunt (see Chapter 5). It is still difficult to judge his impact on the new machinery of the DES, which now had outsiders as Permanent and Deputy Secretaries and a non-political Minister of State: if the secondment had been for a longer period, or if it had been followed immediately by other such appointments, we would perhaps now be in a better position to form a judgement.

The joint number two was Reg Prentice (b. 1923) who had been educated at Whitgift School, Croydon, and the London School of Economics. He had been unsuccessful in elections in 1950, 1951 and 1955, but won East Ham North in 1957. He was appointed Minister of State at the DES in October 1964 with responsibility for schools under Michael Stewart. A year later, when Lord Bowden gave up his responsibility for higher education under Crosland, Prentice was switched to the higher-education portfolio. In April 1966, however, Wilson moved him to the Ministry of Public Buildings and Works, and eight years later he was returned to the DES as Secretary of State. Prentice was very much a gradualist. On the public-school issue, for example, he was always in favour of integration rather than abolition and on comprehensive secondary education favoured persuasion rather than compulsion.

There were five other Ministers of State between 1965 and 1970. Edward Redhead (1902-1967), the MP for Walthamstow since 1956, had been a junior Minister at the Board of Trade before taking up his post at the DES in 1965. Like George Tomlinson in the Attlee government, Redhead had completed his schooling at an old elementary school and brought to the department that same set of fundamental beliefs in the rights of the individual to have access to good schools which had characterized the fervour of the 1940s. He was succeeded in 1966 by Goronwy Roberts (b. 1913, universities of Wales and London), the MP for Caernarvon since 1945 and previously the Minister of State at the Welsh Office. Alice (later Baroness) Bacon (b. 1911) was a Leeds MP from 1945 to 1970. She was educated at Normanton High School and Stockwell College, where she trained as a teacher. As an NUT member, she had been active in her opposition to Labour Ministers of the 1940s, becoming one of the most outspoken critics of the Wilkinson-Tomlinson policies. By 1950 she had become the principal voice of the NUT teachers in Parliament, hurling hostile national executive and conference resolutions at the ministers on every possible occasion. The committee on comprehensive schools which she chaired in 1950-51 resolved that 'the tripartite system of education does not provide equality of educational opportunity and is therefore out of tune with the needs of the day and with the aspirations of socialism' (Barker, 1972, p. 95). In opposition in 1952 she had taken the view at the party conference that the Labour Party had not given enough thought to education while in office, partly because it devoted so much energy to the reform of the social services, and partly because politicians (backed by civil servants) had come to assume that the 1944 Act had created sufficient change for at least a decade. She came to the DES in 1967 after three years at the Home Office.

Shirley Williams (b. 1930) was the daughter of Sir George Catlin and Vera Brittain. She had been educated at St Paul's Girls' School (among other schools on both sides of the Atlantic) and Somerville College, Oxford, and was the first female president of the Oxford Labour Club. After graduating, she studied at Columbia University in New York before taking up posts as a journalist on *The Financial Times* and as a teacher in Ghana. She became General Secretary of the Fabian Society, and after unsuccessfully contesting one by-election and two general elections, she was elected MP for Hitchin in October 1964. She immediately became PPS to the Minister of Health, and by 1966 she was appointed to a junior post in the Ministry of Labour. In 1967 she was promoted to Minister of State at the DES, where she remained until October 1969, with responsibility first for schools and then for higher education. For the last few months of the second Wilson government she served in the Home Office. Ironic as it now seems, she was widely predicted to become the first woman Prime Minister.

The final appointment at this level was Gerald Fowler (b. 1935), who after Northampton Grammar School and Lincoln College, Oxford, had taught in the universities of Oxford and Lancaster until he was elected MP for The Wrekin in 1966. In 1967 he was given a junior post in the Ministry of Technology, and in October 1969 he replaced Shirley Williams as Minister of State for Higher Education. As the youngest minister in Wilson's government, his nine-month stay in this post was thought at the time to have prepared him for a brilliant political career. A prolific writer, he brought to the DES a specialist knowledge:

> Any account of the distribution of power within the educational world must recognize the influence of groups other than the teachers' unions and the local authorities. Not least among them are the educational psychologists and sociologists. Their influence in converting the Labour Party and Labour Ministers [*NB*] to the view that the eleven plus examination could never accurately measure the ability and potential of children, and that in consequence the comprehensive system was the only viable form of secondary school, was perhaps decisive.
>
> (Fowler, in Lello, 1979, p. 29)

But his early optimism was later to turn sour: 'In the sixties there were beliefs in the value of educational investment in producing greater social equality and the value of educational investment in increasing the rate of economic growth. Both of these beliefs proved to be equally fallacious' (Fowler, in Broadfoot, 1981, p. 5).

Three politicians held the post of Parliamentary Under-Secretary. James Boyden (b. 1910) had progressed from elementary school to King's College, London, where he received a BA in history in 1932. He was a schoolteacher from 1933 to 1940, and after service in the war he taught at Durham University. He was elected MP for Bishop Auckland in 1959, retaining the seat for twenty years. He was at the DES from 1964 to 1965, before being promoted to the Ministry of Works and the Ministry of Defence. During his time in opposition he had pressed for maintenance allowance for 15-18-year-olds after the Crowther debate. He was replaced by Denis Howell (b. 1923, Handsworth Grammar School), who combined his schools role with that of Minister of Sport, a post which, like Minister for the Arts, from time to time was housed at the DES. For the last few months of this government Joan Lestor joined the team, with Wilson claiming particular pleasure in her appointment because it meant that all the posts at the DES were now filled by former teachers.

THE CIVIL SERVANTS

The new Department of Education and Science, formed in April 1964 in response to recommendations in the Robbins report, had for its first Permanent Secretary Sir Herbert Andrew (1910-85). He had arrived at the ministry in July of the previous year as a Deputy Secretary and designate Secretary. The new Department had additional responsibilities. In addition to its traditional obligations to schools, further education and teacher training, it now exercised extended influence over the University Grants Committee, library services, the arts and museums, and, not least, the whole area of civil science. To this more complex government department, Andrew brought substantial experience. He was a product of Manchester Grammar School and Corpus Christi College, Oxford (mathematics), and had been with the Board of Trade from 1938 to 1963. His career was thus in this respect similar to that of his predecessor, Mary Smieton (who had come from the Ministry of Labour).

> [Andrew] had no previous government experience of education, and he remained throughout his six years' sojourn a somewhat detached figure who saw his role more as a manager, keeping the department on an even keel, than one called upon to make any strong personal contribution to policy. What he did bring was an acute personal awareness of changes taking place elsewhere in Whitehall and Westminster, and how this would affect what had, till then, been a relatively cosy and non-political world of education.[2]

Throughout the 1964-70 administration the key posts of the Deputy Secretaries were held by (Sir) Toby Weaver (b. 1911), Harold Rossetti (1909-83) and Jack Embling (b. 1909). After Clifton College and Corpus Christi College, Cambridge, Weaver had taught for a couple of years before becoming an LEA education officer from 1936 to 1939. After the war he joined the ministry in 1946, rising to the rank of Deputy Secretary in 1962. He left the DES in 1973 to become a visiting professor of education at universities on both sides of the Atlantic. Weaver chaired a number of committees which produced reports that still carry his name - the Weaver Report of 1957 on maintenance allowances, the Weaver Report of 1966 on the government of colleges of education, and the Weaver Report of 1970 on a Teaching Council for England and Wales. Of all the Deputy Secretaries, he perhaps became the best known and certainly the most widely read.[3] Embling also joined the ministry in 1946, and, like Weaver, brought with him substantial previous experience of significant value to his post: after graduating from Bristol University, he had been a schoolteacher from 1930 to 1944 and an LEA officer from 1944 to 1946. He served as a Deputy from 1966 to 1971 before returning to teaching (in universities) from 1972 to 1976. Rossetti was a civil servant from 1932 to 1969, working mostly in the Ministry of Labour. He joined Education during the transfer from ministry to department and was a Deputy Secretary for six years.

(Sir) Cyril English (b. 1913) replaced Percy Wilson as Senior Chief Inspector in 1965. He had a BSc in engineering, had taught in the technical education field before the war, and had joined HMI in 1946. As the first top HMI to possess a technical background, he seemed admirably placed to be serving during Harold Wilson's white-hot technological revolution. Unfortunately his period in office lasted only two years, and he left to become Director General of the City and Guilds and to work on the Industrial Training Act. The new top HMI from 1967 to 1972 was William Elliott (b. 1910), perhaps cast more in the mould of the Roseveare tradition - St Paul's School and Queen's College, Oxford, where he read classics. He had taught in schools for three years before being recruited to HMI in 1936, and, with experience as Chief Inspector for Secondary Schools behind him, he was apparently well placed to influence the growth of the comprehensives.

POLICY

The first Queen's Speech of the Wilson administration in 1964 referred to new developments in higher education, in teacher supply, comprehensive education, and the establishment of a Public [i.e. independent] Schools Commission. None of this came as a surprise since it had all been widely publicized in advance. But if in 1945 the Labour Party had been fortunate in coming into office immediately after the 1944 Act, then it was equally fortunate in 1964 in being able to follow up the optimism and expansionism of three major reports: Crowther, Robbins and Newsom as well as the setting up in that year of the Schools' Council. As one of the latter's close observers has stressed,

> given the representative nature of the Council it was inevitable that it should be a political institution. What was remarkable was that, on the whole, it worked through consensus not conflict. It was the only forum where all the educational bodies met, on neutral territory, to discuss matters concerning the curriculum, rather than salaries, conditions of service and professional policy.
>
> (Plaskow, 1985, p. 2)

Its chequered career, however, failed to fulfil the early optimism which heralded its arrival. The growth of a new national body in education undoubtedly created certain tensions in the DES which finally surfaced fifteen years later.

'Ministers are likely to start from the assumption', Rose (1984, p. 27) has asserted, 'that manifesto intentions are practicable as well as desirable. The stronger they are as politicians *vis-à-vis* their civil servants, the more arguments they will require before abandoning these intentions.' As far as the four main items of the Queen's speech were concerned, it must be said that the new ministers encountered little opposition from political or civil service critics on either the enlargement of higher education or the increase in teacher supply. The DES had inherited the optimism and expansionism of the Eccles-Boyle decade. Building more schools, polytechnics, and colleges and filling them with more pupils, students, teachers, and lecturers could easily be measured, and growth can always be interpreted as progress. For the DES, aggrandizement became a way of life. As the number of ministers increased, so also did the number of civil servants. In 1964 the birth rate reached its highest point since the end of the First World War, and the DES annual reports throughout the 1960s continued to point to the challenge thus created. Just as the ministry's optimism of the 1940s had been fuelled by the need to build new and better classrooms, so the optimism of the 1960s was bolstered by demographic imperatives.

But growth is not the same as change. When it came to the reorganization of secondary schools and the investigation of the independent sector, expansiveness changed to inhibition, confidence to uncertainty, exhilaration to exhaustion, and optimism to suspicion. Although both of these issues concerned the same problem, that is, how adolescents should be educated, the DES managed to separate them as political problems by dealing with the comprehensives through advisory circulars and with the independents via the well-tried tactic of setting up a committee of inquiry, thus effectively removing the whole matter from parliamentary discussion.

The DES circular 10/65 *requested* LEAs to prepare and submit plans for the reorganization of secondary education on comprehensive lines. These could include 11-18 schools, two-tier schools (11-14, 14-18, etc.), 11-16 schools followed by sixth-form colleges, and middle and upper schools. There were many people in the 1960s who hoped that schools could effect social reconciliation; indeed, they believed that this was their major purpose. The concept of the *common school* in secondary education was simply an extension of the common primary school system that seemed be widely accepted as entirely wholesome and effective. It is possible, however, to point to two distinct and separate attitudes among supporters of the comprehensive school that emerged during the 1960s.

For most Labour supporters and many Conservatives, the comprehensive school simply provided more individual freedom. It did this, firstly, because it allowed the individual pupil free access to secondary education without selection, and, secondly, because it provided a far greater range of courses than had ever been possible in relatively small grammar, technical or modern schools. It was believed at that time that the comprehensive school could effectively respond to 'the demands by individuals for education as a means both to improve economic prospects and to a richer and more constructive life'. This, as we have seen, was the view of the Labour government's 1965 National Plan, but it was a concept embraced equally by the Conservatives, or at least those who occupied the middle ground of their policy-makers. Bright, clean, well-equipped palaces were springing up all over the country. Pupils were now offered such a wide range of curricular choices that brochures had to be provided for parents, and evenings set aside for choosing options. In practice, consensus politics in education continued to flourish, for 'the school system . . . is exceedingly strong in its ability to generate and sustain its own policies. The continuities are far stronger than are the changes' (Kogan, 1978, p. 47). Even when, as we shall see later, the consensus was broken after the next election, the momentum of comprehensivization still resulted in the doubling of the number of pupils in such schools by the end of the Conservative government in 1974 compared with the number at the end of the Labour government in 1970.

The second distinctive attitude among the pro-comprehensive lobby was represented by other Labour supporters, for whom the purpose of the comprehensive school was socialization, with a corresponding lessening of talk about opportunities for the individual and an increase in the pursuit of the culture of collectivism and equalization. Thus, the comprehensive secondary school had already achieved the status of a political football both within the separate parties and between them. It was a ball, moreover, that continued to be kicked around in a conspicuously unproductive manner throughout the next decade. As Marwick has indicated, 'Although the potential for mobility through the educational system was greater than it had been in the 1930s . . . the whole system still very much replicated the division of social structure into working, lower-middle, upper-middle, and upper classes.'[4]

By the time we reach October 1969, for what proved to be the last session of this Wilson Government, it was still proposed to introduce a bill 'to require laggard local authorities to come into line with Government policy requiring the *preparation of plans* [my italics] to reorganize secondary education on comprehensive lines' (Wilson, 1974, p. 721). In the event, when Parliament was dissolved in May 1970, no such bill had arrived. As for Wilson himself, he had by now developed some enthusiasm for comprehensive secondary schools: 'I was greatly impressed by what I had found in this [Linthwaite] and other comprehensive schools; how the very size of the school and staff gives pupils a far greater freedom of choice, in permutating subjects for "O" and "A" levels - one of the under-publicised achievements of comprehensive secondary education' (*ibid.*, p. 739).

By 1970 some 30 per cent of secondary pupils were attending comprehensive schools. But if secondary reorganization had made only modest progress during the remaining years of the Labour government, the Public Schools Commission had got absolutely nowhere. Set up in December 1965 (again under the chairmanship of Sir John Newsom), the commission was asked 'to advise on the best way of integrating the public schools with the state system of education'. In October 1967 the Commission received amended terms of reference so that it could also consider the intrinsically related question of the direct-grant grammar schools. The Commission's first report was published in 1968, and its second report (under the chairmanship of Professor Donnison) followed in 1970, the year in which there was a change of government. Thus, the 1964 election proposals received nothing but further discussion during the six years of the Labour government. When Labour returned to office in 1974 it did nothing to revive the Newsom recommendations, but implemented part of Donnison's by discontinuing the grant-maintained grammar schools from 1975.

Secondary education was not the only subject on which the DES received official reports. In August 1963 Sir Edward Boyle had asked the Central Advisory Council to inform him on the developments in primary schools. The committee formed under the chairmanship of Lady Plowden did not produce a final report until January 1967. There was some justification for this, since the report was not only very wide-ranging, but based on substantial research. It quickly achieved the status of a talisman for progressive primary education. Its influence was in fact greater among teachers than within the DES, since it endorsed ideas that professional practice was already tentatively exploring. In fact the DES had no real need to ask Plowden to reveal information that was already available from HMI. Nevertheless, the high profile of the report did provide primary teachers with an injection of confidence that lasted until the early 1980s, when suddenly 'Plowden methods' were blamed for all the ills of the British educational system. Some of the recommendations were given government support: the notion of educational priority areas was put in place almost immediately; the development of more middle schools was supported; an expansion of nursery education took place in the 1970s; and parents were formally encouraged to participate in the educational process. Other recommendations took much longer to achieve: it was not until 1980, for example, that the requirement that all new teachers should have passed O-level Maths and English was introduced. And some were lost in discussion.

From the perspective of the 1980s Shirley Williams cited the problem of nursery assistants as an example of the apparent and undesirable power of pressure groups to influence the DES without being accountable to the electorate in a general sense. She believed that only the teachers' union stood between government policy to provide a massive increase in nursery education and its implementation. The Plowden recommendation that nursery classes should be staffed by nursery assistants (with six months' training), who would be supervised by qualified teachers at the ratio of one to four or five, apparently had her personal support as well as that of the DES. The teachers' viewpoint, however, was not based on the usual prejudices of self-interest. The professional associations were not protecting the interests of their members since there were very few qualified nursery teachers in the workforce at the time. Their concern centred on the very deep conviction, widely supported by psychologists, that the learning development of 3-5-year-olds was of crucial importance and required as much genuine professional help as, say, sixth-formers preparing for university entrance. At a pragmatic level, there was also a fundamental flaw in the Plowden recommendation, since most nursery classes would be located within existing infant schools, which could normally accommodate only one such class. A qualified nursery supervisor would thus have to relate to four or five different schools at the same time. Ironically, there is more of a case to be made for assistants, especially those based in learning-resources centres equipped with computer-assisted learning packages, being employed on post-16 courses than there can ever be in programmes designed for young children.

For many readers the Plowden Report will always mean Lady Plowden's 1967 report. But, curiously, it was the other Plowden Report, by Lord Plowden in 1961 on the management and control of public expenditure, which had the more immediate effect on the DES in 1967. For it was then that the DES belatedly established a small planning branch to advise on the strategic allocation of resources in an attempt to replace the somewhat piecemeal approach of the past. For the next twenty years the financial planning of the DES was to become increasingly sophisticated as successive governments moved towards Public Expenditure Surveys and annual White Papers on departmental running costs. The planning branch was faced with an immediate problem. The government had set 1970-71 as the year in which a school-leaving age of 16 would come into effect, and the DES annual report of 1967 proclaimed that 'preparations to raise the school leaving age . . . gave further stimulus to a growing movement towards curricular reform in the schools'. But in January 1968 the cabinet decided that the UK's economic position could not justify such an increase in the educational budget, and a new date of 1973 was proposed. The planners were therefore faced with a question mark over the not insubstantial problem of when to provide for an extra year of secondary students.

Two other reports surfaced towards the end of this period: the Dainton Report on *The Flow of Candidates in Science and Technology into Higher Education* (1968) and the Haslegrave Report on *Technician Courses and Examinations* (1969). Neither of these achieved any real prominence at the time, and therein lies their significance. Science and technology had become political slogans when Wilson arrived at Downing Street. The formation of the DES itself, the provision made by the Nuffield Foundation for science teaching, and the enthusiasm for science of the newly formed Schools Council and the Council for National Academic Awards might have been expected to have led to an improvement in the educational system. But Dainton was actually confronted with a general decline in science in secondary schools and Haslegrave with an unsatisfactory approach to technology. The problems surrounding science and technology teaching in the UK were both financial (science and technology were more expensive to teach) and attitudinal (the arts offered a broader education). Looking back at the late nineteenth century, Correlli Barnett (1986, p. 230) has cogently argued that

> the development of technical schools and colleges in Britain had been stultified by the same combination of prejudice against state intervention and lack of local government organs. In vain did the Royal Commissions of the 1860s, 1870s and 1880s amass their evidence about the excellence of European technical education and call for Britain to repent of her neglect before it was too late. The nearer a proposed blueprint approached the Swiss or German model, the less acceptable to political and industrial opinion it proved.

Barnett (p. 223) lays the blame for the anti-science prejudices fairly and squarely at the doors of the nineteenth-century romantic idealists, Thomas Arnold, J.S. Mill and Newman.

> On state-funded elementary and secondary education in Britain the long-term impact of that triumph of 'liberal education' in the Victorian debate was clear and decisive: the intellectual and emotional stream can be traced from its spring in the romantic movement, especially religious revivalism, all the way down to the broad current of British national schooling . . . It was not just a question here of the general influence exerted by the convictions that had come to prevail among the intelligentsia and informed public opinion at large by the second half of Victoria's reign . . . it was that the development of state education in Britain at critical

> junctures fell directly to members of that governing élite which had been moulded by the Arnoldian public school and Newmanian Oxbridge.

That same governing élite still formed the administrative core of the DES, and thus the responsibility to create new patterns of curriculum development remained mostly in the hands of the cultivated generalist who found unacceptable the Dainton recommendation that all sixth-form studies should include some science and mathematics. Not until the early 1990s did such radical ideas for the curriculum again reach the public domain. When Herbert Andrew concluded his annual DES report in 1964 he employed language resonant with nineteenth-century traditions and which remained pervasive throughout the 1960s: 'There is evident,' he reassured his readers, 'a conscious striving after that pursuit of the balanced man which has engaged education at decisive stages in the evolution of the Western tradition' (DES, *Year Book*, 1964, p. 33). Unfortunately the 'balanced man' formed an insufficiently high proportion of school productivity, and the UK's economic decline continued to be celebrated in the champagne of educational self-delusion.

Outside the DES, events were taking place that were to have both a direct and indirect effect on the development of educational policies in the next decade. Not long before the 1966 election, the Labour government had set up a wide-ranging investigation of the Civil Service under the chairmanship of Lord Fulton, the Vice-Chancellor of Sussex University, and a former Oxford don in philosophy and political science. Like many other academics of his generation, he had experienced Whitehall from the inside as a civil servant during the war. The Fulton Report was published in June 1968, and its implications for the reorganization of the DES, as for all the other government departments, were substantial, impressive and of formidable significance to the whole machinery of the government of education. Wilson (1974, p. 540) received the report with undisguised enthusiasm:

> The committee laid great stress on two developments I had repeatedly pressed. The first was a freer two-way movement between the civil service and other areas of our national life, such as private and public industry, local government and the professions. The second was the development of regionalism ... [with, for new recruits] ample opportunities ... which would bring them into contact with the public.

In the Fulton/DES context, two names were particularly crucial. One was Lord Boyle, a member of the Fulton Committee and the former Minister of Education. The other was Norman (later Lord) Crowther-Hunt, a key member of the Fulton committee, and later a Minister of State at the DES from October 1974 to January 1976. The committee, therefore, had direct access to the views of perhaps the most gifted politician to work in education since Butler, and also (and perhaps of even more importance for the future) to the investigatory skills of Crowther-Hunt, who was later to find himself in the unique position of being able to bring to the DES the fruits of Fulton's wisdom. As far as the outcomes of Fulton are concerned, it is appropriate to leave the analysis until Chapter 5, when it will be relevant to take account of Crowther-Hunt's later ministerial perspective on the matter. For the present, it will be enough to summarize Fulton's recommendations:

new recruitment programmes looking for specialists with 'relevant degrees';
career specialization;
a civil service college;
a civil service department;
unified grading system for civil servants;
increased exchange between civil servants and industry/professions;
departmental planning units involving specialist advisers.

Another aspect of the government's election policies which might have had a considerable impact on education was regionalism. In the early stages of the Wilson administration, plans were introduced to encourage the 'maximum regional devolution of Government departments' (Wilson, 1974, p. 64). It was proposed that education (together with other aspects of social planning, industrial planning and communications) should form an element of the work of the Regional Economic Planning Councils which were being established by the newly created Department of Economic Affairs, with George Brown as its Secretary of State. Regional educational provision would be a contributory component brought into planning by representatives both from the LEAs and from the regional universities. The universities, moreover, were to be provided with research contracts to help establish the nature of regional priorities. The idea of regionalism in the organization of education has cropped up at various times since 1945. It has always failed to secure a foothold for two main reasons: firstly, because it has been seen by the LEAs as an extra layer between them and the DES; secondly, because Whitehall has not wished to lose its grip on education in England. The fact that Welsh schools have traditionally been administered by the Welsh Office, Scottish schools by the Scottish Education Department, and schools in Northern Ireland by the Northern Ireland Office means that the British education system is already regional. Perhaps if England were to have been divided into six or seven regions (just as HMI divisions are), and if the universities and higher education generally had been added to such regional responsibilities, the DES might have been better placed during the last twenty years to exercise a coordinating role in policy development and evaluation rather than the confused managerial role that it has blindly pursued with such destabilizing enthusiasm. But that would be another story.[5]

It was, perhaps, in one of his election broadcasts for the 1970 campaign that Wilson's personal view emerged of what six years of Labour government had achieved: 'This is the first government,' he proclaimed, 'which is spending more on our children's education than on armaments and defence.'[6] But there were other achievements. In the Robbins-recommended expansion of higher education, there were now more universities and CNAA polytechnics and colleges, and the establishment of the Open University was a major achievement.

Following Newsom, the process of rationalizing secondary education and the discrediting of the eleven-plus selection procedures were well under way. Plowden had signalled the innovations in primary schools and the expansion of nursery education. Finally, the establishment of the Schools' Council had begun to make some impact on the level of educational debate at the DES.

But what of the DES itself? During the years 1968-70 a Commons Select Committee under the chairmanship of Fred Willey had undertaken two monumental tasks. The first was an exhaustive investigation of 'student relations' and the problems brought to light by the widespread student unrest both at home and abroad. The second was an inquiry into teacher training (which led eventually to the establishment of the James committee; see Chapter 4). When, in April 1970, the chairman asked the direct question, 'Who controls the curriculum?', Sir Herbert Andrew replied in these terms:

> The curriculum is not under central control . . . we have a concern with and influence upon the proportion of teachers who are trained . . . but the concept of curricula is a matter on which HMI gives advice but over which we do not exercise control. We may occasionally offer a comment or piece of advice of a very general kind . . . generally the academic side is not under the control of the Department any more than other parts of the education system.[7]

This neat summary defines the political situation precisely. Despite Eccles and his Curriculum Study Group, Boyle and the Schools Council, Crosland and his circulars, and Short and his proposed replacement of the 1944 Act, the DES had managed somehow to retain its distance from education policy as opposed to schools' management for another decade.

NOTES

1 Speech delivered at the North of England Education Conference, January 1966, and reprinted in Crosland (1974), p. 207.

2 *The Times*, 23 August 1985. See also Andrew (1964).

3 See the Bibliography for further information.

4 That is, modern, grammar, direct-grant and independent-HMC schools. Marwick (1982), p. 60.

5 For government statistical purposes, England is often divided into eight regions. With their 1986 populations this would create the following pattern: South-East 17.3 m, North-West 6.4 m, West Midlands 5.2 m, Yorkshire and Humberside 4.9 m, South-West 4.5 m, East Midlands 3.9 m, North 3.1 m, and East Anglia 2.0 m.

6 Wilson (1974), p. 787. See also Lapping (1970) and Stacy (1975).

7 House of Commons Select Committee on Education and Science (1970), *Report on Teacher Training*, p. 419.

Chapter 4

'Mine eyes do itch: doth that bode weeping?': the Conservative government 1970-74

Encouraged by the opinion polls, good municipal election results and a successful by-election, Harold Wilson decided to call a general election on 18 June 1970, some nine months before his term would have finished. A month of intensive electioneering focused for some and trivialized for others the main policy differences between the parties. In the party conferences of the late 1960s Labour had continued to devote protracted discussions to a whole range of educational topics, top of which remained secondary school reorganization, but which also included quite detailed recommendations on the education of the handicapped and maladjusted, on school meals and milk, on playgroups and nursery schools, on grants for pupils wishing to stay on at school after 15, and on the further improvement of both primary and secondary school buildings. The Conservatives had continued to condemn what they called the 'hasty and ill-considered imposition of a comprehensive system', and latched on to the Labour government's evident failure to provide sufficient financial resources for the current expansion including its deferment of raising the school-leaving age to 16.

When the manifestos were published, the Liberals in *What a life!* promised to improve the out-of-date primary schools, to increase nursery and further education provision, and to support non-selective secondary education, provided that options beyond the 11-18 model were encouraged. In *A Better Tomorrow* the Conservatives identified the fundamental problem of all the UK's social services as the shortage of resources. It proposed to shift educational spending towards the primary sector (including nurseries), and for secondary education the party now accepted that selection at the age of 11 was invalid. With *Now Britain's Strong - Let's Make It Great to Live In* (a slogan that surely deserved the derision it quickly attracted), Labour deliberately linked education with social equality and predicted the introduction of an Education Bill 'to replace the 1944 Act'. It claimed that 75 per cent of the LEAs had already submitted plans for secondary reorganization and that measures would be introduced to make sure the remaining 25 per cent followed suit. There was no mention of discontinuing the independent sector.

Just before the election the *TES* published statements by both Edward Short and Margaret Thatcher, the shadow Education Minister. Short wrote of ending selection in secondary schools, increasing nursery provision, expanding higher education, providing maintenance grants for the 15-18-year-olds, and a new Act 'to set targets for the next 30 years'. Thatcher, by contrast, dwelt almost entirely on the past achievements of the previous Conservative epoch, extolling the virtues of the Schools' Council, the Newsom, Plowden and Robbins Reports, and the great contribution of Eccles and Boyle to policy development.

In the light of subsequent events, much of her statement now seems particularly ironic. Particularly interesting were two assertions: that 'building techniques and design were revolutionised to the great benefit of both education and the public purse', and that 'education is essentially a humane service dealing with human and social problems'. In Chapter 6 we shall encounter the Audit Commission's view, expressed with considerable vigour in both 1988 and 1991, that the building mistakes of the Eccles boom had simply created 'a time bomb waiting to go off'; while terms such as 'humane service' entirely disappeared from the vocabulary of Thatcherism. But perhaps the most surprising single item in the statement was one of omission: not a single reference was made to the comprehensives or the eleven-plus. As a result of the general election, the Conservatives, with 46.2 per cent of the votes, won an overall majority of 31, with Labour polling 43.1 per cent and the Liberals 7.5 per cent.

THE POLITICIANS

When Prime Minister Edward Heath appointed Margaret Thatcher Secretary of State for Education, he set in motion a series of events which led to his own political downfall. Yet, traditionally, the DES was seen as, if not a graveyard for political aspirations, at least a lay-by. No Minister or Secretary of State for Education since the war had become a party leader, although Butler, Stewart and Crosland had subsequently held top cabinet posts, and Shirley Williams was for a time a joint leader of the SDP. Thatcher was to remain at the DES for the duration of the Heath government[1] (three years and nine months), making her uninterrupted stay in office the longest since George Tomlinson's under Attlee. In the same period five junior ministers filled three posts.

Margaret Thatcher (b. 1925) entered Parliament in 1959 after Grantham Grammar School and Somerville College, Oxford, had led her first to a career as a research chemist and then to the law. By 1961 she had already become a junior Minister in Pensions and National Insurance. In opposition she was given a variety of jobs, shadowing ministers in Housing, the Treasury, Fuel and Power, Transport, and finally, though briefly, Education after Boyle had relinquished the post in 1969, the year in which the first of the *Black Papers* appeared.[2] She was thought by her DES staff to possess 'an innate wariness of the civil service, quite possibly even a distrust . . . [her actions] were quite unlike anything we'd come across from predecessors and later on I think we saw that this was only the beginnings of the revelation of a character that we'd have to get used to and that we hadn't run into before' (Pile, in Young and Sloman, 1986, p. 24). One of her biographers has pointed to

> her difficulty with the style and practice of the Civil Service. It was uncongenial to her, especially that of the Ministry of Education which was traditionally inward-looking and academically minded. She was quick to judge, quick to decide and quick to act. A brisk argument, which she would begin, was perfectly acceptable to her. But when after a decision had been taken she was presented with more argument and more delay in getting something done, she become impatient and did not conceal it. Her

> civil servants ... were not used to dealing with a woman minister, and found her self-confident and sometimes abrasive approach disconcerting and confusing.
>
> (Harris, 1988, pp. 55-6)

As a matter of fact, her Permanent Secretary had been recruited to the ministry in the days of Ellen Wilkinson and had served under Florence Horsburgh in the early 1950s, as had three of the Deputy-Secretaries, Paul Odgers, John Hudson and Edward Simpson.

There were times, especially during her first two years in office, when she was generally regarded as an unpopular Minister. She was often in conflict with teachers, students and LEAs, and, as later events proved, with other members of the cabinet. It was also true that

> education is not usually an exciting or a glamorous political subject, and her views about it were not such as to be able to alter this ... If at the beginning of her stint as Minister of Education most people would not have thought of her as a future Prime Minister, by the end of it they would have seen nothing to cause them to change their minds.
>
> (Harris, 1988, p. 57)

We may need to remind ourselves, however, of the level of turmoil that the DES faced at the start of her period in office. In the space of only three years Margaret Thatcher was the *fourth* Secretary of State; there had been five different Labour junior Ministers, and two new Conservatives; there was also a change of Permanent Secretary and on top of all this there were radical policy changes that were marked 'action this day'. But Thatcher's 'self-sufficiency was quite remarkable. Most senior civil servants feel that their principal objective or role is to offer ministers sound, balanced, neutral advice on the facts ... I don't think she needed any of that. She never seemed to need any help' (Harris, 1988, p. 25). She rapidly acquired a reputation for incessant devotion to her ministerial duties, and 'she showed very little interest in anything outside the Department's brief ... she devoured that, she mastered that down to the last statistic and the last comma' (*ibid*, p. 59). She came to be regarded as

> clever in the sense that she was able to absorb an immense amount of information ... But this may only have been the result of a competent ability to remember things ... and did not necessarily prove that here was an enormously sophisticated intellectual mind ... I do not think she ever showed an enormous intellectual brilliance in any field. And the wisdom that comes from having to make the right decision when there is nothing else to guide you is not something I noticed her possessing.
>
> (*ibid*., pp. 62-3)

It is sometimes difficult to separate Margaret Thatcher as Education Minister from Margaret Thatcher as Prime Minister, just as it had been with Butler the Minister of Education and Butler the Chancellor of the Exchequer.

Certainly when she was at the DES she continually sought more money from the Treasury for the expansionist policies of the 1972 White Paper, even during the aftermath of the oil crisis. It was, after all, still the fashion for ministers to fight for their corner. Moreover, the Heath cabinet was more concerned with entry into Europe, the price of oil, the Irish question and industrial relations than it was with education policy, much of which continued to rumble on unchanged from the 1960s. As for Margaret Thatcher herself, one editorial at least seemed particularly apt: 'She has commanded more respect than affection ... she remains an extremely determined politician and contender for office in a future government' (*TES*, 8 March 1974).

Heath did not appoint a Minister of State for Education,[3] preferring to slim down the number in government. The two posts of Parliamentary Under-Secretary were first filled by Belstead from the Lords and van Straubenzee from the Commons. Lord Belstead (b. 1932) was an hereditary peer who continued the Eton and Christ Church connection at the DES between 1970 and 1973, but who brought to his office four years' experience as a teacher of history in a small preparatory school and extensive knowledge of farming in Suffolk. He was, however, destined later to become a minister at the Home Office and Leader of the House of Lords in the Thatcher governments. His replacement at the DES was another hereditary peer, Lord Sandford (b. 1920), who after Eton had served in the Navy until 1956 before being ordained in the Church of England in 1958. He joined the government in 1970 as a junior at the Ministry of Housing and was transferred to the DES in the last year of the Heath administration.

After Westminster School William van Straubenzee (b. 1924) served in the Army. He had been elected as MP for Wokingham in 1959, and immediately gained experience of education matters by acting as Eccles's PPS from 1960 to 1962. From 1968 to 1970 he was an active member of the Commons Select Committee on Education and Science, a duty which was an invaluable apprenticeship for the tasks ahead.[4] In 1969 Heath made him a spokesman for education, and between 1970 and 1972 his DES brief was higher education. On his appointment he said, 'We must encourage teachers and emphasize their importance. I firmly believe in a *national enquiry* into teacher training which is thorough-going and *swift* - as opposed to a two- or three-year Royal Commission' (*TES*, 3 July 1970). In the event, the James Report did not appear until December 1972.

When van Straubenzee was promoted to Minister of State at the Northern Ireland Office in 1972, he was replaced by Norman St John-Stevas (b. 1929), a barrister educated at Ratcliffe and Fitzwilliam College, Cambridge, and the MP for Chelmsford since 1964. His actual period of responsibility for education was brief as he was soon given the post of Minister of State for the Arts, but he acted as shadow Education Minister during the Wilson-Callaghan governments of the 1970s. When the Conservatives returned to government in 1979, however, he was made Leader of the House, and thus yet another apprenticeship in education was squandered. He was replaced by Timothy Raison (b. 1929), yet again a product of Eton and Christ Church, Oxford. He had been the editor of the *New Scientist* from 1956 to 1961 and of *New Society* from 1962 to 1968, and a member of the Central Advisory Council on Education between 1963 and 1966. Raison was elected MP for Aylesbury in 1970 and became Parliamentary

Under-Secretary at the DES in December 1973. His stay of fewer than three months, cut short by the general election in February 1974, leaves him a contender both for the record shortest stay at the department and possibly for its greatest individual loss. His experience in working on the Plowden Report, with ILEA and with the Youth Service Development Council might have made him a valuable long-term investment in education, but when the Conservatives returned to power in 1979, he was overlooked. We must make the most, therefore, of a useful summary of his views which he thoughtfully provided while in opposition and which reveals in its elegance of argument a natural succession to Boyle's enlightened imagination.

The main planks of Raison's argument (1979) were these: that 'the Secretary of State acts as the guardian of the education system, rather than its administrative head - though of course he has a crucially important role in winning resources for education and then in determining their allocation (p. 15); that 'the question of whether the Department has an ethos and policy-orientation of its own is an interesting one, but I doubt whether such an ethos depends on the legislative and administrative framework within which it operates' (p. 17); and that 'whatever else one may say about the education pattern, it has been normally fairly sensitive; and while its effectiveness certainly needs to be improved, sensitivity is a valuable ingredient of achieving this. The antennae of the DES are fairly responsive; the isolation of the DES about which other government departments grumble is not isolation from education on the ground' (p. 18).

Raison rejected reforms which proposed a private corporation or removal from local government (like the NHS) or regionalism, in that they would, he then thought, simply provide an extra layer. He recommended the revival of the Central Advisory Council, to be chaired by the Secretary of State, with the DES Planning Unit available to serve the council (p. 19). He was critical of using funding to LEAs as a way of enforcing DES policy and favoured local decision-making after general government allocations.

Raison was at his best, however, in dealing with the balancing act that was demanded of liberal politicians from both major parties in their approach to state intervention in the curriculum. On the one hand, he, like Shirley Williams, recognized that in secondary schools the provision of unlimited curricular options created as many problems as it solved. On the other hand, he (again like Williams) recognized only too clearly the dangers of a state-determined curriculum, with its highly undesirable political overtones. He believed that the Secretary of State already had the powers to influence the curriculum through approval mechanisms for secondary examinations, and that, through a revived Central Advisory Council and a properly working Schools' Council, improvements in curriculum planning were within reasonable, if not easy, reach. In the light of the assessment regulations of the 1988 Act, it is worth noting that in 1976 Raison suggested that appropriate testing points might be at the ages of 8, 11 and 14 'to provide information about the progress of the individual child . . . information, for use within the system only, about the school and the class within the school . . . and national statistics'.[5] Raison later became the chairman of the Education, Science and Arts Committee (ESAC) for two years from December 1987.

THE CIVIL SERVANTS

The arrival of Margaret Thatcher at the DES in June 1970 preceded by only six weeks the official retirement of Sir Herbert Andrew, the Permanent Secretary since the formation of the department in April 1964. His replacement had in fact been appointed in the first week of May, some two weeks before the announcement of the general election. The new man, (Sir) William Pile (b. 1919), was therefore brought in early to ease the double problems of transition created by changes of Secretary of State *and* Permanent Secretary. He had been a Deputy Secretary at the Home Office since 1967 and Director General of the Prison Service since 1969.[6] Unlike the two previous appointments (Andrew and Smieton), however, Pile had already gained substantial experience of the Ministry of Education to which he was first recruited in 1947 after serving in the Army throughout the war. Apart from a short period in the Cabinet Office, he progressed steadily within the department until 1966. His transfer to the Home Office provided him with the crucial opportunity of reaching Deputy Secretary level well before his fiftieth birthday, and of working with the Home Secretary, James Callaghan, during the socially turbulent years of the late 1960s.

Pile had been educated at the Royal Masonic School and St Catherine's College, Cambridge. He was to remain at the DES until 1976, experiencing the very different styles of Margaret Thatcher, Reg Prentice and Fred Mulley as Secretaries of State. We have a first-hand account of the workings of the DES from his own pen (written in 1975 but not published until 1979). The flavour of his writing and the essence of his beliefs are revealed in the opening pages:

> An education department of state like the DES has both to try to influence the historic development of the education service and to respond sensitively to external events. It works to shape the environment in which it discharges its task and the environment shapes the policies, procedures and personalities of those in the Department. The history of that developing environment is therefore inexorably a part of the life and character of the Department.[7]

Pile believed that there were twelve 'salient trends and factors' which could be identified in postwar British educational planning. We need to pay special attention to this list, for it represents the nearest we can get to an official 1970s interpretation of events, and it reveals some of the priorities and prejudices that were brought into play 'to influence the historic development of the education service'. These were the twelve 'trends and factors'

demographic trends
population movements
children's health
technological change
deprivation
the explosion of knowledge
the impact of the media

the development of educational research
changing ideas about the nature and aims of education
the ideal of equality
the demand for participation
the scarcity of resources

The extent to which the DES would be deeply concerned with demography and regional variations is not unexpected, though the fact that they are placed at the top of the list does perhaps illustrate the extent to which the DES traditionally saw itself as reactive rather than proactive. That the DES should historically have been centrally concerned with children's health (and, relatedly, the provision of school meals, milk, clothing and transport) is again, in the context of the 1944 Act, unsurprising; but the fact that such responsibilities had not been passed to another more appropriate department (such as the DHSS) in the restructuring of 1964 is still a matter of concern.

By technological change, Pile was referring to technology in society rather than technology (especially computing) in learning processes. 'A technologically advanced society,' he declared, 'requires from the education system a greatly increased output of qualified scientists and technologists, and of supporting technicians and craftsmen' (Pile, 1979, p. 14). No doubt this was a 'salient trend' in the early 1970s: it had been so in the 1870s, as Barnett abrasively emphasized in *The Audit of War*. What is lacking in Pile's account is why so little action had been taken on this matter throughout his career at the DES. It was not, after all, until the 1988 Act enforced, through the National Curriculum, the teaching of both science and technology throughout the 11 years of compulsory schooling that the DES did more than offer platitudes and palliatives on this crucial national problem.

'On deprivation', Pile wrote, 'there has been wider recognition that [many] areas constitute a special problem for social policy generally, and for education in particular', but again he said little about how such problems had been tackled in the past or should be approached now. The 'explosion of knowledge' and 'the impact of the media' are phrases that now seem peculiarly dated, but the issues in terms of curricular adaptation are still with us. As for the development of educational research, one is glad to see it mentioned, even if the reality has been a sustained policy of distancing the department from academic research that would be unthinkable in the Treasury or the departments of the Environment, Health or Trade and Industry.

Pile acknowledges that the 1960s had brought some shifts of emphasis to the 'nature and aims' of education, particularly in relation to the post-Plowden curriculum. 'Such an approach,' he wrote, 'implies an educational system designed to take account of the needs and interests of children . . . to encourage each child to realize its [*sic*] own potential rather than simply to assimilate knowledge or instruction in skills.' For Pile, the three most significant implications of these ideas during his period of office in the 1970s were 'the designs of school buildings . . . the development of the curriculum and the training of teachers' (Pile, 1979, p. 19).

In respect of the 'ideal of equality', Pile concedes that the notion of equality of opportunity had been reinforced, via Plowden and Halsey, with the idea of 'positive discrimination for the deprived and underprivileged'. He is quick to point out, however, that 'where resources are scarce, there is room for argument as to the extent to which resources should be devoted to the underprivileged at the expense of the able, and many would argue that a too exclusive preoccupation with the social aim of education in promoting equality may result in a neglect of other aims such as the pursuit of quality and excellence' (*ibid*, p. 2). Phrases such as 'room for argument' and 'many would argue that' may be interpreted by many as pure Sir Humphrey-speak for 'over my dead body'. When Max Morris (as president of the National Union of Teachers) met him in the context of a meeting with Margaret Thatcher, he 'treated the teachers' protests with lofty and amused contempt' (Morris and Griggs, 1988, p. 2). The pursuit of quality and excellence, became, of course, the theme tune of the 1980s. Others have argued, however, that where resources are scarce (and when have they not been in the public sector?), the deprived and underprivileged do have first call on services, for the 'privileged' already have access to an enormously supportive private education system.

Participation and accountability are defined by Pile as 'demands' rather than as rights, and he notes that 'successive governments have shown themselves aware of these aspirations'. The level of participation is consultation (without obligation), in which 'the Department is usually ready to receive representations from organizations . . . and not infrequently consults them when new policies are in preparation'. For Pile, participation clearly does not mean partnership, a slogan that was to gain currency in the 1980s. Of course such consultative procedures, including even the reports of parliamentary committees, could be, and generally were, ignored with impunity. Finally, on the resources issue, Pile laments that in the welfare state, education has had to compete with housing, health and other social services, to say nothing of the defence budget and the problems of inflation. 'There can be few,' he declares with resignation, 'who have been engaged in the administration of education in this period who have not sometimes felt condemned to work for ever in a Looking-Glass country, where it was always necessary to run faster to stay in the same place' (Pile, 1979, pp. 21-2). Who in this context, we may ask, was Alice and who was the Red Queen? And did the Red Queen's cries of 'Faster! faster!' get her into Downing Street?

If we compare these components of policy with those emphasized both in the party conference resolutions and in the election manifestos of the period, we can begin to understand some of the ways in which the politicians and bureaucrats interacted. The 'historic development of the education service' is a process of infinite complexity, in which, like the characters in Lewis Carroll's earlier masterpiece, we can never be sure that people mean what they say or say what they mean. And we also need to keep an open mind on a general concern articulated by Tony Benn (1989, p. 62):

> The civil service sees itself as being above the party battle, with a political position of its own to defend against all-comers, including incoming governments armed with their philosophy and

> programme ... Civil service policy is an amalgam of views that have been developed over a long period of time and in the development of which the civil service itself has played a notable role. It draws some of its force from a deep commitment to the benefits of continuity ... To that extent, the Permanent Secretaries could be held to prefer consensus politics and hope they would remain the basis for all policy and administration.

At Deputy Secretary level, the new recruits were Paul Odgers (b. 1915), Claud Wright (b. 1917), John Hudson (b. 1920) and Edward Simpson (b. 1922). Odgers was educated at Rugby and New College, Oxford, and had been recruited in the old Board of Education days in 1937 when its presidents were still peers of the realm. His career took him to the ministry and then the DES, and after widening his Whitehall experience in the late 1960s he returned to the department as a Deputy from 1971 to 1975. By contrast, Wright (Charterhouse and Christ Church, Oxford) reached the DES for the first time on his appointment as Deputy in 1971. His career in the civil service since 1939 had been entirely connected with the War Office and the Ministry of Defence. He was to remain at the DES until 1975. Hudson had joined the Ministry of Education in 1946 after the City of London School and Jesus College, Oxford. He held the position of Deputy from 1969 to 1980. Simpson had come to the civil service with a first in Mathematics from Queen's University, Belfast. He had joined the Ministry of Education in 1947 and, with three short periods elsewhere in Whitehall, had worked his way up the DES's promotion ladder until he reached Deputy Secretary in 1973, a post which he held until his retirement in 1982.

The new chief HMI (now formally designated a Deputy Secretary) in 1972 was Henry French (b. 1910), at 62 the oldest such appointment. A product of a Brighton grammar school and Woolwich Polytechnic, he had specialized in engineering, but had no schoolteaching experience. His work as an HMI had concentrated on further education and engineering, like that of his predecessor Sir Cyril English, with whom he also shared the distinction of remaining for only two years in post.

THE POLICIES

In the twenty-year life of the Ministry of Education between 1944 and 1964, the British education system had been dominated by a single characteristic, and that was growth. In 1964 the rising birth rate had topped the 1 million mark again for the first time since the end of the First World War. In turn, primary schools, then secondary schools, then further and higher education institutions had struggled to keep up with demand. By the end of the 1960s there were more pupils and students, more teachers and lecturers, and more buildings and building programmes than at any time before. The mood of politicians, administrators and teachers was almost unremittingly optimistic. Expansion was the key word and speeches were littered with the vocabulary of extension, development, enlargement and widening opportunity. That the growth in educational provision had in fact never kept up with the growth in population and that the UK was already dropping behind most of the leading industrial countries in post-16 education were factors which most politicians chose to ignore.

But when Lord Butler published his memoirs, *The Art of the Possible*, in 1971, he was able to take a reasonably dispassionate view of the fate of the 1944 Act, in which he had been so personally involved during the war. From the peace of the Master's Lodge at Trinity College, Cambridge, and from the perspective of the years before the oil crisis, he listed the following as unfulfilled promises:

nursery schools - still inadequate provision;
further education day-release schemes - still only voluntary, and taken up by less than 50 per cent of 15-18-year-olds;
raising of school-leaving age to 16;
secondary schools - muddled response to their development;
religious education - perfunctory provision.

How do these 'faults of omission' tie up with the policies of Heath's government and Thatcher's tenure of the office of Secretary of State? In respect of nursery education there was a marked surge in provision. In the 1972 White Paper, *Education: A Framework for Expansion*, it was proposed to reach Plowden targets by 1981. The DES became very enthusiastic about nurseries: in 1970 there were 17 per cent of 3- and 4-year-olds using LEA resources, but by 1975 this figure had already risen to 28 per cent and by 1980 to 39 per cent. Although these fell far short of the White Paper's recommendations, they were, in the light of the 1973 oil crisis (created by the Arab-Israeli war and leading to a quadrupling of oil prices), a valuable step in the right direction.

The priority given to nursery education may in fact have reduced the opportunities for the development of further education. The 1944 vision of providing ample educational support, including maintenance grants, to 15-18-year-olds made very little progress. By contrast the long-delayed plans to raise the school-leaving age to 16 were implemented in September 1972. But if Butler was right to describe the development of the secondary schools as muddled, it was certainly to remain so throughout the 1970s. When Margaret Thatcher arrived at the DES in 1970, some 30 per cent of secondary school pupils were in comprehensive schools, and when she left in 1974 the proportion had risen to some 60 per cent. This happened notwithstanding her very first action as Secretary of State, which was to issue Circular 10/70 withdrawing Crosland's famous Circular 10/65 on comprehensives. This was hardly surprising given the time it actually takes for an LEA to put into place any scheme of reorganization. In some cases LEA plans initiated when Edward Boyle was in charge were only just reaching completion.[8] But a muddle it was, and a muddle it was to remain until the 1990s, a situation which was equally characteristic of Butler's last heading, the status of religious education.

The 1972 White Paper, *Education: A Framework for Expansion*, looked for growth at every level of service but ironically preceded a period of sustained and disabling contraction. At the time, however, it seemed to perpetuate the optimism of the 1960s. However, as Deputy Secretary Edward Simpson was to point out, 'The response to the White Paper was not wholly favourable. In particular, it was critized . . . for having so concentrated on logistics as to exclude consideration of the nature and quality of what lay at the heart of the matter, what was taught, and how.' But it was his view that the caution of the 1970s stemmed from the fear of reawakening the storm that had greeted Eccles's attempt to establish the Curriculum Study Group at the DES during the previous Conservative government some ten years earlier (Simpson, in Ransom and Tomlinson, 1986, p. 23). This view was endorsed by the Prime Minister (Heath) himself, who claimed that 'those of us who have been concerned in Parliament with the problems of education have concentrated too much in recent years on organization and finance, on bricks and mortar. I believe that most people in this country are more concerned with what is taught in schools than with how schools are organized.'[9]

In the same year the DES also published two major reports. The James Report, *Teacher Education and Training*, had been initiated in 1970 and thus *belonged* to the Thatcher team, but the Halsey Report on *Educational Priority* had been commissioned in 1967 soon after the publication of the Plowden Report and was therefore an *inherited* report initiated by the Opposition. They were therefore received with entirely different levels of interest and enthusiasm. The James Report led to a major reorganization of teacher education, the merging of teacher training with other undergraduate studies, and the replacement of the the former Area Training Organizations by Regional Councils. The implementation of this report unfortunately coincided with the belated realization that the declining birth rate meant fewer teachers, and so the report came to be equated with recession rather than improvement. Just one year after the James Report the Advisory Committee on the Supply and Training of Teachers began a systematic programme of reducing the supply of teachers. In the case of the Halsey Report, only volume 1 appeared in 1972, the remaining four volumes waiting until 1974-5. To the extent that it was in support of increased preschool provision, the report was well received by the DES. But its recommendations about the the needs of deprived children in Educational Priority Areas, and the advantages of providing coordinated services shared by the DES and the DHSS led to the usual dragging of Whitehall feet. Similarly, the new Manpower Services Commission set up in 1974 was asked to look after training schemes for the 16-19-year-olds independently of the DES.

Raising the school-leaving age was something of an empty gesture. It was done to prove that Conservative action was louder than Labour words. But an extra compulsory year at school was not necessarily what every teenager longed for. Leah Manning, a Labour MP from 1945 to 1950 and a past president of the National Union of Teachers, a body which had always been in favour of the school-leaving age being raised to 16, recognized, like many other teachers, that 'it will need all our ingenuity and sympathy and best teaching techniques to overcome the reluctance of some young people to stay at school until the age of sixteen' (Manning, 1970, p. 177). Teachers slowly, often reluctantly, often painfully, began to recognize that if children must attend schools for 11 years, the least that can be offered them is coherent progression in their learning. The fight for more and more secondary education, which had started in the 1920s, did not achieve its goals in 1972, nor were the hopes of the liberal community fulfilled during the rest of the 1970s. It was not enough simply to provide more of what, for perhaps half the children in secondary schools, was already unacceptable.

The inevitable slide into the abyss of an assessment-led curriculum now seemed, however, irreversible, except, perhaps, to a few writers, of whom Bernard Crick (1977, p. 14) may now seem prophetically clear-minded:

> Is it right or wise to keep 15 and 16 year olds full time in school against their will, often with few visible results, except increased alienation ... It is fairly natural ... for some people to work, in the ordinary sense of the word. The dilemma would be less if governments had followed the logic of the Industrial Training Acts of the late 1940s and had extended ... some spasmodic or even continuous day-release for education throughout working life ... Until we cut down in secondary education, we cannot take away the stigma of unwanted compulsion from most people's education and begin to spread resources more evenly through life.

But, unfortunately, such common-sense attitudes attached to themselves no political glamour, no allure for Whitehall, and little enthusiasm from the teachers' unions, who saw in the extra numbers provided from the ages of 15 to 16 something of an antidote to counteract the disease of falling numbers. We must turn now to an investigation of how another government faced the same set of issues in the latter half of a decade that proved much more turbulent than was generally predicted at its start.

NOTES

1 It is intriguing to speculate whether Thatcher's political career would have been the same if, as fellow cabinet minister Peter Walker contended, Heath had carried out his idea of transferring her to the number two position at the DTI.

2 C.B. Cox and A.E. Dyson, eds (1969), 'Fight for Education: A Black Paper', published by the Critical Quarterly Society.

3 However, Norman St John-Stevas later held that rank as Minister for the Arts.

4 The wide-ranging and exhaustive investigations of the Select Committee into student relations during the 1968–69 session resulted in a report of commendable breadth of vision. It was followed in the 1969–70 session by an almost equally in-depth analysis of teacher training.

5 Raison (1976), p. 49. A further perspective on his thinking can be gained from Raison (1975) and Raison (1979).

6 It is difficult to establish whether or not this post was thought to be an ideal preparation for his new responsibilities with schools.

7 Pile (1979), p.v. Two important alternative views of the DES at this time are provided by Locke (1974) and Lukes (1975).

8 For interesting perspectives on this, see Rubinstein and Simon (1973), Stacey (1975), and Saran (1973).

9 Speech at the Conference of the Society of Education Officers, January 1973.

Chapter 5

The Mad Hatter's Tea Party: the Labour governments 1974-79

There had been four autumn conferences since the 1970 election, in which the Conservatives had followed the usual pattern of congratulatory resolutions, and Labour had continued to press for innovations, some constructive, others mere fantasy. The only Conservative pressure was that the government 'should do everything possible to increase the range of choice in education in both state and independent schools', as stated in a 1973 resolution, perhaps in response to the growing realization that the DES during Thatcher's period of office had given approval to an ever-increasing number of comprehensive schemes.

The Labour conferences had carried a number of resolutions which were much more contentious. In 1970, for example, the National Executive was asked 'to formulate plans for merging all Independent, Direct Grant and Grammar Schools into a fully comprehensive system of State education', and this call was repeated in 1971 and 1972. Another resolution in 1971 anticipated some of the 1977 Taylor Report recommendations concerning the powers of elected governing bodies, but went further in urging that all secondary schools should elect staff and pupils to councils which would advise on the curriculum, on teaching methods and on organization. In 1972 a resolution was carried which expressed Labour policy in its fundamentalist mode:

> Conference believes that the co-relation between class origin and educational attainment in this country indicates that a fundamental reallocation of resources in education is imperative. Conference therefore instructs [*sic*] the NEC to effect a total reappraisal of education policy believing as it does that the basic objective of education should be the development of the potential of each individual and not the preparation of the individual for his future role in the capitalist system.

In 1973 it urged the reform of education for the 16-19 age group and looked to the abolition of all peripheral expenses attached to schooling such as the cost of milk, meals, uniforms, travel and materials used in classrooms.

In the context of a strike-ridden winter, Parliament was dissolved on 8 February 1974, a general election for the 28th having been announced on the previous day. This gave the parties just three weeks to campaign, during which time the only real issue was the central one of 'who runs the country?' The titles of the manifestos underlined this concern: for the Conservatives the promise was *Firm Action for a Fair Britain*, for Labour *Let Us Work Together: Labour's Way out of the Crisis*, and for the Liberals *You Can Change the Face of Britain*. Thus, although the parties had had well over three years to determine their education policy, they all found themselves in much the same position: as editorials were quick to point out, compared with the general election of 1964, education was no longer an election issue.

The evolution of education policy within the party system nevertheless reveals its progress at elections, even if it is noticed by only a few. After three years and nine months of Margaret Thatcher's uninterrupted reign at the DES, it was hardly surprising that the Conservative manifesto would demonstrate the continuation of her own policies. For Labour, the party conferences had, as usual, indicated the trends in the party's thinking, though not the actual content of its manifesto. The Liberals again provided policies that, in keeping a balance between left and right, nevertheless revealed some examples of independent thinking.

All three manifestos shared a substantial area of common ground. Nursery education was a priority for everyone, followed closely by improved provision for special educational needs and (within the current economic circumstances) the maintenance of access to further and higher education. In contrast, Labour and the Liberals were in favour of non-selective secondary schools, while the Conservatives maintained their customary stance on a mix of grammar and comprehensive schools. As far as independent schools were concerned, Labour favoured all forms of tax relief and charitable status being withdrawn (but said nothing of abolishing the private sector), while the Liberals and the Conservatives defended the situation as it was. The Conservatives expressed their continuing disquiet about truancy and indiscipline, and the Liberals looked for a major reorganization of the curriculum in such a way as to provide a more realistic final three years for non-academic pupils in secondary schools, and also for the establishment of much closer links between the universities and the public-sector polytechnics and colleges.

The result of the February election was indecisive: Labour gained 301 seats from 37.2 per cent of the votes, while the Conservatives gained 296 from 37.9 per cent. By October a second election was in full swing. The election slogans were now *Putting Britain First* (Conservatives), *Britain Will Win with Labour*, and *Why Britain Needs a Liberal Government*. Although, as would be expected, there were few changes of emphasis in the intervening six months, there were some details that invited interest at the time and continue to do so today.

For example, the Conservatives (perhaps in the light of the Liberal manifesto in February) were now showing a more than general concern for the problems of 15-year-olds in school by suggesting opportunities for the taking up of an apprenticeship or training during the last year at school. Even more significantly, they were now mentioning the establishment of a professional council for teachers to regulate their own affairs. The Labour Party gave added emphasis to compulsory, paid day release for school-leavers, and the Liberals reinforced their February proposals. The result of this election was that Labour won 319 seats against 276 for the Conservatives, but with an overall majority of only three.

By the time the October manifesto had been translated into the Queen's Speech, all that was left was the following brief statement: 'My government's education policy will continue to give priority to areas of greatest need and to children with special difficulties. Particular attention will be given to a fully comprehensive system of secondary education and to nursery education.' A *TES* survey showed that among teachers and lecturers, 37 per cent said they would vote Conservative, 30 per cent Labour and 27 per cent Liberal. In the event, the electorate as a whole gave Labour 39 per cent, the Conservatives 36 per cent and the Liberals 18 per cent.

THE POLITICIANS

Among those elected to Parliament in 1974 there were 76 teachers. In the Labour Governments of 1974-79, there were as many as three different Secretaries of State and three different Ministers of State, one of whom served for two separate periods, and three Parliamentary Under-Secretaries. The longest-serving politician at Elizabeth House was Margaret Jackson (Beckett), who held the post from March 1976 until the election in May 1979.

There was some surprise when Reg Prentice was appointed Secretary of State instead of Roy Hattersley, who had been the opposition chief spokesman from 1972 to 1974 and the drafter of the party's education policy in the manifesto. Presumably, this was on the grounds of his experience as a Minister of State in the DES between 1964 and 1966, but in spite of the fact that he had not been directly involved in education for eight years (see Chapter 3). In the event, Hattersley became Minister of State at the Foreign and Commonwealth Office from 1974 to 1976. Just as Crosland had issued circulars about comprehensive schools in the 1960s, so also did Prentice in the 1970s. Both knew at the time that since a circular was only advisory, they would have to resort to other pressures if LEAs failed to take the DES's advice. Eventually Prentice's successor, Fred Mulley, had to force through the 1976 Act.

Fred (later Lord) Mulley (b. 1918) was an example of the determination which characterized so many Labour MPs from non-professional backgrounds. His first in PPE at Christ Church, Oxford, was followed by a research fellowship at Cambridge and a call to the Bar in 1954. He was a Sheffield MP for over 30 years and held ministerial posts in various departments continuously from 1964 until 1979 whenever Labour was in power. His tenure of this office at the DES from June 1975 until September 1976, however, must in many ways be regarded as one of the most uncomfortable since 1945, perhaps rivalling Patrick Gordon-Walker's unhappy nine months in the previous Labour government. Mulley's fifteen months' stay at Elizabeth House is now chiefly associated with the Tameside judgment (see p. 77), just as Gordon-Walker's transient incumbency is associated with the Hendon case. An editorial comment in the *TES* summed up Mulley's first year in office in these terms: 'When he was appointed, nobody expected much of him, so perhaps nobody is too disappointed. He was the beneficiary of a Wilsonian reshuffle aimed mainly at paying off other debts and spiking other guns' (*TES*, 11 June 1976). But he was not without a sense of humour. When he was attacked in Parliament for not having anticipated the surplus of teachers that was developing in the late 1970s, he replied that 'to suggest that the reorganization [of initial teacher training] should have taken place earlier, or should have been more severe, is to suggest, in my view, a degree of certainty about the future that even the Old Testament prophets would not have aspired to' (*TES*, 4 June 1976). On another occasion in the Commons, he was asked by a member why there were still Victorian primary schools in the member's constituency in urgent need of renovation. 'It is a little hard in the present economic circumstances,' he replied, 'that I should be asked to put right this year all the shortcomings of the past 75 years' (*TES*, 7 May 1976). When he departed to the Ministry of Defence in September 1976, the best that Janet Fookes (the indefatigable chairman of the Select Committee investigating the DES) could say of him was that 'he was totally blinkered and too preoccupied with providing resources to be able to look ahead.'[1]

Shirley Williams was appointed Secretary of State in September 1976 and held the office until the general election in May 1979 (see Chapter 3). She was greeted 'as the logical heir to the Crosland-Boyle inheritance' and as capable of re-creating the sense of idealism that was perceived as then missing from the DES (*TES*, 24 September 1976). At the very point of her return to the DES, the Fookes Report was published.[2] It made four major recommendations: that the Secretary of State should take part in shaping the curriculum, but not in controlling it; that the DES should make more documents available to the public and should encourage wider debate; that a Standing Education Commission of employers, trade unionists and academics should be formed; and that DES planning should consider broad, long-term issues and not just the allocation of resources. Williams was immediately reported as supporting all the Fookes recommendations (*TES*, 1 October 1976). During the period from March 1974 when the DES had been led by Prentice and Mulley, she had been Secretary of State for Prices and Consumer Protection. It was undeniable, therefore, that she brought to the DES impeccable political credentials, a sharp intellect, and wide-ranging government experience, including previous and valuable experience as number two at the DES. Everything was set for a period of triumphant leadership in British education, perhaps paving the way for reform, for restructuring, for the imaginative reshaping of a system which at all levels from primary to university was creaking and groaning. All that happened was the 'great debate'.

As an example of the story of what might have been, the following is typical. In the summer of 1978 Williams persuaded the cabinet to agree to a proposal that had remained dormant since the 1944 Act. It will be recalled that the Butler Act had attempted to encourage 15-18-year-olds to stay on at school, or in the proposed county colleges, by providing them with maintenance allowances. In 1974 a Select Committee had recommended that educational maintenance allowances should be provided for 16-18-year-olds.[3] The October 1974 manifesto included promises to provide paid day release to the same group. However, the development outside the DES of the Manpower Services Commission's Youth Opportunity Programme had created a glaring anomaly in that young people who left school to study on this course received a substantial weekly allowance, whereas young people who stayed on at school received nothing. Williams asked the cabinet to agree to the implementation in 1979-80 of a maintenance scheme that would apply across the board to students pursuing full-time courses. In the event, the proposal was lost in the turmoil of 1979, and not taken up by the new Conservative government.

Shortly after the 1979 election defeat (in which she also lost her own seat), Williams spent some time as a visiting fellow at Harvard, where she was able to reflect on her period in office. 'For the last six years,' she wrote (1981, p. 13), 'I have been engulfed in the work of government. Anyone who has ever been a minister . . . knows that the job leaves little time for thought. One lives on the dwindling resources of past reading and past thinking.' Is this admission an indictment of the machinery of government or simply the statement of yet another Minister who saw the waves closing over her head? The chapter on education in her book is deeply disturbing, for it reveals the enormous gap that had arisen between thought and action. As the reader wades through a catalogue of good intentions and sound educational thinking, there is the risk of forgetting that what is being presented is, yet again, not the hopes and aspirations of professional commentators on British education, but the ideas of someone, rare in our society, who was actually in a position to make such ideas operational.

By the time she left office, about four out of five children attending secondary schools were in comprehensives. But she recognized that 'the comprehensive reform . . . is controversial mainly because it is widely believed that academically able children suffer from being educated together with their less able contemporaries. The debate has centred on systems, not on schools.' By this she meant that it is difficult to make generalizations about secondary schools, for schools vary tremendously, as do classes within them. She saw it as her role to ensure that the system was working by concentrating attention on what was actually going on in individual schools and in individual classes. In other words, she was talking about curriculum evaluation and teacher appraisal. 'Politicians,' she acknowledged, 'shy away from the question of what makes a good school, because they prefer to explain things in terms of systems. It makes reform so much simpler . . . But system changes only take one part of the way to success. The rest depends on the people in the school' (Williams, 1981, pp. 163-4). The curriculum was indeed an area she heavily involved her department in during her tenure of office, but it was still at the debating level, rather than the action level. She was able to cite the 'divorce between the thinkers and the makers, those that study and those that do' (*ibid.*, p. 166) as one of the UK's most serious problems, and yet did little to reform the curriculum while in office. Again, in respect of teacher appraisal, she was able to point to 'the nasty question of what is to be done with poor teachers', but made no provision for a systematic programme of monitoring. On the question of staff development, she understood the need for serious in-service education, even going so far as to insist that 'regular in-service training should be a requirement for promotion' (*ibid.*, p. 163), while doing nothing towards introducing the appropriate circular or legislation.

There were other issues. 'The dilemma posed by the public prestige and size of the independent sector in British education is acute', but it was a dilemma, however acute, that was to remain untouched (Williams, 1981, p. 157). 'Nursery schools should become the hub of a whole group of services for the young child, including health visitors, child-care workers, mother-and-baby clinics and resources and advice centres', but where was the legislation or the funding? 'If the Open University, the further education colleges and the resources of higher education were brought together, a system of continuing education could be established in Britain', but, again, what action did the government take to create such a sensible line of development?

If it is true that *everyone knows that the job leaves little time for thought*, then it is the role of Ministers that must be questioned, and questioned closely. In this we have the help of an insider. Norman Hunt (b. 1920; later Lord Crowther-Hunt) read history at Cambridge just before and immediately after the war. Since 1952 he had been a Fellow of Exeter College, Oxford, where he taught politics. He had served on the Fulton Committee between 1966 and 1968, acted as a constitutional adviser to Harold Wilson, and served as a member of the Kilbrandon Commission on devolution. Having been made a peer in 1973, he was available to serve as Minister of State in October 1974 when Gerald Fowler, who had been in post for only seven months, was surprisingly moved to the Privy Council Office. Crowther-Hunt's considerable experience of the university sector could be usefully employed by appointing him Minister for higher education. It will be recalled that Wilson had given Lord Bowden a similar opportunity in 1964. The use of members of the House of Lords as serving ministers, though not particularly popular with Labour back-benchers, provided the technocratic Wilson with opportunities, which possessed familiar transatlantic associations, for bringing specialists into his government.

Crowther-Hunt's two earlier books, *Whitehall and Beyond* (1964) and *Personality and Power* (1970), provide some indication of the critical stance which he took, and the freshness of his approach to politics. What he witnessed in office, however, and which he recorded in *The Times Higher Education Supplement* in May 1976, later enlarged upon in *The Civil Servants* (Kellner and Crowther-Hunt, 1980), went much further in generating a fiercely analytical approach to government. He had been strongly in favour of a regional basis for education, suggesting that the Secretary of State should relinquish much of his responsibilities to second-level governments whose principal function would be to draw up a five-year development plan for their region. For example, his view of the teacher-training cuts (with which he had to deal during his time at the ministry) was that the DES should simply set targets and let the LEAs (or regional committees of the LEAs) get on with it. But the DES would not give up its desire to manage the entire system of higher education. His known views on these and other Fulton Report matters made him, of course, a target for the civil service when he was in office.

In addition to Crowther-Hunt, the other Ministers for Higher Education were Fowler and Oaks. After the 1970 election, Gerald Fowler had found himself without a seat and without a job (see Chapter 3). However, he was soon snapped up by Huddersfield Polytechnic and then the Open University, during which time he usefully developed further his academic and professional interest in the relationship between education and politics. In March 1974 he regained both his seat and his office, only to be replaced by Crowther-Hunt in October. His third stint in the same job came in January 1976, but when Callaghan shuffled his Ministers in September of the same year, he again found himself out of office. By December of that year he was writing speeches with titles such as 'Fewer resources must not mean less commitment . . . strategy goals and objectives of the Labour Party', a sure sign that his departure from office was at least in part connected with the underfunding of higher education. There are also some hints that Fowler did not agree with the popular theory, enshrined in Callaghan's Ruskin College speech, which proposed that manpower planning ought to be the basis for education planning. 'Many politicians believe,' he wrote later, 'that the theories are still good, but the practice was bad. Put a different way, it was felt that the education system had somehow failed the nation. What in fact was wrong was the theory' (Fowler, in Broadfoot, 1981, pp. 14-15). After the 1979 election he moved to a full-time, distinguished career in polytechnic administration.

Fowler, who was only too well aware of the tensions within government, was also fond of referring to the 'sub-government', by which he meant the LEAs, teachers and parents. 'Any Secretary of State, and his junior Ministers,' he insisted, 'must seek to keep a balance between the competing interests in the educational sub-government. To that extent, and in a quite informal sense, they are accountable to that sub-government' (Fowler, in Lello, 1979, p. 28). It was a relationship which was to be severely undermined in the next decade. Fowler remained throughout the 1970s a prolific contributor to educational journalism. Typical of his independence of thought was his attitude to degree courses. His experience of higher education did not lead him to encourage every 18-year-old to read for a BSc. Industry, he believed, 'needs its due supply of responsible and enlightened young people educated to consider problems dispassionately and to reach conclusions on evidence rather than prejudice' (*TES*, 7 May 1976). He believed that postgraduate specialization was essential. It must be remembered, of course, that British degree programmes were, and have remained, traditionally shorter than some Continental and US equivalents, and that three years *plus* one-year courses allow for both breadth and depth.

Gordon Oakes (b. 1931) had been educated at a grammar school in Widnes and Liverpool University where he read English. In 1956 he qualified as a solicitor and was elected MP for Bolton West in 1964, serving as a PPS at the DES to Shirley Williams between 1967 and 1969. In the new Labour administration of 1974, he joined the Department of the Environment and was promoted to Minister of State for Higher Education in September 1976. With his boss, Shirley Williams, he remained in post until the 1979 election. His preoccupation with the public-sector institutions is well known. He claimed,

> The polytechnics have forged close links with industry and business ... their courses are not conceived in academic isolation but are seen as education in the context of broadly equipping the student to make a contribution to, and earn his living in, some aspect of society's life. The importance of this link between education and industry cannot be overstated.
>
> (*TES*, 29 October 1976)

There were three junior Ministers in the period, Armstrong, Lestor and Jackson. Ernest Armstrong (b. 1915) started teaching in 1937. After a long and successful career as a headmaster he became the MP for Durham North-West in 1964 and represented this constituency until he retired in 1987. He was an NUT-sponsored MP, and had joined the opposition front-bench team on

Education only during the latter stages of the Heath administration. In the Parliamentary debate on educational finance which took place in January 1974, he had said, 'I believe we are facing a crisis in education - a crisis of educational thinking as well as in the supply of the necessary resources. Education is threatened not only by cuts, but by a lack of confidence in the future and also by disillusionment. We must give education greater priority in the future than we have done in the past' (*TES*, 25 January 1974). It is the business of opposition spokesmen to see crises all round them, but only two months later he was in office facing these same problems. His career in the DES as a Parliamentary Under-Secretary, however, was short-lived, for after only fifteen months in office he was transferred by Wilson to the Department of the Environment. At least his experience as a headmaster was exploited to the full when he served as Deputy Speaker in the Commons from 1981 to 1987.

Elected MP for Eton and Slough in 1966, Joan Lestor (b. 1931) had risen quickly in Parliamentary circles. She had briefly been at the DES in 1969-70 and was sensibly retained as an opposition spokesperson on education throughout the Heath government. Wilson reverted, however, to his usual path of discontinuity by sending her to the Foreign and Commonwealth Office in 1974. In June 1975 she was brought back to the DES as a Parliamentary Under-Secretary in place of Armstrong. She was the first nursery teacher to reach the secondary-dominated DES. Alas, her stay was brief: the financial cuts announced in January 1976 led to her resignation in February. In a subsequent speech she asserted that 'the argument that the cuts are not real cuts but only cuts against further development is nonsense ... teachers are not being replaced, pupil-teacher ratios are worsening, building maintenance is being curtailed ... libraries and the youth services feature prominently in many of the local authority cuts' (*TES*, 28 May 1976).

To replace Joan Lestor, the Prime Minister selected Margaret Jackson (b. 1943, later Beckett), the MP for Lincoln since 1974 and a PPS to Judith Hart. She had been educated at Notre Dame High School in Norwich and Manchester College of Science and Technology, where she had later become an Experimental Officer in the Department of Metallurgy. 'Many people who, like me,' she said in the House, 'started out their careers with practical experience of the shopfloor may not realize that they can use this experience, if they have suitable technical qualifications, to help children develop practical skills' (*TES*, 7 May 1976). As the schools Minister, she was regularly faced with breakdowns in the system. On one occasion soon after her appointment, she was presented with sustained and aggressive questioning about the alleged increase in truancy in secondary schools. Her retaliation was immediate and direct: 'It is important that MPs should consider whether what they said would contribute to an understanding, and would help the problem, or would make it worse' (*TES*, 7 May 1976). She admitted, however, that the raising of the school-leaving age to 16 had contributed to the truancy predicament. Although proposed in the 1944 Act and supported, half-heartedly, by both major parties, the extra year at school had always been something of an enigma. The teachers' unions had been divided about its feasibility, and many commentators had felt that it was tactically a mistake to force unwilling adolescents to endure an 'extra year' before most schools had really developed a coherent and structured curriculum that demanded five years' progression, rather than the four-plus-one pattern that emerged in practice in the early stages.

'Contributing to an understanding of the problems' is perhaps a fair evaluation of her work at the DES. As we have already noted, she was the longest-serving MP at the DES during the Wilson-Callaghan government. She did, however, have to work within the rigid hierarchical structure that the civil service continued to impose upon junior Ministers. As one of her ministerial colleagues indicated, 'all Members of Parliament are equal, each having stood for election and reached the House of Commons on merit. But in government . . . there were top-dogs and dogs-bodies, the insiders and those who fetched and carried' (Rogers, 1980, p. 11). The notion that a junior Minister is an apprentice is understandable, but wasteful. Unless senior Ministers can delegate specific tasks to their juniors, and unless Permanent Secretaries can work to their instructions as well as to the Secretary of State, the overloading that Shirley Williams complained about will continue to increase. In Margaret Jackson's case, the apprenticeship really led nowhere. After losing her seat in the 1979 election, she returned to Westminster in 1983 as Margaret Beckett, MP for Derby South and party spokesperson for health and social security, and, later, shadow Chief Secretary to the Treasury.

THE CIVIL SERVANTS

For the first two years of the Labour government Sir William Pile continued as Permanent Secretary.[4] His replacement, Sir James Hamilton (b. 1923), was the third Permanent Secretary to be appointed to the DES from another government department. His previous post had been in the Cabinet Office, which together with the Treasury had become the prime channel for key promotions.[5] He took over from Sir William Pile on 1 June 1976 at what has since come to be seen as a dramatic moment in the conduct of DES affairs. It is also a matter of controversy. Bernard (later Lord) Donoughue, who was head of the Downing Street Policy Unit under both Wilson and Callaghan, asserts (1987, p. 110) that 'Downing Street intervened, with the full support of the Cabinet Secretary, to secure a change at the top of the Department of Education. The existing Permanent Secretary was transferred to a more appropriate department.' Since at that time the Head of the Civil Service was not the responsibility of the Cabinet Secretary, and since the appointment of all Permanent and Deputy Secretaries was handled by the Head of the Civil Service and the Prime Minister, and not the Cabinet Secretary, the grounds for Donoughue's interpretation seem uncertain.[6] In the event, Pile became Chairman of the Inland Revenue, in a much larger department of the more prestigious and central offices of the Treasury.

When Prentice, Fowler and Armstrong arrived in March 1974, Pile and his Deputies, Hudson, Odgers, Simpson, and Wright, were obviously in a very well-established position.[7] The almost immediate exchange of Fowler for Crowther-Hunt, and the replacement of Prentice and Armstrong (by Mulley and Lestor) in June of the next year helped to exaggerate their permanence and to reinforce Pile's view of the nature of the civil servant's contribution to policy development.

And whatever variations there were in the attitudes of the politicians, Pile's gradually strengthening view, expressed in his evidence to the OECD and in his own book, was that the DES could not continue to evade a measure of responsibility for the curriculum. But Hamilton represented an entirely different type of appointment to high office in the DES. Previously, Smieton and Andrew had been drafted into the top post at the DES from other departments, but Hamilton was by no means a regular administrative civil servant.

After reading civil engineering at Edinburgh University, he had become a scientific officer in the civil service, and this career led him to become the Director General of the Concorde Project when Fred Mulley was Minister of Aviation. It was also Mulley, now Secretary of State for Education, who approved his appointment to the DES after Hamilton had gained significant experience and advancement at the Department of Trade and Industry and as a Deputy Secretary in the Cabinet Office. He had been educated in the state system (as were his children) and in many respects brought an entirely new attitude to the DES. It was perhaps ironic that Crowther-Hunt, who might have perceived Hamilton as a Fulton Report man, had left the DES only some six months before his arrival.

Within a month of his appointment, however, it became clear that Hamilton was a DES hard-liner. The role of the DES, he asserted, 'must mean more than seeing that teachers, buildings and other resources are available on whatever scale the country can afford. It must mean, I believe, a much closer interest by the department in the curriculum in its widest sense, the assessment of performance and even the relation of teaching method to performance' (echoing Heath's speech in January 1973).[8] Since the DES presumably already exercised *a close interest* in the curriculum by virtue of the reports of its 450-plus HMI, it is easy to see that *interest* was simply a euphemism for *control*. As justification, he pointed to the alleged 'growing chorus of discontent from parents, teachers and employers about the education provided in a minority of schools, colleges and universities'. What he chose not to acknowledge was that the growing chorus also included an articulate minority who felt betrayed by the actions of both major political parties in destroying a flourishing educational system by constant and increasing financial cuts since 1968.

By 1979 Hamilton had developed the Department Planning Organization in such a way that the Policy Steering Group (which he chaired himself) filtered all the recommendations of the Policy Groups, which in turn were chaired by Deputy Secretaries. The 'Planning Unit' which serviced these important committees did contain (in addition to administrative staff) HMI, economists and DES-appointed researchers, but the *control* of planning remained firmly within the grasp of the senior civil servants. Again, this was far from the Fulton model. During this period the DES gradually and systematically weakened the role of the Schools' Council. Hamilton was accused by John Mann, its Secretary between 1979 and 1983, of managing to make only one three-hour visit to the Council during his entire seven years in office, and of being the chief architect of the Council's destruction (Plaskow, 1985, pp. 189-91). Was this in line with Shirley Williams's view of widespread consultation?

Together with Sir William Pile, the four Deputy Secretaries during the

Heath administration, Hudson, Odgers, Simpson and Wright, remained in post when the new Labour government took over. Subsequently, Odgers was replaced by Alan Thompson and Wright by Walter Ulrich. They represented very different career paths. Thompson (b. 1920) had left Queen's College, Oxford, to pursue an uninterrupted career at the Ministry of Education and DES, reaching the post of Deputy Secretary in 1975. Ulrich (b. 1927) had been in the civil service since 1951, but his first post in the DES was as Deputy Secretary in 1977, he having spent the previous two years in the prestigious Cabinet Office (from where his immediate boss, James Hamilton, had also sprung).[9]

Sheila Browne (b. 1924) was Senior Chief Inspector from 1974 until 1983, having spent one year as Deputy SCI and only twelve before that as an HMI. After reading Modern Languages at Lady Margaret Hall, Oxford, she had gained experience of university, but not school-, teaching. She claimed for herself, and for many HMI that she later appointed, that familiarity with schooling could be picked up 'on the job' (*TES*, 29 November 1974). In the event, her lack of school experience was compensated for, at least in part, by the clarity and sharpness of her thinking about HMI as an organization, which she believed should report independently of the Assessment and Performance Unit (APU), which had just been established at the DES. While Browne was in office, the number of curriculum publications published rose dramatically. As a senior local authority administrator observed, this

> admits of two explanations. The first is that there are messages which require much emphasis, the second that such a flurry of activity may have been designed to avoid less welcome, over-prescriptive, even damaging initiatives by politicians in the wake of the Great Debate . . . One has to conclude that the presence of the Senior Chief Inspector, not to mention her strong-willed adherence to principle, has been of enormous significance to the work of the schools during a period which seemed about to drive the schools in a wrong direction. She has been able to argue her case in a way that is perhaps unrivalled by any of her distinguished predecessors.
>
> (Brighouse, in Harling, 1984, p. 92)

Concerning the role of HMI in the late 1970s, Browne herself observed that

> no one is obliged to do as they say but all concerned in education are likely to pay attention to their reports. The awareness of this has to mark all HMI's work, making him constantly alert to what may be read into his words, his silences, and his choices. He must always remember that the heart of the matter is to collect and communicate evidence so that those with real responsibility for decisions are in a better position to make them.
>
> (Browne, in Lelo, 1979, p. 39)

'Those with real responsibility' ought in the end to be the elected representatives in Parliament. To what extent did they receive such evidence and how were they equipped to exercise such responsibilities?

THE IMPLEMENTATION OF POLICY

An interesting perspective on the DES and its ministers has been provided by Lord Donoughue, who worked for both Wilson and Callaghan as Senior Policy Adviser and Head of the Downing Street Policy Unit. 'Education,' he claimed, 'was surprisingly rarely at the centre of the Labour Cabinet's attention; no education matter was on the agenda of Harold Wilson's Cabinet throughout our first year in government and in the following year it was still a rare occurrence.' He reiterated the Whitehall view that the DES had little power, and that it was traditionally led by other than senior members of the cabinet. His own judgement was that 'Education policy was conducted by the local authorities and the teachers' unions, with the DES, as Harold Wilson once commented to me, being little more than a post-box between the two . . . In my dealings with the NUT at the time I never once heard mention of education or children' (Donoughue, 1987, pp. 109-10). Donoughue's strictures lead us to a number of recurrent questions. Was the failure to bring educational matters onto the cabinet agenda, at least until Callaghan's Ruskin College speech, the fault of the Prime Minister, or the fault of the Secretary of State, or in the nature of political priorities? Was education no longer a key aspect of the welfare state as it had been for the postwar generation of Labour MPs? If the DES was simply *a postbox*, was that necessarily a bad thing? Was the party frightened of the teachers' unions, from which many of its own MPs were drawn, in some cases with sponsorships? Did not the Schools' Council, in practice, provide the appropriate forum for the discussions that Donoughue did not find being held in Downing Street? It will be recalled that the first Wilson government in 1964 thought seriously about the advantages of operating the education service on a regional basis, with reduced powers and responsibilities for the DES. Perhaps it was only when Wilson's policies gave way to Callaghan's that the possibilities of centralism and increased power at the DES became manifest?

There were, nevertheless, certain events which were politically significant and did provoke controversy. In April 1974 the DES had issued Circular 10/74 requiring local education authorities to submit plans for removing selection procedures for entry into secondary schools, thus revoking Margaret Thatcher's Circular 10/70 and re-establishing Anthony Crosland's Circular 10/65. Until May 1976, Tameside LEA had been under Labour control, and long-term plans had been made to bring in a full comprehensive system from September of that year. The local elections had, however, brought in a Conservative administration, which immediately revoked these plans and introduced a hurried selection procedure for immediate operation. Mulley invoked his powers under Section 68 of the 1944 Act, which allowed him to exercise overall authority over LEAs where he thought they were behaving 'unreasonably'. This was challenged through the courts as far as the Law Lords, who decided that Tameside was not acting unreasonably.

By November 1976 the new Act requiring LEAs to admit children to secondary schools 'without reference to ability or aptitude' was law, and, as we now know, subsequent events led to the 1979 Act revoking this requirement yet again. What was of importance about the 1976 events, however, were three particular features: that an Act of Parliament remains subject to interpretation in law; that the advice given to an inexperienced Secretary of State (at least inexperienced in the field of education) by his department was insecure; and that the relationship between local authorities and Westminster was, at that time, demonstrably fragile. The year 1976 is often seen as the year in which Callaghan's Ruskin College speech signalled the tightening grip of central over local government in terms of the curriculum, but the Tameside case was equally a watershed in the development of government controls over LEAs. In both areas the growth towards centralism was encouraged by both major parties, the Labour Party in the 1970s and the Conservative Party in the 1980s. The consensus of centralism became a conspicuous feature of the educational landscape.

In March 1976 Harold Wilson retired as Prime Minister, to be succeeded in April by James Callaghan. It was unusual for a Prime Minister to make a speech on education, and exceptional for such a speech to discuss the curriculum. Thus, when Callaghan used an invitation to speak at Ruskin College, Oxford, in October 1976 as the opportunity to close the gap between concepts of what should be taught in schools and concepts of what he perceived as the proper responsibilities of government, he commanded the attention of the education world. In fact what he had to say was entirely predictable, and the *TES* labelled it an anticlimax. The Labour Party had already published, in a May issue of *Labour Weekly*, a strong argument in favour of the raising of school standards, and Callaghan himself had introduced the subject at the Party conference in September. Pile had hinted at the need to strengthen the DES in his report to the Select Committee, and Hamilton had introduced the subject at his first major speech to the Association of Education Committees. But the immediate background to the speech included four events which must be taken into account: the leaking of the DES *Yellow Book* and the publication of the Auld Report, Bennett's book on the primary curriculum, and Willmott's report on GCE.

Headed *School Education in England - Problems and Initiatives*, the *Yellow Book* was meant to be a confidential memorandum to the Prime Minister. It was a 63-page report prepared by the DES under seven main headings: the nature of the primary curriculum; standards in secondary schools; the chaos of the sixteen-plus examinations; the perceived failure of the Schools' Council to assist in their improvement; the problems of the 16 to 19 age group; the contribution of HMI; and the willingness of the DES to take a leading part in reform. It was leaked to the *Guardian* and *TES* shortly before the Oxford speech. As a document on the politics of education, it soon became a collector's item:

> It will be good to get on record from Ministers and in particular the Prime Minister, an authoritative pronouncement on the division of responsibility for what goes on in school, suggesting that the Department should give a firmer lead . . . and should firmly refute any argument . . . that no one except teachers has any right to any say in what goes on in schools. The climate for a declaration on these lines may in fact now be relatively favourable. Nor need there be any inhibition for fear that the Department could not make use of enhanced opportunity to

> exercise influence over curriculum and teaching methods: the Inspectorate would have a leading role to play in bringing forward ideas in these areas and is ready to fulfil that responsibility.
>
> (*TES*, 15 October 1976)

Of overriding importance to observers of the machinery of government was not that the report was critical of schools and the Schools' Council, but that it was prepared *in secret*. The relationship between government, HMI, LEAs and schools depends upon mutual trust and open access to information. Sir William Pile, who had been Permanent Secretary until 31 May 1976, could not at the same time claim to head an organization famed for, and proud of, its 'openness' while engaging in the preparation of clandestine documents that denied all the accepted principles of consultation that he vowed to espouse. Callaghan had asked for the report soon after taking up office in April (it reached him in July), but it is widely believed that the DES had already been working on this paper. The transfer of responsibilities between Pile, who had been with the DES, on and off, for nearly 30 years, and James Hamilton, who was entirely new to educational administration, came at an awkward, not to say sticky, moment. In the context of the OECD and Fookes Reports, the *Yellow Book*[10] case provided ample supporting evidence for the many critics of the DES.

Phrases which were employed in the report, such as 'authoritative pronouncement', 'firmly refute any argument', 'enhanced opportunity to exercise influence', and 'ready to fulfil that responsibility', display both a deeply uncertain identity on the part of the DES, and at the same time a scarcely concealed ambition to rule the world. It is not surprising that the education system was in such turmoil. Analysts have since pointed to the fundamental attitude that was revealed in this pantomime:

> Leading members of the Department did not fully share the politician's concern to vocationalize the curriculum for what was perceived to be the 'non-academic' section of the school population . . . the desire to exert direct influence over the curriculum was more important than the *precise nature* of its form and content.
>
> (Chitty, 1988, p. 329)

The Schools' Council case was particularly unsavoury. From its inception in 1964 until 1970, the Council had worked in partnership with the DES. Even after 1970, when the Council had gained a level of independence, one of the Joint Secretaries continued to be supplied by the DES. There were, therefore, ample opportunities for the exchange of views. But as one of the officers of the Council observed, 'The role played by DES officials and HMI was always enigmatic . . . there was very little continuity of representation of DES personnel, and few of them understood the nature of curriculum development anyway. HMI were strangely reticent in policy committees . . . It was only when the notorious Yellow Book appeared . . . that the real views . . . of those in the DES surfaced' (Plaskow, 1979, p. 3). Crowther-Hunt, as a Minister for higher education, had no cause to come into contact with the Schools' Council, but he would undoubtedly have recognized the same 'insidious operation of civil service power at its most triumphant'.

The chairman of the Schools' Council, Sir Alex Smith (who had been pressured by the Wilson government to take on the job), was incensed by the *Yellow Book* in general and its glorification of HMI in particular.

> What has HMI ['this most powerful single agency'] been doing during the decade or two during which these [alleged] weaknesses have been developing? . . . The report shows that there is a clear need for a firm appraisal of the performance of HMI, yet it contains not a word of criticism of it.

The Ruskin College speech had given the impression that the Schools' Council had not grasped the problem of preparing school-leavers for employment. Smith's response was magisterial:

> The purpose of education is to produce an educated and not a servile people, and I regard it as an essential fundamental characteristic of an educated nation that it should understand, support, and take pride in the means whereby it earns its living.
> (*TES*, 29 October 1976)

The Auld Inquiry had carried out an investigation on behalf of ILEA into the activities of teachers at the William Tyndale Junior School in Islington. The media had created a storm over the apparently eccentric styles of teaching practised in this school, and the case gave ammunition to supporters of the *Black Papers*, who had remained largely uncomprehending of post-Plowden curricular development in primary schools, and who therefore were unable to differentiate between examples of good and bad practice in this sector. Neville Bennett's book *Teaching Styles and Pupil Progress* similarly attracted the attention of critics of the primary curriculum. In this case, however, the research material simply raised questions that were common among observers of primary practice, questions that related to techniques rather than principles. Alan Willmott's preliminary report for the Schools' Council had similarly hinted at falling standards in GCE. Throughout the summer the pages of educational journals became littered with accusations and counter-accusations, while the popular daily press simply hurled abuse at schools and teachers in general.

The gist of Callaghan's speech was this: 'There is no virtue in producing socially well-adjusted members of society who are unemployed because they have not the skills' (*TES*, 22 October 1976). He laid great emphasis on the economic needs of the country as he saw them. 'I am concerned . . . to find complaints from industry that new recruits from the schools sometimes do not have the basic tools to do the job that is required.' The 'tools' that a school-leaver should have acquired were 'to be basically literate, to be basically numerate, to understand how to live and work together, and have respect for others and respect for the individual'. There is no doubt that Callaghan was influenced by accusatory statements from industrialists about the educational standards of the workforce they were recruiting. What was surprising about his reaction was that he chose to bypass the DES. If there was a real educational problem, it would have been the duty of HMI to 'observe and report' its real nature, and for the DES to negotiate with the LEAs on how to remedy the situation. Many wild charges were thrown at schools, especially about their presumed failure to teach the 'basics', by which was usually meant mathematics and English language. It would have been very rare, however, for any secondary school to fail in providing compulsory and substantial lessons in these subjects throughout the entire 11 to 16 age range. Unlike the industrial models of productivity, however, schools have never been able to guarantee the product, for, as part of the overall educational process, schooling represents only a minority element of the measures that need to be taken by the individual learner.

The nature of the Ruskin College speech was interpreted in a variety of ways at the time. Perhaps the following examples will adequately demonstrate the contrasting reactions:

> His intervention was more important for the change in policy it signified than for the precise words he used. It marked a major change in the attitude of government towards the curriculum and the location of responsibility for the content of education. It called the bluff of the more extreme exponents of the teacher-controlled curriculum, and initiated a programme of consultations aimed at bringing the curriculum back into the public arena.
>
> (Becher and Maclure, 1978, p. 10)

> The change in formal stance towards the teachers was an important shift for the leader of the Labour Party to register. By arguing the necessity for external controls on teaching and teachers, he both signalled an 'open season' on educational issues, in which teachers would fare badly, but also assumed a position ... which was difficult to distinguish from that of the *Black Paper* authors.
>
> (Centre for Contemporary Cultural Studies, 1981, p. 218)

While the first analysis was broadly in tune with middle-ground opinion, the second emphasized the failure, as the writers saw it, of the Wilson-Callaghan governments to deliver a socialist education programme. The first underestimates the impact government intervention was to have on moderates in the teaching workforce, while the second, despite its often lucid and penetrating analysis, fails to come to terms with both the political realities of a hung Parliament and the self-regulating nature of the DES mechanisms. The authors of the second view come near to acknowledging the problem when a little later (p. 246) they admit that 'we face a deeply contradictory situation: a strong but *internal* growth of radical intellectual work and groupings ... but lacking ... a strongly popular educational role and connection.' This signals the profound dilemmas that were to overtake the Labour Party while in opposition in the 1980s.

What, then, was the nature of the relationship between the *Yellow Book* and the Ruskin College speech? It would be wrong to think of the former as a draft of the latter. Although we can presume that the DES memorandum would have been thoroughly studied by Downing Street, it certainly did not provide the structure of the Oxford speech. Callaghan had 'outlined concerns and raised questions' chiefly about the effectiveness of schooling as a means of improving the British economy. As the *TES* unkindly pointed out at the time, 'he has whistled up weasel words to exploit popular prejudices . . . he has sought to divert popular indignation . . . from his own management of the economy to the teachers' management of the curriculum' (22 October 1976). The DES memorandum, on the other hand, was chiefly concerned with its bid to control the educational system. Moreover, it was not in the style of the DES to think about education in other than the traditions of romantic idealism: inside most senior civil servants lurked still the aspirations of Arnold, Mill, and Newman. The notion that schools should produce persons specifically trained for particular jobs was deeply alien to public-school and Oxbridge men who had reached the top of the civil service by virtue of their role as civilized generalists.

The Ruskin College speech was followed by the episode called the 'Great Debate' by the government, which, in practice, was neither great nor a debate - more a half-hearted regional dissemination of DES schemes. The main topics 'allowed' for set-piece expositions were the curriculum, monitoring and assessment, teacher training, and school and working life. Among teachers and LEAs the 'great debate' succeeded only in provoking great hostility. When Shirley Williams published *Education in Schools*, it was described as a consultative document. But in a very important sense, the key issue among its wide-ranging set of proposals was not up for discussion at all. It concerned her own role (combined with the Secretary of State for Wales): 'They [meaning both Secretaries of State] must draw attention to national needs if they believe the education system is not adequate in meeting them.' The 1977 Green Paper therefore represents the formal arrival of central government intervention in matters which, broadly speaking, had been traditionally left to the good sense of teachers, working within a framework of public examination systems and the demands of employers and higher education. The DES 'had co-operated in maintaining the myth of a teacher-centred curriculum' (Becher and Maclure, 1978b, p. 11) since 1944, but the new realism was a direction that was to be followed relentlessly in the 1980s and especially by two of her successors, Sir Keith Joseph and Kenneth Baker. Once again a change of government seems to have made very little difference to the main thrust of policy, reminding us of Pile's inevitability concept of the 'historic development of the education service'.

The main points in the Green Paper were concerned with the curriculum, assessment, the management of teachers, and the relationship between school and working life. It was, however, on the evaluation of the curriculum that most attention was focused. In the ten years that had elapsed since the Plowden Report, the so-called 'child-centred primary curriculum' was thought to have become a liability in all but the most expert hands. What was wanted, it was suggested, was child-centred learning within an agreed curriculum framework. In the secondary sector it was argued that an 'overloaded curriculum' had not ensured that (in addition to mathematics and English) all pupils were following a coherent course in science and a modern language. Since the Green Paper was essentially a product of traditional DES and HMI thinking, it did not contain any major surprises.

If, however, we turn again to Donoughue's version of the circumstances surrounding the publication of the Green Paper, we cannot help noticing a different and challenging perspective. He insists upon certain features of the affair that were not common knowledge at the time: that the Green Paper had been asked for by Callaghan when he had called Mulley to Downing Street in May 1976; that Shirley Williams was unhappy about the Prime Minister's intervention in her department;[11] that the DES officials were less than rapturous in their enthusiasm for the demand for a Green Paper; that the draft (which did not appear until June 1977) was seen by the Policy Unit as 'sparse in content and deeply complacent in tone' and 'represented Whitehall at its self-satisfied, condescending and unimaginative worst'; that it had ignored the Ruskin College speech and 'Great Debate' almost entirely; that the DES was divided between the older generation of officials, who still believed in reaching agreements with the LEAs and the teacher unions, and the younger interventionists; and that Sheila Browne had 'conducted a thorough investigation of [Donoughue's] motives and objectives' between the Ruskin College speech and the publication of the Green Paper (Donoughue, 1987, p. 112).

The Green Paper was followed by other government inquiries about what the LEAs were doing with the curriculum (DES Circular 14/77), and also by DES attempts to improve its image, such as *How the DES Is Organised* (1977). Consultative procedures became fashionable even though serious doubts have been expressed about their effectiveness. Maurice Kogan's definitive 1975 study of interest groups in education analysed the relationship between many influential groups (which were still in place in 1977) and the government. These included the local authority associations (such as the Association of Education Committees, the County Council Association, and the Association of Municipal Corporations), the teachers' associations, the parental groups (such as the Campaign for the Advancement of State Education and the Nursery Schools' Association), the churches, and numerous research groups. It became required reading at the time, and even now needs to be studied by those who wish to have a clear insight into the circumstances which influenced the Wilson and Callaghan administrations.

It would be an unenviable task to attempt to summarize Kogan's findings, but with the changed perspective of the 1990s, it is possible to draw attention to three elements which seem of as much significance now as they did at the time, and which amplify the themes of this book. As we have seen, ministers at the DES can become so entangled in the department's slow-moving machinery that it is not uncommon for them to reflect departmental policy rather than party policy, although the former is often disguised as the latter. Back-bench MPs of the government party, on the other hand, may remain unentangled and unseduced. They may also have more time than do ministers to gather the views of their constituents. They can therefore enjoy the privilege (and pleasure) of 'giving ministers a rough time', as Kogan (1975, p. 151) so aptly puts it. It would not be stretching credibility too far to suggest that Labour back-benchers are more prone to this pastime than Conservatives. This attitude, coupled with the small majorities, the incessant ministerial changes, and the decline in public expenditure meant that the 'rough times' were fairly frequent between 1974 and 1979. And this says nothing of the part played by opposition MPs.

Of course Ministers have to answer formally presented questions for which their civil servants have prepared formal answers. But, as we have seen earlier, the department's official answer may not always represent the personal views of the Minister, and he or she may not have been given the time to demand further revisions of a statement. 'Parliamentary Questions make ministers healthily vulnerable. If they are not quick on their feet, if they cannot see trouble coming, the Parliamentary Question exposes them' (Kogan, 1975, p. 160). Gerald Fowler (in Lello, 1975, p. 13) said that they may 'expose the inadequacies of a Minister or of his policies. But they test only a particular form of adequacy, namely the ability to defend oneself for a very brief period within the context of Parliamentary procedures and conventions.' Fowler, unlike his colleague Crowther-Hunt in the Lords, had to deal with the hurly-burly of the Commons. 'No Minister worth his salt,' he emphasized, 'is likely to fail this test. It is too easy to give answers which are soothing or belligerent, as occasion demands, and which may, *although not obfuscating the truth, fail to reveal the whole of it*' (my italics). Such tendencies to obfuscate are the everyday habits of senior civil servants, and the two weeks that they have to prepare a Minister's answer to a question placed on an Order Paper gives them plenty of time to polish their practised skills in 'being economical with the truth'. The Secretary of State is, in any case, normally required to answer questions only once a month, and junior Ministers usually present answers only to less important questions late at night in an almost empty chamber.

To return to Kogan's three elements: the second matter of continuing significance is the role of Parliamentary debates. In Kogan's view (1975, p. 163), they normally 'offer undefined and imprecisely applied pressure on governments rather than help determine policies'. During the 1974-79 period, however, the government's tiny majority often depended on the goodwill and support not only of all its own members, but also of Liberals and other MPs. The 1976 Act was therefore particularly vulnerable to amendment. Fowler, who had held office at the time, acknowledged (in Lello, 1979, pp. 15-17) that this bill took longer in committee stage than any other education bill since 1944, and that its passage through the Commons depended on agreements being reached on a number of amendments. Nevertheless, the 1976 bill, with its highly charged policies on secondary schooling and its precarious progress through a hung Parliament, was exceptional. Much more controversial policies have passed through Parliaments in which the government had a commanding majority without encountering the obstacles that accompanied this bill.

The third element is the potential value of the Select Committee system. In 1975 Kogan pleaded for the strengthening of its powers, including the right to demand rather than request that Ministers *and* civil servants appear before the committee with full documentation. If the Select Committee system is to function properly as an investigative monitoring and evaluation process, then it will have to be given more powers, and more administrative back-up. During the 1970s, at least, the work of Parliamentary committees was constantly obstructed by stonewalling civil servants, and their reports were received by the DES with barely concealed contempt.

Alongside the flurry of interest in the curriculum that we associate with the Green Paper, another publication appeared in 1977 that was to have widespread implications for the running of schools. It was the Taylor report, *A New Partnership for Our Schools*. What lay beneath the rhetoric? What was the 'old' partnership? And what was meant by 'partnership', new or old?

The Taylor Committee had been established in 1975 'to review ... the management and government of maintained schools ... including [their] composition and functions, and their relationships with LEAs, with headteachers and staffs ... with parents and the local community at large'. Its recommendations gave new-style governing bodies not only more power over the management of schools, but, crucially, and in line with Ruskin and the Green Paper, power to influence (if not determine) the curriculum. The 'implications' referred to above only gradually became apparent in the 1980s when the report was hijacked by Sir Keith Joseph. Just as the 1977 Green Paper was to lead inexorably to the curriculum reforms of the Conservative 1988 Act, so also did Taylor's ideas (generally welcomed by Shirley Williams) inevitably influence the management reforms of the same 1988 Act. What we were to witness once again was Sir William Pile's *systematic thinking, formulation and implementation of policy*, in which party perspectives made little or no difference.

There is a tendency among some commentators to suggest that the use of the word *curriculum* in many DES and HMI documents of this period is evidence of government interference with the rights of LEAs or schools, or teachers in classrooms. Such a view overlooks the earlier work of the Schools' Council and such writers as Stenhouse in the 1960s and early 1970s in the UK, and Tyler, Schwab and Phenix (among others) in the US in the 1960s. What we were witnessing in the late 1970s and increasingly in the 1980s was the extraordinary sight of the DES catching up with its reading, and rapidly disseminating summaries of it to the outside world.

But the Schools' Council's brief had been to look after examinations as well as the curriculum in general, and its ineffective attempts to restructure examinations at eleven-plus are seen by Christopher Price (an outstanding chairman of the Education Select Committee) as its greatest weakness (Plaskow, 1985, p. 174). It had first set up a committee to investigate the issue in 1968. It took until July 1970 to produce a recommendation in favour of a single examination to replace GCE and CSE. Amazingly, these proposals did not reach Shirley Williams until 1976, who promptly set up the Waddell Committee to go over the same ground again. 'The major responsibility for the delay', in Price's view, 'arose from Mrs Williams' assiduous procrastination - a chronic disability from which she had suffered all her political life' (Plaskow, 1985, p. 174). It was not until a change of government brought first Mark Carlisle and then Sir Keith Joseph to the DES that the sixteen-plus proposals were eventually accepted, and not until much later, in Kenneth Baker's time, that pupils actually sat the new GCSE. The delay of twenty years, however, may seem to many readers as fairly standard practice in the process of developing and implementing policy in education, and the blame in this case cannot, surely, be laid entirely at the door of the Schools' Council.[12]

In spring 1976 the arrival of the the Assessment and Performance Unit (APU) at the DES was a clear sign that central government wished to play its own central role in the development of the curriculum and in the control of teaching. The terms of reference required the APU 'to promote the development of methods of assessing and monitoring the achievement of children in school, and seek to identify the incidence of underachievement'. Very quickly an elaborate mechanism of committees and monitoring groups was set up, with membership being drawn from teachers, advisers, HMI, academics, LEA officers and representatives from teachers' and lecturers' unions, supported by DES administrators and statisticians. During the years which followed, it became clear that the APU's chief interest was in mathematics, languages, and science, and these subjects featured centrally in the development of the National Curriculum and the 1988 Act. What was unclear at the time, and was to remain structurally untidy for many more years, was the relationship between the APU and the routine work of HMI and LEA advisers, which in turn raised a whole series of questions about the interrelation of HMI and these advisers, and between both groups and academic researchers in the topics they were monitoring.

The flow of major reports to the DES during this period reached dangerous proportions. In addition to Taylor, there were investigations into the teaching of English (Bullock, 1975), the management of higher education (Oaks, 1978), special educational needs (Warnock, 1978), and secondary school examinations (Waddell, 1978). Bullock, Warnock and Waddell had all been set up by the previous government, illustrating once again that many events in the management of education seem to possess their own momentum. Bullock and Warnock seeped into the system little by little without the need for much government intervention. Oaks became entangled in the change of government in 1979. Waddell's recommendation that the CSE exams should be merged with the GCE to form the GCSE took exactly ten years to achieve.

THE POLICY SYSTEM AND THE MACHINERY OF GOVERNMENT

Since the DES was the channel through which the Labour government's education policy inevitably had to be steered, it is not surprising that it frequently came under attack during and after the life of the Wilson-Callaghan administrations. 'In recent years it has been demoralised and has not yet discovered how to play its role. It has simultaneously been accused of being non-participative and yet too captive to its pressure groups; dictatorial but too unclear of its purposes; reactionary but at the same time committed to a soft view of education' (Kogan, 1975, p. 151). It would be easy to argue that these conflicts and confusions were those that were created by radical changes of direction on the part of the politicians. But such an analysis would be totally inadequate. With the possible exception of the secondary-comprehensive-school issue, education policy had remained strikingly bipartisan in practice, even if the rhetoric of policy presentation created a different impression from time to time, and especially at party conferences. The mythology of the partnership between central and local government, and between both of these and the major pressure groups of parents and teachers, suffered bouts of disintegration throughout the 1970s, some of which was caused by poor communication. 'Where a department never explains, and is never obliged to explain,' concluded McPherson and Raab (1988) in their study of the Scottish Education Department, 'the prospects for explanation and accountability are bleak. But, where a department or government has to explain in order to govern, there is at least a prospect of improvement in explanation and in governability alike' (p. 501).

We have already seen that Lord Crowther-Hunt was in a unique position to evaluate the work of the DES. His academic background, his Fulton Report involvement, his record as a constitutional adviser and his ministerial experience all combined to equip him with the necessary skills to penetrate the fog of bureaucratic deviation. He set out very clearly what he believed to be the principal weaknesses of an unresponsive system.

The classic accountability model of *advice - decision - action* (in which the civil servants give the advice and take the action while the decisions are made by ministers answerable to a democratically elected Parliament) he saw as suspect. 'But what,' he asked, 'if power does not reside exclusively in the hands of the directly elected representatives of the people? What if non-elected civil servants can, and often do, thwart or modify the will of ministers and Parliament by devising and operating policies of their own?' (Kellner and Crowther-Hunt, 1980, p. 204). It was because the classic model was seen to be inadequate that the Fulton Report suggested so many modifications to the system. However, 'it might well be said that what actually happened after the Fulton Report shows the insidious operation of civil service power at its most triumphant. Not only did civil servants successfully block the key Fulton proposals, but whilst doing so, they actually had the audacity to claim they carried out most of them' (*ibid.*, p. 205).

The Fulton Report had suggested a number of ways of introducing outside influences into the ministries, but 'most of these recommendations ... were either ignored, distorted, or watered down. Instead the Civil Service has acted to preserve, and even strengthen the citadels of its power' (Kellner and Crowther-Hunt, 1980, p. 205). The notion that the DES should have a planning unit (to include specialist educational advisers from outside the department) and that it should be led by a senior policy adviser had the intended outcome of coherent strategic planning by experts with direct access to the Secretary of State.[13]

In Crowther-Hunt's view, the top civil servants saw this as a process which would undermine their authority. John Hudson, the DES Deputy Secretary, confirmed to the Fookes Inquiry: 'It is true that at present we do not have within the DES ... advisers who are fully qualified in relation to any project ... We do not see them as being essential ... not at present or in the foreseeable future' (*TES*, 21 May 1976). In the DES a *Departmental Planning Organization* had been established in response to Fulton, but instead of using external expertise, this committee consisted almost exclusively of the Permanent-, Deputy-, and Under-Secretaries. 'This,' said Crowther-Hunt, 'was the very opposite of what Fulton had in mind ... There was not a specialist among them, none of the experts that were the essence of the Fulton proposal - no educational psychologists or sociologists, no counterparts of professors of education, for example' (Kellner and Crowther-Hunt, 1980, pp. 207-8).

The traditional DES view has always been that of course it does employ experts - 430 HMI in 1975 to be precise. Now, clearly, this is not an answer that satisfied Crowther-Hunt, or Fulton, or the Organization for Economic Cooperation and Development (OECD) in 1975, or, to any extent, the House of Commons Expenditure Committee 1975-76 (Fookes Committee). And when HMI was the subject of further investigation between January 1981 and March 1983 (the Raynor Report), the whole issue of the nature of 'independent professional judgement' was sidestepped. What else, after all, could be expected than that 'the insidious operation of civil service power at its most triumphant' would be seen in action once again? Sir Derek Raynor may have coordinated the report, but it was largely drafted by N. W. Stuart, a career civil servant, who first joined the DES in 1964 and who by 1988 had been promoted to Deputy Secretary. If it can be argued that it was in the clear interest of the DES to have it believed that not only did the department already maintain a body of independent professional advisers, but, furthermore, that it acted upon such advice, then it was hardly likely to encourage an adverse report on HMI.

The OECD report (1975, p. 30) had accused the DES of secrecy, passivity and conservatism, and of being held back by the 'inertial power of historically enshrined goals' of the civil service. 'A permanent officialdom,' the report contended (p. 29) 'becomes a power in its own right. A British department composed of professional civil servants who have watched the ministers come and go is an entity that only an extremely foolish or powerful politician will persistently challenge or ignore. The prestige, acquaintanceships, and natural authority of leading civil servants give them a standing in the civil forum often superior to that of their *de jure* political superiors.' A year later the Fookes Report was highly critical of the DES, and although it could be argued that the DES was more than happy to enter into curriculum planning, and, in a limited way, to encourage debate, it totally rejected the notion of a Standing Education Commission (on the grounds that it would be 'ineffective'), and completely misunderstood the notion of long-term strategic planning. The *TES* labelled the DES response as 'more like a public relations exercise than a genuine attempt to consult' (26 November 1976).

Of the 1975 and 1976 reports, Lawton and Gordon (1987, p. 27) highlighted that 'the two main complaints were that the DES was excessively secretive and that it lacked an adequate planning organization . . . the publication of the two reports in the same year undoubtedly stimulated the DES into a more open stance in policy making.' The stream of DES and HMI publications since 1976 is certainly evidence of a more 'open stance', but it scarcely represents an incursion into strategic planning in the sense that Fulton had in mind. The time-honoured role of HMI has always been to observe and report. It has been independent only in the sense that its observations and its reports have been carried out with the appropriate levels of dispassionate integrity long associated with HMI. It has never really carried out, nor claimed to be carrying out, a forward-planning role.

If HMI is not a strategic-planning group, then neither is it full of educational experts in the sense that Crowther-Hunt suggested above. HMI as a body has never claimed that it contains among its members 'the counterparts of professors of education'. Indeed, quite the opposite. It is a matter of pride to HMI that most of its members are drawn more or less directly from the ranks of schoolteachers.[14] In the context of HMI there is also a need to unpack the meaning of the term 'professional'. No one would doubt that, as a body of men and women charged with an often difficult and demanding brief, its members behave professionally in the sense that they bring knowledge and experience of teaching to a wide variety of problems with sensitivity and detachment. But HMI is not part of the teaching *profession* as such. Its members do not regularly teach in schools, colleges, polytechnics or universities. Nor do they enter into exchanges with those who do. Nor do they participate in the rough and tumble of educational research, or have to defend their views as equals in academic debate. They can be seen therefore as professional, but not *of* the profession. Their very existence depends on their being distanced *from* the profession. As Lawton and Gordon (1987, p. vii) found when writing their brief study, members of HMI 'were all very conscious of the Official Secrets Act'. This very secrecy, of course, excludes them from the profession.

Senior Chief Inspector Sheila Browne (in Lello, 1979, p. 35) believed that the accountability of HMI was 'beset by misunderstanding, myth and wishful thinking.' The *misunderstanding* related to the perceptions of some teachers and some politicians that HMI was there to judge rather than to advise; the *myth* was centred on a semi-romantic view that at some earlier time, all HMI had been able to have a personal and specialized relationship with every institution; the *wishful thinking* was that HMI could make schools more cost-effective. While emphasizing HMI's responsibilities towards the teaching profession, she nevertheless remained abundantly clear about allegiances. 'Like all Civil Servants,' she wrote (p. 40), 'HMI must be seen to work within current policy. In their dealings with local authorities and schools, they are often called upon to explain its implications or to comment on how it is proposed to implement it.' *Working within current policies and explaining implications* may seem inevitable to HMI, but it is neither what Fulton had in mind nor is it what the teaching profession deserves. Even if one accepts the rider that 'this sort of involvement still stops short of advocacy and propagation', the growing impression that HMI gave during the late 1970s, and with ever-increasing emphasis in the 1980s, was that it was simply the messenger of central government.

Thus, the Fulton recommendation concerning policy advisers had again been 'ignored, distorted, or watered down', to repeat Crowther-Hunt's memorable comment. When he gave evidence to the Fookes Committee, he described the DES as 'essentially passive and negative rather than active and positive' (*TES*, 14 May 1976). But his criticisms of the DES were not confined to the lack of proper planning mechanisms. He had first-hand experience of the 'pernicious practice of ministerial musical chairs':

> I had responsibility for the whole of further and higher education ... I stayed in the job only fifteen months, which was not long enough to develop and see through any major new policies, even though it was soon abundantly clear to me that our overall strategies in this area needed fundamental appraisal. The

> fact that Reg Prentice was replaced by a new Secretary of State after I had been there eight months enabled the Civil Service to fight back against some of the new initiatives I had got under way with Reg Prentice's blessing. Yet my stay was just about par for the course.... So where can you really expect the balance of power between ministers and their officials to lie?
>
> (Kellner and Crowther-Hunt, 1980, pp. 211-12)

Pile served for some seven years as Secretary. The Deputy Secretaries in 1975 - Hudson, Odgers, Simpson and Wright - had between them no fewer than nineteen years' experience *at that level*, and substantial further DES experience at lower levels. This balance of power equation cannot be blamed with any justification, however, on the civil service. The 'pernicious practice' is the consequence of the *politicians'* musical chairs, and no one else's. If the Prime Ministers of both the major parties did not incessantly (to use another metaphor) play snakes and ladders with their colleagues, this aspect of the problem would not exist.

Even if Ministers were to stay in office for a longer period, however, there would still remain an imbalance in the governmental process. Ministers, except for those few from the House of Lords, have to exercise all the duties of MPs and party members. Fulton made it clear that the sheer volume of papers arriving at their ministerial desks creates a marked tendency for politicians to become dependent upon departmental recommendations. 'If a minister accepts his officials' advice and he is challenged,' observed Crowther-Hunt, 'he at least knows he can go back and get all the supporting evidence he wants ... But if he strikes out in a direction of his own choosing, he can all too easily find himself alone and lost' (Kellner and Crowther-Hunt, 1980, p. 218).

When he was a Minister, Crowther-Hunt found that the politicians were normally excluded from the drafting stages of proposals. In the *advice - decision - action* model a crucial element of the process is the timing of the presentation of the evidence. Crowther-Hunt noted that it was common for Ministers to be 'faced with having to make quick decisions in the space of hours - and sometimes even minutes - on the basis of recommendations that civil servants had been chewing over for months among themselves' (*ibid.*, 1980, p. 219).

If Lord Crowther-Hunt is relentless in his attacks on the DES, then so also is Sir William Pile in its defence. It is comparatively rare for outsiders to be spectators of gladiatorial combat between ministers and mandarins, but the publication of Pile's account of the DES in 1979 and Crowther-Hunt's in 1980 invites onlookers to witness scenes of extraordinary piquancy. Not that either author refers to the other directly, or for that matter attempts to respond to arguments in other than covert terms.[15]

> It is ministers and ministers alone ... who are ultimately responsible to Parliament for national policies for education ... It does not follow that all new national policies for education originate with ministers ... Individual ministers may come to office with their own considered ideas on policy. Moreover, it is increasingly common for new educational policies to feature in the election manifestos ... [but] the department's senior permanent

> officials also have a role in policy making ... The Department's permanent staff has in recent years become increasingly equipped through the departmental planning organisation, to undertake systematic thinking about national policy objectives and their resource implications, and to identify longer term issues that may require policy decisions by ministers ... HMI have in recent years come to be more closely associated with the formulation as well as the implementation of policy.
>
> (Pile, 1979, pp. 35-6)

So there we have it. So much for the Fulton, OECD and Fookes Reports. Ministers are responsible, but perhaps for little more than getting the legislation through Parliament; they must not think it is their ideas that really matter, even if, or perhaps especially if, some similar idea appeared in a manifesto. The mandarins (with a bit of help from HMI) will do the *systematic thinking, the formulation and the implementation of policy*, while the ministers go off and busy themselves in their constituencies or, as in Lord Crowther-Hunt's case, the University of Oxford.

No less fascinating is the exchange of gunfire over openness and secrecy. As we have seen, OECD and Fookes accused the DES and HMI of unjustified levels of clandestinity. A fascinating example of this came to the surface when John Hudson, Pile's most senior Deputy, gave evidence to the Fookes Committee. Janet Fookes asked for DES planning documents to be made available to her committee. Hudson refused on the grounds that they had been written 'in confidence'; he then gave a lengthy explanation of Whitehall's 'rules', saying that 'the practice had grown up in the context of the political and parliamentary system. *It also served the needs of the administration* [my italics] ... Much public business was often a matter of delicate negotiation which would be inhibited if the papers were easily accessible' (*TES*, 21 May 1976). Referring to the failure of the DES to respond effectively to the Select Committee's report, Kogan (1975, p. 143) summed up the general dissatisfaction within educational circles: 'The DES could be allowed to get on with its decision-making but defend policies in advance and explain more detailed actions, if necessary, in retrospect. Education does seem less subject to political scrutiny than other zones of public policy'.

There was clearly a fundamental conflict of thinking about the nature of 'openness' and 'confidentiality'. For example, Pile devoted a whole chapter of his book to an explanation of how widespread his department's consultations and disseminations have been. Indeed, he believed (1979, p. 43) they provided 'a common universe of discourse within which debates on national educational issues can be pursued'. When Lady Plowden and Lord Robbins gave evidence before the Fookes Committee, they questioned the value of the whole DES consultative machinery, since it concentrated especially on the teachers' unions and the LEAs, and mostly excluded specialists from the academic and industrial worlds (*TES*, 6 February 1976). There is a characteristic and pervasive ambiguity about Pile's style when he observes (in Harling, 1984, p. 85) that 'It is *probably fair to say* that the Department *is as conscious as any department of central government* of the need to promote *continuous consultation* with its local authority and other partners *on all major issues* of policy and resource allocation' (my italics).

Pile returns to the 'common universe of discourse' with some enthusiasm in the final chapter of his book. While acknowledging the existence of 'successive ministers bringing with them into office explicit political commitments (and occasionally educational convictions)', and modestly recognizing the contributions of civil servants in providing 'professional skills, accumulated knowledge, and a concern for the continuity of things', he nevertheless believes, that 'more deep-seated forces' are at work. 'The obscure tides of moral, social and economic change which have run with singular strength in the postwar years have in this sense been the main determining factors' (Pile, 1979, p. 228). In this adventure into the metaphysical, the message is still abundantly clear: we are invited to confess that the *obscure tides of change* are most likely to be comprehended by the *department* with its *concern for the continuity of things*.

A further dimension of the whole messy political/administrative problem was identified by Maurice Kogan (1975, p. 147) when he pointed to 'one of the paradoxes of the system', namely that

> parties in opposition have clearer ideologies, or commitments to large scale change, than parties in power. Once in power, a minister must relate to the total system of interest groups, many of whom, in education at least, are anxious to hasten rather than to arrest the death of ideology. The total government machine led by the Treasury favours consistency and coherence rather than idealism and adventure. The government department serving a minister is concerned to sustain gradualism and continuity that take so long to identify and nourish, and put to work.

Consistency, coherence, gradualism and continuity, especially in relation to budgetary constraints, are matters to which Pile attached considerable significance. In his analysis the bulk of educational expenditure 'is predetermined by basic demographic factors . . . At any given point the residue is small and leaves little room for manoeuvre. However, the further ahead that this distinction between basic expenditure and the remainder is projected . . . the larger the area of choice is seen to be' (1979, p. 58). The opportunities for changes of policy are therefore severely limited not only in financial terms, but also in procedural terms. When a new government comes into office, the 'residual' budget has already been earmarked for perhaps the next two years. Consultations have been made, and promises extracted. It hardly gives a new Secretary of State much room for implementing his or her own policies in the early stages of the administration, and, as we have seen, the chances of a Secretary of State staying in office long enough to determine radical usages of the residual funds, let alone of the bulk of the educational budget, have been minimal.

There is often only a very fine line to be drawn between manifesto rhetoric and mandarin rhetoric. The 1978 official DES Annual Report listed four themes that it claimed had dominated departmental thinking and actions. They were: the extension of educational opportunity and participation; the improvement of the quality of education; the management of the education system in the face of a dramatic decline in the number of children; and the provision of educational support for the government's industrial strategy. The reader could be excused for confusing these bland generalizations with the manifestos of any of the political parties. 'The quality of education is inseparable,' the report goes on to state in the very broadest terms, 'from the quality of teaching in our schools. In 1978 the Department concentrated on two major aspects of this problem: the need to maintain an effective teaching force in the face of falling school rolls and the need to improve the quality of individual teachers ... On the second, the increasing importance of induction and in-service training was ... reflected in financial planning.'[16]

The Labour governments of the period 1974-79, in coping with the problems of small or non-existent majorities in the House, the IMF emergency, the resulting public expenditure cuts, and the pressures exercised by a number of trade unions, may have lost their way in the development of a coherent education policy for schools and for higher and further education. At the same time it has to be recognized that the White Paper of 1972, *Education: A Framework for Expansion*, had set in motion, according to Pile (1979, p. 59), budgetary programmes extending as far as 1981. In other words, Margaret Thatcher, as Secretary of State for Education, had approved financial strategies in 1972 which were still partly in place when she became Prime Minister in 1979. But only partly: for the 'wider events' of the oil crisis and rapidly falling birth rate had 'pulled the foundations from under the logistics of the 1972 White Paper', as the Deputy Secretary Edward Simpson later confirmed (in Ransom and Tomlinson, 1986, p. 23): 'Taken together, these developments of 1974 were to lead the Secretary of State and the department into very unfamiliar territory.'

When Shirley Williams returned to the DES in 1976, she certainly found it not only unfamiliar but hostile territory. In the 1960s she had been faced with the problem of how to cope with more and more pupils, needing more and more teachers and resources. This may have created its own difficulties, but expansion is always easier to manage than contraction, for 'the main objective may no longer be held in common. Those concerned only to forward the education service's interests may see falling demand as an opportunity for further qualitative improvement, which the government with their wider financial responsibility will feel obliged not just to moderate, but to deny.' In the late 1970s, therefore, the 'management' of declining numbers led the DES into 'areas which had previously been the LEAs' exclusive concern' (Simpson, in Ransom and Tomlinson, 1986, pp. 23-4).

There was, then, a major and unresolved problem for the Labour Party's education policy. As we have seen, at the very heart of Pile's concept of the DES is its forward-planning capacity, and the belief that its essential function is

> that of resource planning for the education service as a whole: that is, the formulation of objectives, the framing of national policies best calculated to meet these objectives, the undertaking

> of long term costings of policies in a way that enables ministers to choose their priorities, and the task of effectively presenting the consequential resource needs within central government.
>
> (Pile, 1979, p. 59)

When the ongoing budget allows for only marginal investment in new initiatives, and when that margin is further reduced by Treasury cuts, the 'long-term costing of policies', in which Pile and the DES took such pride, may become a trap rather than a solution. Are we, therefore, faced with irreconcilable contradictions? On the one hand, politicians, following the Fulton line, clamoured for coherent strategic planning, supported by external educational advisers. On the other hand, since such planning must inevitably (from a budgetary point of view) span a substantial period of time, governments are bound to encounter acute short-term operational difficulties, and with the IMF agreements they were undeniably acute. Since governments may last fewer than five years, and ministers may last less (perhaps considerably less) time than three years, we are back to the machinery-of-government problem yet again. As has been correctly observed, 'The more that official estimates dominate the context in which policies are made, the more these estimates are likely to become self-fulfilling prophesies and, conversely, the more that opportunities to develop the system in different ways will be neglected' (Salter and Tapper, 1981, p. 102). If we are to find a way out of this labyrinth in the future, then it is not new education policies that we shall need, but new structures at the very heart of government.

NOTES

1 When finally presenting the report of her committee, *TES*, 24 September 1976.
2 House of Commons, *10th Report from the Expenditure Committee, Session 1975–6, Policy Making in the DES* (1976). Dame Janet Fookes MP was a former teacher and chairman of the Education, Arts and Home Affairs Sub-Committee of the House of Commons Expenditure Committee 1975–79.
3 House of Commons, *Third Report of Expenditure Committee* (1974).
4 See Chapter 4 for a discussion of his earlier years.
5 In 1978 the external view of the DES was summed up in Kogan's critical appraisal: 'although the DES is exceedingly powerful within the education service, within the civil service it is regarded as a little separate. It has the appearance of a Vice-Royalty, something akin to the style of the British Raj in India, a prestigious part of the main system but somewhat remote from it . . . The civil servants in the department have not been in the mainstream of Whitehall. The response of different heads of the civil service has been to introduce permanent secretaries from the outside, and some at least have taken time, usually until their day of retirement, to understand the issues' (1979, pp. 150–1).
6 Chitty (1988) appears to accept uncritically Donoughue's version of this episode.
7 Subsequently, Odgers was replaced by Alan Thompson, and Wright by Walter Ulrich.
8 *TES*, 2 July 1976, reporting a speech made at the Association for Education Committees at Scarborough.
9 For an account of the open hostility that existed between Ulrich and the Schools' Council see John Mann in Plaskow (1985), pp. 188–9.
10 Some readers may have confused this title with *The Yellow Book: An Illustrated Quarterly*, the first volume of which appeared in April 1894, and which documented the 'decadence'

of Aubrey Beardsley's Aesthetic Movement. Although both publications were intended for a restricted readership, any similarities in the content are purely accidental.

11 She repeated her view that the Secretary of State did not have detailed responsibility for curricula, and that state control would be 'a long step backwards' (*TES*, 5 November 1976).

12 For further discussion of this point, see a valuable perspective provided by Geoff Whitty, 'State policy and school examinations 1976–1982', in Ahier and Flude (1983).

13 Raison had also suggested a revived Central Advisory Council; see Chapter 4.

14 For further discussion of this, see Lawton and Gordon (1987), pp. 118–19.

15 Pile's book had in fact been completed in 1975, and much of Crowther-Hunt's chapter on the DES had appeared in articles in 1976.

16 Department of Education and Science, *Annual Report 1978* (HMSO 1978).

Chapter 6

'My story being done, she gave me for my pains a world of sighs': the Conservative governments 1979-92

In the conferences that had taken place since the general elections of 1974, the two main parties had tackled educational issues in strikingly different ways. The Conservative resolutions, which had returned to the brevity of the early 1960s, laid emphasis on only one concern - the raising of standards in schools. In 1976 the Conservatives had called for the 'immediate introduction of minimum standards' (as if education were like agriculture or industry), and in 1977 had introduced the term 'national standards', which ten years later became linked with the 'National Curriculum'. The Labour conferences, in spite of the fact that Labour was in government, became more and more critical of education policy. The resolutions became longer, the range of issues wider, and the defeated motions more numerous. Only two themes remained constant and unchallenged, the provision of nursery education and the abolition of selection in secondary schooling. Almost everything else was ignored or resisted.

Throughout the 1950s and 1960s the political parties always claimed to be encouraging the expansion of teacher education in order to cope with the rapidly growing population of schools. The total school population grew, it will be recalled, because of three major factors: the growth in the birth rate, the raising of the school-leaving age, and the increased numbers of pupils electing to stay on at school after they had reached their 16th birthday. The first two factors had predictable outcomes, but the take-up of places in the 'new sixth forms', as they were called,[1] was variable. As the birth rate declined equally rapidly in the 1970s, the parties had to think of strategies that could first reverse the growth in teacher training, and then redistribute the existing workforce in schools. The manifestos of 1979 revealed Labour as the supporter of universal comprehensive secondary schools, reduced class sizes, an end to subsidized independent schools, more nurseries, and an increase in access to, and financial support for, 16-19 education; and the Conservatives in favour of the repeal of the 1976 Act, a Parent's Charter and an expanded assisted-places scheme for the independents.

In many respects the Conservatives' 1983 education proposals were simply a continuation of the strategies already in place and traded on assertions such as 'giving parents more power is one of the most effective ways of raising educational standards'. But when the Conservatives won their biggest majority in an election since the war, they did so, if Rose's analysis is correct, not on the basis of their own departure from the norms of British political policies, but because their main opponents themselves chose to depart from the middle ground: 'In a free society, any political party has the right to be as different as it wishes from its political opponents. But it cannot expect to win a general election if it chooses to be too different. The price it pays is not only its own exclusion from office but the confirmation in office of its distrusted Adversary' (Rose, 1984, p. 161). Before we ask if this was true in the case of education policy, we must first pay due attention to the role of the Alliance parties in this election. The Conservatives won the 1983 election by a landslide because they were able to take advantage of the confusion in the minds of the electorate about who was actually occupying the middle ground. Only 42 per cent voted Conservative in 1983, to produce a majority of 144 seats. Compare this with 1964 when Labour, with a bigger share of the votes at 44 per cent, achieved a majority of only four seats.

The games-playing titles of the 1987 manifestos told the whole story. The Conservatives had been in office long enough to know exactly what they wanted to do, and so *The Next Moves Forward* seemed particularly apt, while Labour's *Britain Will Win* simply raised the question, 'against whom?' and the Alliance's *Britain United - The Time Has Come* proved to be amazingly ironic. The Conservatives promised increased funding and four reforms: the National Curriculum, grant-maintained status for schools, increased parental choice, and local management of schools. Labour emphasized nursery education, a Schools' Standards Council, maintenance allowances for 16-18-year-olds in need, the ending of secondary selection, and increased access to higher education. The Alliance parties revealed plans to create a new Department of Education, Training and Science, to restore negotiating rights to teachers, to provide education and training allowances for the 16-18-year-olds, and to guarantee free further education to adults.

General election results

	Conservatives	Labour	Liberal/Alliance	Overall Conservative majority
1979	43.9%	37.0%	13.8%	43
1983	42.4%	27.6%	25.4%	144
1987	42.4%	30.8%	22.6%	101

THE POLITICIANS

During the 1979-92 period, the DES was to see five Secretaries of State, four Ministers of State, and twelve Under-Secretaries (not including Ministers for Sport or the Arts). Four of the five Secretaries had already run other (mostly larger) departments, but none brought with them any previous DES experience. Two Ministers and two junior Ministers were on their way to cabinet positions; one Minister moved sideways to the Home Office, and one other junior rose to ministerial level in another department. In no sense, therefore, did the DES provide an internal promotion programme for politicians interested in education, although it did provide wider opportunities for a few high-flyers and a quiet retreat for many others.

Four of the five Secretaries of State were lawyers. The first, Mark Carlisle (later Baron Carlisle; b. 1929), had been educated at Radley and Manchester University and was an MP from 1964 to 1987. He had joined the Home Office as a junior Minister in 1970, rising to Minister of State after two years. He was a surprise choice for Education, having had no experience of the portfolio in opposition and little or no direct experience with the education sector during his political career before or after his two years at the DES. The manifesto promises of increased parental choice and higher standards were only marginally tackled - by the 1979 Act repealing Labour legislation on the comprehensives, and by DES documents such as *The School Curriculum*.

In September 1981 he was replaced by another lawyer, Sir Keith Joseph (later Baron Joseph; b. 1918), whose four years and nine months' continuous stay at the DES fell only just short of George Tomlinson's record in the ministry days. After Harrow, Magdalen College, Oxford, and wartime Army service, he had been a fellow of All Souls before becoming an MP in 1956. He was in government from 1959. His career in politics is often described as falling into two quite distinct compartments. As Housing Minister in 1962-64 and Social Services Minister in 1970-74, he was responsible for huge expenditure programmes, which he did much to encourage. However, after a period at the Centre for Policy Studies (1974-79), he emerged as a key exponent of the policy of reduction in government spending, first as Industry Secretary in 1979-81, and then as Education Secretary. Although not previously connected in a formal sense with the politics of education he had from time to time voiced strong opinions on schooling long before his Elizabeth House days. In a speech in Birmingham as shadow Home Secretary in 1974, he had launched an intemperate attack on the schools, which he accused of abusing 'their power and authority to urge or condone anti-social behaviour either on political grounds - against an unjust society, against authority - or as liberation from the trammels of the outmoded family'; and on the universities, which he accused of harbouring 'cuckoos in our democratic nest' (*TES*, 25 October 1974). When the *TES* took him to task for such wild language, he retaliated (*TES*, 1 November 1974) with an article entitled 'Time to Stop the Rot' which became something of a catch-phrase for a while.

Joseph's 1983 White Paper, *Teaching Quality*, probably represents his most characteristic contribution to educational policy. It offered an intriguing mixture of long-term DES strategies developed from the 1970s and the personal idiosyncrasies of an All Souls fellow somewhat ill at ease in the arena of a public education service. Essentially the White Paper looked at four phases of the teachers' careers - how they are selected, how they are trained, how they are managed and how they can be disposed of when necessary. But the White Paper had to contend with falling school numbers and the resulting decline in teacher morale. In practice it asked teachers who were perhaps uncertain of their own futures to give extra time to help in the selection of new entrants; it assumed, incorrectly, that there were more candidates than vacancies for trainees; it wanted good managers in the schools without offering them good salaries; and it failed entirely to find a way of disposing of incompetents. What it did achieve was the almost total breakdown in any further sensible communications between Sir Keith Joseph and the LEAs and teachers. One of the White Paper's suggestions was that teachers should be regarded as belonging to an LEA's workforce in general rather than to the staff of a particular school, in order that they could be moved from school to school as the need arose. Whatever the merits of such an idea, it engendered so much hostility from teachers that any further attempts to encourage their participation in anything other than their minimum contractual obligations were doomed to failure. Not untypical of their attitude was the following reaction:

> Sir Keith's policies are intended to secure obedient teachers and pupils, willing servants of capitalist competition. Teaching will be defined in new contracts and monitored through a complex, hierarchical mechanism of reporting and appraisal. There will be no more voluntary activity, goodwill or professional discretion; only prescribed duties and targets. Pupils will find their every move recorded in profiles and reports; their efforts will be constantly measured against national criteria and fixed standards.
> (Barker, 1986, p. 83)

Joseph had already angered the LEAs and teachers' unions by closing down the Schools' Council in April 1982, despite the Trenaman Report's recommendations of the previous year. Its role as curriculum planner was to be replaced by HMI and DES officers. Not that the Council had ever been a great success. As Christopher Price (in Plaskow, 1985, pp. 171-2) noted, 'throughout the 1970s, it withdrew deeper and deeper into its own private language. One of the reasons why it died was because it had neither projected itself coherently enough nor coopted sufficient allies a decade earlier.'[2] Nevertheless, Price was the first to admit that even he 'had underestimated the rapacious determination of the government to obtain ministerial control over the school curriculum' (*ibid.*, p. 173).

Keith Joseph may or may not have represented Thatcherism at the DES - it is still too close to the event to form a reliable view on the issue. But what he undoubtedly did represent was yet another cabinet minister on the way out and serving time in Education: a list that already included Horsburgh, Lloyd, Gordon-Walker, Mulley and Carlisle. His impact on the DES was well summed up in the following account:

> Education, like health, is an area obsessed with 'cuts', although real expenditure per pupil, class sizes and pupil-teacher ratios reached the best levels ever. Even teachers' pay increased; few teachers believed this. The shock waves from the declining school population did their work. Education had the low morale of a declining industry; and Sir Keith Joseph was made to serve as a hate figure in consequence. Still, when he departed, the school system was visibly as Mrs Shirley Williams had left it in 1979.
> (Vincent, in Hennessy and Seldon, 1987, p. 290)

When Edward Heath lost the election in 1975 for the leadership of the Conservative Party, his campaign manager was Kenneth Baker. It was not surprising, therefore, that when Margaret Thatcher formed her first government in 1979, Baker remained on the back benches. But in 1981 he forced his way into government by inventing and then filling the post of Minister of Information Technology in the Department of Industry. In 1985 he was made Secretary of State for the Environment, and only a year later replaced Joseph at the DES. Baker (b. 1937) was educated at St Paul's School and Magdalen College, Oxford, where he read history, the only non-lawyer among the five.

Kenneth Baker brought to the DES both a determined political ambition (accompanied by a permanent, self-congratulatory smile) and a single-minded political ideology. It was the full-blooded ideology of Thatcherism: pro-individual, anti-state. It was manifested most obviously in the proposals to loosen the grip of local authorities on schools, polytechnics and colleges, and to encourage those institutions, together with universities, to acquire and develop conventional commercial attitudes and manners. However, when it came to the curriculum of schools, the ideological supertanker came to grief on the rocks of old-fashioned British traditionalism. The reawakening of Victorian values led not to a governmental withdrawal from state-led curriculum decision-making, but to the reassertion of the widely held view that everyone knows more about teaching than do professional teachers. Leave it to the common sense of parents and businessmen (it was said), and things are bound to improve. Let them (with the help of the government they elected) tell the teachers what to teach, for schools are there to promote national wealth, and all that unemployment of the early 1980s was simply the result of poor teaching and the development of inappropriate attitudes to an industrial economy. After three years in office Baker left the DES to become party chairman.

They were three not uneventful years. City technology colleges, the abolition of Burnham, changes in university funding, parental choice, opting-out, licensed teachers, student loans, the local management of schools and the National Curriculum are all ideas that will continue to be associated with Baker. Generally speaking, they were all established DES initiatives, but what Baker achieved was the most rapid production line since the DES was formed. Of course many welcomed the speed of events, pointing to the very slow turn-round in the past. But others wondered not only whether so many changes could be accommodated within the system in so short a time, but also what exactly they amounted to. As a *TES* editorial (28 July 1989) said of him, 'He was too good at presentation; what he lacked was substance.'

When John MacGregor (b. 1937) was appointed Secretary of State in July 1989, the general response was 'John MacWho?' He had, however, already established within government circles a substantial reputation for reliability. He had been at school in Edinburgh and at the University of St Andrews before combining a career in politics and the law. After working in the Conservative research department and in Edward Heath's private office, he had entered Parliament in 1974. In government since 1981, he had served in the cabinet since 1985, first as Chief Secretary of the Treasury and then as Minister (a.k.a. Secretary of State) of Agriculture, Food and Fisheries. The question was, how successful would he be in putting into place the consequences of the Reform Act? or, as the *TES* (9 November 1990) put it, 'about making Kenneth Baker's national curriculum dreams fit the reality of the classroom', adding, 'if he has brought a political style to education, it is to try to get people to work with him.'[3] And MacGregor himself sensibly took the attitude that 'there is not much point in trying to invent a radical idea every minute if you have not actually carried through the one before' (*Guardian*, 18 October 1990).

Events that took place in the autumn of 1990 vividly illustrate the nature of the relationship between governmental education policies and the wider spheres of political activity. From the annual party conferences the notion emerged that education was to be the 'big idea'. First at the Labour conference at Blackpool, and then at the Conservative conference at Bournemouth, the party chairmen and the press fostered the illusion that the next general election could be won or lost on the battlefield of education policy. Now, as everyone knows, or should know, no postwar general election has ever been won or lost on a single issue, and certainly not on an issue as narrow as education (or, more specifically, the provision of schooling). It might be argued that the *economy* has been seen as a single election issue, but even if that were true, it would be at a level of generalization that undermines any attempt to use *education* as a similar all-embracing concept.

Nevertheless, there for two or three weeks was education masquerading as the 'big idea'. It will be recalled that there were two much bigger ideas jostling for position at the time: the Gulf crisis and the Chancellor of the Exchequer's announcement, timed to coincide with the climax of the Labour conference, of the UK's entry into the European Exchange Rate Mechanism (ERM). In spite of this, the press managed to keep education in the headlines by the old trick of dealing in personalities first and policies second. John MacGregor had kept a fairly low profile during his first year in office, visiting a lot of schools in various parts of the country and attempting to repair some of the damage inflicted by his predecessor. As a result, his standing in opinion polls published in October showed that he was almost unknown to the general public. Now this may very well be evidence of his devotion to duty as opposed to devotion to self-publicity, but it gave rise to press speculations that he was no longer in favour at Downing Street. His conference speech, notable for its lack of eccentricity and bravado, was greeted with some derision, and ten days later the Secretary of State had a formal meeting with the Prime Minister. This event was variously described as a routine meeting called at MacGregor's request to discuss education finance and the implementation of the 1988 Act Stage 1 Attainment Targets, or as a demand by Thatcher that he either follow the Baker line to the letter or be replaced by a more vociferous exponent of the far Right. We shall no doubt have to wait for the publication of more political diaries to learn more about the circumstances, but, in the event, MacGregor emerged from Downing Street with the news that not only had he won approval for his proposal that testing at the age of 7 should be dramatically reduced, but also that in that round of departmental estimates he had been given £0.5 billion more by way of extra funding. Of course no one knows, or is ever intended to know, whether that meant *more* than the DES was asking for, or *more* than the massively reduced counter-offer made by the Treasury in its bargaining with the so-called spending ministries.

Only a month later MacGregor *was* replaced at the DES by Kenneth Clarke, until then Secretary of State for Health. If education was the 'big idea', it was now in the hands of a department in which the Secretary of State, however politically astute, was brand-new to education policies; a Minister of State who was only three months into the job; one Under-Secretary (Howarth) who had just spent twelve months learning the schools portfolio, only to be switched to higher education in July 1990; another Under-Secretary (Fallon) who had also only three months' experience of government; and, crucially, a new Permanent Secretary who had joined the DES only in 1989. DES *experience* therefore lay in the hands of the Deputy Secretaries and the Senior Chief Inspector, who between them had notched up some 28 years' involvement at that level. The immediate cause, if not the explanation, for this reshuffle was the dramatic resignation of yet another senior cabinet Minister, Sir Geoffrey Howe, the Deputy Prime Minister and Leader of the House. MacGregor became the new Leader of the House (though not the Deputy Prime Minister) and thus left the DES after fewer than fifteen months in office.

Unlike his predecessor, everyone knew the high-profile Kenneth Clarke (b. 1940) with his reputation for challenging almost every assumption of the National Health Service. Why had he been brought to the DES, apparently against his will? Was he expected to confront the teaching profession with the same techniques that he had employed against doctors, dentists, nurses and ambulance workers? Had he been so successful that Downing Street feared the competition? Or had the backlash of the medical profession made his diversion into the sidings of Elizabeth House a sweet revenge on a man who had accused senior consultants of being self-seeking and GPs of being interested only in the size of their wallets?

There were four Ministers of State in this period. Baroness Young (b. 1926) had been brought into the last year of Edward Heath's government as a junior Minister at the Department of the Environment, serving as Minister of State at the DES from 1979 to 1981. She was a product of Headington School and St Anne's College, Oxford, where she had been a contemporary of the new Prime Minister. She left the DES to become a Minister at the Foreign and Commonwealth Office, and held cabinet rank as Leader of the House of Lords and Lord Privy Seal. She was not replaced for four years,[4] that is, not until the arrival of Chris Patten (b. 1944), the MP for Bath since 1979, who had been educated at St Benedict's School, Ealing, and Balliol College, Oxford. He had joined the government in 1983 as a Northern Ireland junior Minister, and in 1985 he was promoted to Minister of State at the DES. The following year, however, he became Minister of State at the Foreign Office; in 1989, Secretary of State for the Environment; and in 1990 chairman of the Conservative Party. He was followed by Angela Rumbold (b. 1932) of Notting Hill and Ealing High School and King's College, London, where she read Law and Art History. Elected to Kingston upon Thames Council in 1974, she became MP from 1982 (by-election) for Mitcham and Morden. The following year she became PPS to Nicholas Ridley (Secretary of State for Transport), and in 1985 Parliamentary Under-Secretary for the Environment before joining the DES from 1986 to 1990, when she moved over to become Minister of State at the Home Office. Tim Eggar (b. 1951), the

MP for Enfield North since 1979, had graduated from Magdalene College, Cambridge, after Winchester. Another lawyer, he had been a junior Minister at the Foreign Office between 1985 and 1989 before being promoted to Minister of State at the Department of Employment. He was appointed to the DES as Minister of State in July 1990, bringing with him his responsibility for TVEI and taking over further education, adult education and the links with the training agency.

The eleven Parliamentary Under-Secretaries normally filled two posts throughout this period, one for schools and one for higher and further education. They also formed three categories of career performance - those who went on to become Secretaries of State, those who reached Minister of State level, and those who returned to the back-benches. Dr Rhodes Boyson (b. 1925), the MP for Brent North since 1974, was a grammar-school boy (as he never failed to remind everyone), who went on to Manchester University and the London School of Economics. A schoolteacher who had been a head since 1955, he became well known as a writer on educational politics from 1969 onwards, and became an opposition spokesman on education from 1976 to the election.[5] He remained at the DES from 1979 to 1982 and was then promoted to Minister of State for Social Security (1983-84) for Northern Ireland (1984-86) and finally for Local Government (1986-87). We can perhaps see the strength of at least one well-aimed comment (Johnson, 1989, p. 112) on such a career: 'How paradoxical that this important early character, apostle of the practical, the basic and the real, failed to survive (in "education") to the pragmatic resolution of our tale!'

In complete contrast, (Sir) William Shelton (b. 1929; Radley and Worcester College, Oxford) had gained substantial experience as a company director. He became the MP for Streatham in 1974, and soon afterwards the PPS to Margaret Thatcher in opposition. His formal connection with education was limited to his time at the DES between 1981 and 1983. William Waldegrave (b. 1946) of Eton, Corpus Christi College, Oxford (where he was president of the Union), and Harvard, became a fellow of All Souls College, Oxford, in 1971 and MP for Bristol West in 1979. He had gained considerable political experience by working in the Cabinet Office in the early 1970s and held the DES post from 1981 to 1983. He went on to the Department of the Environment and then to become Secretary of State for Health. Robert Dunn (b. 1946), the MP for Dartford since 1979, had been in business following his education in state schools. He remained at the DES for five years between 1983 and 1988. Peter Brooke (b. 1934) was a product of Marlborough, Balliol College, Oxford, and the Harvard Business School. He was elected MP for the City of London in 1977 and joined the government in 1981. He spent only two years at the DES before rising to Minister of State at the Treasury in 1985 and Secretary of State for Northern Ireland in 1989. George Walden (b. 1939), educated at Latymer Upper School and Jesus College, Cambridge, had worked extensively in the diplomatic service before becoming MP for Buckingham in 1983. He remained at the DES from 1985 to 1987, but his book *Ethics and Foreign Policy* (1990) may indicate where his interests really lay. Robert Jackson (b. 1946) was educated abroad and at St Edmund's Hall, Oxford (where he was president of the Union), before also becoming a fellow of All Souls. He had been a Member of the European Parliament (MEP) before arriving at Westminster as the MP for Wantage. He joined the DES in 1987. He had responsibility for higher education until July 1990 when he became employment Minister, but he continued links with education by maintaining some responsibilities for the careers service, TVEI, and the training and enterprise councils. Like Jackson, Baroness Hooper had also been an MEP (1979-84) before joining the DES during 1987-88. She was a lawyer trained at Southampton University, who went on to hold further junior posts in Energy and then in Health. John Butcher (b. 1946; Huntington Grammar School and Birmingham University) had been a Coventry MP since 1979 and a Department of Trade and Industry junior Minister before spending a year at the DES in 1988-89.

Alan Howarth (b. 1944), the MP for Stratford-upon-Avon since 1983, was educated at Rugby and King's College, Cambridge, where he read history. He taught at Westminster School from 1968 to 1974 before joining Conservative Party HQ. He held the post of Schools Minister in 1989-90 but was changed to higher education (together with special educational needs (SEN), inner-city policies and youth services) from July 1990. Unlike some of his immediate predecessors, he seemed to take a more traditional view of the nature of higher education: 'I am quite confident', he announced, 'that the system is willing to innovate. I don't think it would make sense if, from this office, I tried to plan for them or impose on them my view of what kind of innovation is appropriate' (*Guardian*, 18 June 1991). On the other hand, Michael Fallon (b. 1952; St Andrews University) rapidly acquired a reputation for feeding the media with instant opinions and quotable remarks, or so it appeared. In a team of four ministers it is perhaps useful to have one junior who can raise controversial issues without the necessary circumspection usually associated with a Secretary of State. As a kite-flyer, Michael Fallon had the enviable characteristic of complete self-confidence. The MP for Darlington since 1983, he had joined the DES in 1990, with responsibility for teacher training and supply, local management of schools, the schools-industry links, careers education, discipline and health education.

During the last stages of the Conservative government, and particularly during the Major administration, Westminster became the scene of widespread splintering within the party. Members, supporters or associates of at least nine different, but perhaps overlapping, groups, sought to secure prominence for a particular point of view. The Centre for Policy Studies had of course been operating since 1975, and, as both Margaret Thatcher and Keith Joseph, its founders, were at the DES, it was inevitable that it should exercise a strong influence on education policy. The No Turning Back Group, founded in 1985 in order to reinforce Thatcherite policies, had Angela Rumbold and Michael Fallon as prominent members. The Conservative Way Forward Group included Keith Joseph and Bob Dunn; the Tory Philosophy Group is thought to have included a number of right-wing MPs, but remained somewhat secretive; the Selsdon Group, the Institute of Economic Affairs, the Adam Smith Institute, and the Bruges Group were chiefly concerned with economic affairs; but the Social Affairs Unit, whose priority was the continued dismantling of the welfare state, attracted members whose inclination was to privatize the whole British education system. Overall, the posts at the DES were dominated by lawyers and businessmen: only two (junior) ministers had been schoolteachers. How did these various talents combine with the permanent staff at Elizabeth House?

THE CIVIL SERVANTS

When Mark Carlisle arrived at the DES in May 1979, he found Sir James Hamilton at the end of his third full year as Permanent Secretary, and four Deputy Secretaries and a Chief HMI who had between them accumulated 30 years of experience at that level in the DES. Hamilton was to stay a further four years, presiding over many of the developments that occurred in DES policy in the early stages of the Joseph regime. On his retirement in 1983, he was appositely described as an 'unrepentant centralist' (*TES*, 24 April 1983). His replacement was Sir David Hancock (b. 1934; Whitgift School and Balliol College, Oxford), who had joined the Board of Trade in 1957 before developing a successful career at the Treasury and enhanced by a spell in the cabinet office. Not since 1952 had an Education Deputy become the Permanent Secretary, and not since Sir William Pile had a Permanent Secretary drawn on substantial previous education experience. The combination of an ex-Industry Minister and ex-Treasury mandarin to run the DES could not have sent a clearer message about the cabinet's perception of the department's future role. Nor was this image much changed with the appointment of Sir John Cains (b. 1933) as his eventual replacement. Educated at Westminster School and Christ Church, Oxford, he was a career civil servant who had joined the Ministry of Supply in 1957 and later the Ministry of Aviation, before establishing himself at the DTI, where he rose to Deputy Secretary in 1983. He then held the post of Permanent Secretary at the Overseas Development Administration of the Foreign and Commonwealth Office between 1987 and 1989.

New appointments at Deputy Secretary level mostly reinforced the new image that the Prime Minister was determined to impose upon the DES. It began in 1980 with the promotion of Richard Bird (b. 1932; Winchester and Clare College, Cambridge), who had arrived at the DES in 1973 after a civil service career of some eighteen years in the Ministry of Transport and the Department of the Environment. Next, in 1983, came Philip Halsey (b. 1928), who undoubtedly represented a significant change in civil service appointments. A University of London BSc, he had joined the DES at Principal grade in 1966 after relinquishing the post of headmaster of Hampstead School. He was promoted to Under-Secretary in 1977 and served as head of the teachers' branch from 1982 to 1986, retiring to become chairman of the School Examinations and Assessment Council. John Vereker (b. 1944; educated at Marlborough and Keele University) was another outsider, who arrived as a DES Deputy Secretary in 1988. He had begun his career in banking and moved into Overseas Development before joining the Prime Minister's office from 1980 to 1983 and then the FCO from 1983 to 1988.

Nicholas Stuart (b. 1942; Harrow and Christ Church, Oxford) was more conventionally prepared for his post. He had joined the DES in its inaugural year of 1964, where, with some interruptions (including Private Secretary to Harold Wilson), he had remained throughout his civil service career. John Wiggins (b. 1938; Highgate School and Oriel College, Oxford), by contrast, was brought into the DES only in 1987 as an Under-Secretary before promotion to Deputy in 1988. His Whitehall experience had included twenty years with the Treasury and two in the Cabinet Office. The new Senior Chief Inspector from 1983 was

Eric Bolton (b. 1935), who, after a grammar-school education and Lancaster University, had been an English teacher for eleven years, a lecturer for two, and an LEA inspector for another two before being recruited to HMI in 1973.

POLICY

During the early years of the Thatcher administration the running of the civil service became the focus of considerable attention. The DES had developed a Department Planning Organization (DPO) with its own policy steering group chaired by the Permanent Secretary, with further policy groups chaired by Deputy Secretaries and a 'Planning Unit' in which the administrators were joined by HMI, economists and researchers. In May 1982 the Financial Management Initiative was launched by the government in a White Paper whose title aptly caught the mood of the time: *Efficiency and Effectiveness in the Civil Service*. By August 1983 the DES had replaced the DPO with SPER (System for Policy Evolution and Review). Whatever the force of these changes, there were, nevertheless, certain constant factors within the DES - the required expenditure cuts, the falling rolls in schools, the steady accumulation of critical HMI reports, and the drive towards centralism - which continued to exercise an overriding influence on all educational planning.

If we look at each of these four factors in turn, we can perhaps begin to form some explanation of the situation in which education found itself during the 1980s. Some have taken the view that 'the fragile progressive consensus based on incremental change and school and LEA autonomy has been replaced by conflict and contention, and the assertion of greater centralized controls' (Ball, 1990, p. 8), while others have doubted whether such 'autonomy' has ever existed, or indeed whether conflict and contention can ever be absent from a matter as important as education. The first of the constant factors - expenditure cuts - although no worse than those which characterized the educational planning of the late 1940s, the early 1950s, the late 1960s, and all the 1970s, was different in one particular: it was perceived by the government as a positive element in its overall economic strategy, rather than the usual temporary setback. The Thatcher cabinets wished to cut public expenditure in order to achieve specific political goals, and since public education represented a major call on public funds, it was bound to be a prime target. The situation, however, was made more difficult by the fact that educational funding was, by the end of this period, provided by the DES, the Home Office, the Department of Employment, and the Department of the Environment as well as the Scottish and Northern Ireland offices. A proliferation of schemes does not in itself prove inefficiency, but the problems of monitoring and evaluation certainly increased alarmingly. Moreover, funding was also being sought from industry for new schemes such as CTCs, thus increasing the variety of sources from which finance could be provided. The 1987 Alliance manifesto plans - to create a new Department of Education, Training and Science - began to appear more significant. Even the interest of the DES in controlling the curriculum may have resulted as much from its loss of financial control of the LEAs to the Department of the Environment as from its enthusiasm for educational theory. As one DES official later admitted, 'discussion along the traditional axis between the Secretary of State and local authorities' education leaders, deprived of its financial aspects, was correspondingly weakened' (Simpson, in Ransom and Tomlinson, 1986, p. 26).

However, it would be a mistake to exaggerate this diversification. In fact, by the end of the second Thatcher government, at least, little perceptible change had overtaken the educational institutions, and it is possible to agree with John Vincent's view (in Hennessy and Seldon, 1987, p. 290) that 'what stands out is how much Mrs Thatcher has left alone. In four central areas of government, namely defence, social security, health and education, there has been no shake-up. There may have been deterioration, and there may have been increased expenditure; perhaps there have been both. But in these four big-spending areas, the landscape would look familiar to Attlee.' By 1985 a period of some 40 years had witnessed no fundamental change in the nature of educational provision. It can be argued, moreover, that even the post-1988 landscape is far from being transformed by the reforming legislation to the extent that its publicists would like us to believe.

The second constant factor - falling school rolls - had, like the first, existed since the late 1960s. In Chapter 4 we noted the emphasis which a Permanent Secretary placed on certain 'given' factors in educational planning such as the size of the school population and the estimates for future numbers in the light of the current birth rate. By 1980 the figure for live births had dropped to about 735,000, that is, to much the same level as that of the 1930s and early 1940s when population growth was at its lowest point (and when most of the thinking that led to the 1944 Act had been taking place). The trend downwards had been consistent since the high point of 1,015,000 live births in 1964. For the Wilson government of that time, and for Anthony Crosland, his Secretary of State, the whole mood was inevitably expansionist. But for Carlisle, Joseph and Baker, the scene was inevitably one of contraction, and that would have been true even if the economic policies of their Prime Minister had not also constantly emphasized the need for public expenditure cuts.

By 1980, the estimates for children entering reception classes in infant schools by 1985 were roughly 145,000 down on the 1970-75 figures. Translated into classrooms, this meant that almost 5000 would be surplus to requirements by the end of the decade. Managing contraction is usually a difficult and unsavoury task, on which much has already been written.[6] It is enough now simply to indicate the scale of the problem. In the UK as a whole, the decade 1978-88 saw a marked trend in all sectors. The numbers of schools were as follows:

	Primary	Secondary	Special
1978/9	26,850	5585	2018
1987/8	24,482	5020	1900
% reduction	9%	10%	6%

(Central Statistical Office: *Annual Abstract of Statistics 1990*)

In other non-statutory areas such as adult education, the decline in provision was very marked: 51 per cent institutional closures took place, although reorganizations and mergers account for at least part of this decline.

The birth rate in the UK had reached a peak in 1964 and a trough in 1977. This meant that by the early 1970s the demand for places in infant and first schools was at its highest. By the mid-1970s the maximum numbers were just reaching the secondary schools, and by 1980 the surge had reached the final years of compulsory schooling. Thus, although the mid-1980s was expected to see a climax in the demand for university places, it was quite clear, and indeed had been so since the late 1960s, that school rolls would decline. Perhaps the only uncertainty was in respect of the actual steepness of the decline. We can, therefore, look at this problem from a non-partisan point of view since DES policy on this matter was carried out during both Labour and Conservative administrations.

When the DES published its *Pupils and School-Leavers: Future Numbers* in 1982, it predicted that the decline in the school population would go on until 1991. Research at the time suggested that 'the climate of educational planning is one of falling school rolls combined with financial constraints and changes in central-local relations' (Walsh *et al.*, 1984, p. 4). On the face of it, therefore, it was not surprising that the DES chose to close schools, reduce the supply of teachers and curb teachers' wage demands. But the same DES report also included 1996 projections, which took into account a new *rise* in the birth rate and a *growth* in demand for school places in the later 1990s, and by 1990 the Office of Population Censuses and Surveys was estimating the following:

	1991	2001	% increase
Children 14 years and under (UK)	11.08m	12.08m	9%

The choice that the DES had throughout the 1980s was in fact quite clear: either to seize the opportunity of replenishing and refurbishing the system, particularly in the period 1975-85 while the overall problem of coping with increasing numbers was temporarily in abeyance, first in the primary and then the secondary sector; or to slim down the education service still further. Both Labour and Conservative governments took the latter course. During the Joseph period in particular (1981-86) negotiations between the DES and teachers were therefore carried out in a climate of decreasing teacher numbers and all the associated organizational and social problems that surround an insecure workforce.

The third constant factor in the DES was the accumulation of critical reports from HMI. In 1982 Joseph announced that, from March 1983, HMI reports on schools would no longer be confidential but would be published and widely circulated. In a consumer economy, it was argued, parents were the consumers whose rights must be protected. By exposing the weak schools, HMI would provide parents with the most precious of Thatcherite objectives, the so-called freedom to chose. At the same time the White Paper *Teaching Quality* added further to HMI powers. HMI had traditionally *advised*, but these proposals now gave it powers of *approval*, indirectly in the schools and directly in teacher training. In both the public-sector colleges (polytechnics, institutes and colleges) and, now for the very first time, the university departments of education, HMI was the gatekeeper of accreditation.

The nature of HMI reporting, however, became a political issue in its own right. HMI had stepped, or was pushed, into the public arena ever since the 'great debate'. A succession of publications - *Ten Good Schools: A Secondary School Inquiry* (1977), *Primary Education in England* (1978), *Mixed Ability Work in Comprehensive Schools* (1978), *Aspects of Secondary Education in England* (1979), *A View of the Curriculum* (1980), *Schools and Working Life* (1981), *Education 5-9* (1982) - had managed to look rather like blueprints for government approval. But at the same time the Senior Chief Inspectors had continued to claim the inspectorate's independence from government. However, 'one of the problems with education is that nearly everyone considers himself or herself to be an expert on the subject. Civil servants and politicians are therefore tempted to interfere in, and pronounce upon educational matters in a much less inhibited way than they would where medical or technical expertise was involved. HMI serve to constrain this tendency to some extent, although they are sometimes less successful than other professional educationists would wish' (Lawton and Gordon, 1987, pp. 151-2).

Reporting is always open to interpretation. In the past, *confidential* reporting had been the subject of *confidential* interpretations. Only extreme anxieties had been made public. But quasi-public investigations inevitably changed the relationship between teachers and HMI, which now was perceived as acting on behalf of the government. It has been correctly observed (Dunford, 1988b, p. 315) that 'traditionally HMI has reported to the Government on an educational system that is organized by other people. As the Secretary of State increases his own power in the system, the inspectors will be reporting more directly on Government policy', a situation which few HMIs looked forward to with any relish.

HMI was itself the subject of investigation. Some three months before the 1983 June election, the Raynor report on HMI (started in January 1981) had been published. Sir Derek Raynor had been attached to the cabinet office to undertake a number of 'efficiency' investigations. His role in this report was supervisory rather than executive, and much of the responsibility for the survey fell to Nicholas Stuart, soon to be promoted to Deputy Secretary at the DES. The terms of reference were characteristically Thatcherite:

> To consider and report on the role, organization, staffing and effectiveness of HMI in England and Wales, including the main priorities of work to be undertaken, the arrangements for collaboration between the Inspectorate and the rest of the DES and the Welsh Office, taking account in particular of the following:
>
> 1. the responsibilities and policies of the Secretary of State;
> 2. the present and prospective needs of all components of the education service;
> 3. the role of LEAs and their staffs and of other educational agencies;

4. government statements of policy relating to the quality of education and to the Inspectorate;
5. the government's plans to reduce public expenditure and Civil Service manpower.[7]

As we have already seen in Chapter 5, the report did not succeed in significantly changing the role of HMI, nor did it contribute to re-establishing the previously harmonious relationship between the LEAs (and their employees) and the government. Raynor failed to deliver the controls which many Ministers yearned for, and, as Lawton (in Morris and Griggs, 1988, p. 168) has put it so clearly, 'emphasis on the machinery of control . . . has served to confuse the real issues of quality . . . The tragedy of the last ten years has been that the attention of teacher educators has been diverted from real questions of quality to bureaucratic issues of time and content requirements which seem to have taken on almost theological importance.' Similarly, the attention of HMI has been diverted from observation and advice to quantification and control. And when HMI annual reports themselves revealed major shortcomings in the resourcing of education, many government supporters felt that the time had come to replace the Inspectorate with accountants.

Behind the thrashing about over curriculum control was old Black Paper mythology, constantly repeated in the party conference resolutions, that standards were falling. In fact this was clearly not the case:

School-leavers: England, Wales, Scotland and Northern Ireland
[Highest qualifications in 000s]

	1975-76		1985-86	
All school-leavers	823		871	
With 2 or more A levels	109	13.2%	127	14.5%
With 1 A level	31	3.7%	34	3.9%
With 5 or more O levels*	68	8.2%	95	10.9%
With 1-4 O levels*	209	25.4%	231	26.5%

[at grades A-C]*

These figures obviously represent a modest improvement in all categories, achieved by a larger workforce of teachers: 19.9 pupils per teacher in 1975/6 as against 17.4 in 1985/6. Of the 14.5 per cent qualified to take up courses at universities, polytechnics and colleges of advanced further education, only 12.2 per cent found places. What the undercurrent of mistrust actually represented was a dissatisfaction with the undeniable *modesty* of the achievement. What the pioneers of the 1944 Act were looking for would have been something that could, with justification, have been called an *impressive* improvement.

In the White Paper, *Better Schools* (1985, ch. 2), the government's view that 'Education at school should promote enterprise and adaptability in order to increase young people's chances of finding employment or creating it for themselves' should be seen in the light of a stated objective: 'to help pupils to acquire understanding, knowledge and skills relevant to adult life and employment in a fast-changing world'. And therein lies the problem. If the world is so fast-changing, how can a curriculum be based on the aims and objectives of hitting the moving target? The reality is that modifying a curriculum is inevitably a slow process. If one wants different outcomes at the end of an eleven-year compulsory curriculum, the planning, implementation and delivery of a new structure is unlikely to be achieved in a time-scale that can never have the target in sight long enough to provide a rational framework for development. No doubt it would be possible to create courses of study that had titles such as 'Coping with Change', or 'Developing Strategies for Decision Making', or 'Creative Problem Solving', but they would be very unlikely to have received DES approval, for at the heart of its thinking was the desire to return to a traditional and conventional curriculum with well-tried and well-defined subject differentiation, as, indeed, the arrival of the National Curriculum later proved.

The 1988 Act did little to enhance the position of teachers. As Lawton (in Morris and Griggs, 1988, pp. 155-6) has stressed:

> Teachers in state schools occupy a number of positions which are in direct conflict with current Conservative ideology, and, in particular, they appear to enjoy security of employment and are not susceptible to 'normal' market forces. In Conservative eyes the state schools also tend to be seen as second-best, cheap alternatives for those who cannot afford independent schools, but they are, nevertheless, expensive. Thus the Conservative solution has been to cut the system down in size and make it more cost-effective.

It is, however, not enough to say that the political perspective is derived from the independent schools, although, as we have seen, with one notable exception, every Conservative Secretary of State (or Minister) since 1945 has attended an independent school. What is equally significant is that nearly every Permanent- and Deputy-Secretary has come from the same background. This does not carry the implication that all senior civil servants are Conservatives: but it does suggest a certain remoteness from the public sector, a remoteness, aloofness, and distancing, furthermore, which civil service in-house training does nothing to dissipate. 'It has been convenient,' Lawton argued (in Morris and Griggs, 1988, p. 166), 'for the DES and (some) members of HMI to support this policy, partly because it increases their own power of influence. The DES bureaucrats, in the interest of efficiency and good administration, want a more uniform system with less autonomy for individual institutions; members of HMI, who see themselves as the professional experts on teacher training, want to modify the procedures so that their advice carries more weight.'

We have looked at three of the four permanent factors which influence the conduct of educational affairs in the 1980s - expenditure cuts, the falling rolls in schools, and accusations of falling standards - and now we can turn to the last, the drive towards centralism. It is perhaps unnecessary to point out that the education service has got caught up in the more general conflict between central and local government in the UK over financial strategies. Rate-capping and other devices and controls have inevitably brought the funding of education to centre-stage. But, as late as 1986, Edward Simpson, the former Deputy Secretary, could say (in Ransom and Tomlinson, 1986, p. 24), 'The understandable concern that a centrally imposed curriculum might be intended has found no ground to take root in, and the "framework concept" still fits the new developments.' And when Kenneth Baker did impose a national curriculum only two years later, even he continued to deny strenuously that this was a centralist manoeuvre. It is obvious, therefore, that centralism is a difficult concept to grasp. Since LEAs already depended for the bulk of their resources on central funds, and since most curriculum decisions were made not by LEAs but by schools strongly influenced by the demands of external examination boards (themselves gripped by the demands of universities), it could be argued that the DES was simply rationalizing a system that was in desperate need of tidying up. There were, furthermore, no proposals to change the status of teachers and lecturers to that of civil servants, employed by the DES.

At the same time, the moves to provide 'opting-out' schools with direct government funding created a *de facto* situation in which the centre controlled every aspect of a school's activity, even if, technically, the teachers became the employees of a governing body rather than the DES. In such circumstances the only real freedom is to join the independent sector and to charge fees, an option which is not available to the overwhelming majority of schools. Nevertheless, since an escape route from central control not only exists but is actually encouraged by some back-bench Conservative MPs, the argument that centralism was the sole purpose of government legislation in the 1980s, seems somewhat wide of the mark. The other argument that centralism is just a tactic designed to fulfil the strategy of a totally independent school enterprise is, I think, inadequately supported by the evidence.

* * *

Whatever else can be said of the DES during this period, it cannot be accused of inactivity. While it is not the purpose of this book to form a record of historical events, it may, nevertheless, be helpful to outline the scale of endeavour:

The Education Acts and Reports	
1979	Act repealing 1976 Act on comprehensives
1980	Act providing for assisted places scheme, parental choice, parents on governing bodies, capping of Advanced Further Education pool
1981	Act providing for special educational needs; Rampton report on West Indian children White Paper, *New Training Initiatives*; Trenaman Report recommends continuation of Schools' Council

1982 Cockcroft Report on mathematics; Thompson Report on coordination and funding of youth services

1983 White Paper *Teaching Quality*

1984 Act providing grants to LEAs for DES-approved options

1985 Swann report on education of minorities; Lindop report on higher education
White Paper, *Better Schools*

1986 Act concerning school governing bodies and Local Management of Schools
Act controlling funding of in-service courses for teachers

1987 Act abolishing teachers' pay negotiating rights
White Paper, *Higher Education: Meeting the Challenge*

1988 Kingman report on the teaching of English
Reform Act: National Curriculum, parental choice, grant-maintained status, City Technology Colleges, polytechnics removed from LEAs, funding of universities and polytechnics

1989 Elton report on discipline in schools

1990 Circular 9/90 on assessment for English, mathematics and science; Act on student loans

1991 White Papers on *Education and Training for the 21st Century* and *Higher Education: a New Framework*

The 1979 Act is now generally seen as no more than a political gesture. Because the 1944 Education Act was the product of a coalition government, there was a strong consensual agreement about the implementations of its aims. As we have seen, the only topic that raised significant conflicts between the parties for a quarter of a century was the comprehensive school issue, and even this was only illusory, for the gathering momentum of school-building programmes and local authority reorganizations ensured the growth of this type of secondary school irrespective of which party was in office. By 1979 roughly four out of five pupils attending secondary schools were at a comprehensive school. Yet when the opinion polls asked, 'Should we bring back the grammar schools?' not only did an expected 80 per cent of Conservative voters say yes, but 41 per cent of Labour voters agreed, with only 32 per cent opposing the idea (Rose, 1984, p. 40). Perhaps some of the 27 per cent 'don't knows' among the Labour group recognize that the same question might have been put differently: 'Should we bring back the secondary modern schools for seven out of ten pupils?' And, as Barker (1986, p. 83) has so rightly put it, 'it was the educational disadvantages of the modern school and the unsatisfied demand for grammar-school education, not the equitable structure of Britain, which provided both the force and the context of the campaign for reform.' Of course the basic weakness of opinion-poll questioning is thus revealed, but it is neither this issue nor the grammar-school issue as such that demands our attention. What we know about the comprehensive school provision for the 80 per cent is that it had taken the education system some 40 years to reach that stage, and that it was, for administrative reasons, unlikely that the steps taken could be retraced in the period of the next government, or even two governments.

But the proposals which eventually led to the 1988 Reform Bill were not seen in the same light at all. Firstly, they were strongly linked (by politicians and public alike) to Thatcherism, and thus to the aspirations of the Treasury rather than the DES. Secondly, they were seen as proposals for a third-term government, and, thus, far removed from the agreements of the 1970s. The Education Reform Bill became the 1988 Education Reform Act in July. It was an example of pantechnicon legislation hurriedly packed by a transient Secretary of State. Containing over 200 sections, it ranged over a very broad landscape of educational legislation and included both minor *miscellaneous provisions* and major financial reforms. At its heart, however, was the National Curriculum and its associated assessment schemes. The widespread accusation made at the time was that it was the result of feverish short-term planning based solely on hard-line Thatcherite doctrines. Was this true?

The general characteristics of DES behaviour patterns that have become apparent in this account so far do not match up with concepts such as speed of innovation, rapid changes or reversals of policy, quick solutions to structural problems, or even unpredictability. It would consequently be rash to assume, as many have done, that most of the so-called reforms had not been in circulation for many years. Our concerns are not, therefore, with the arguments for and against the individual requirements of the Act, but rather with such questions as: Did the proposals emerge from previously argued positions? Were the proposals consistent with manifesto commitments? Were the 'normal' DES procedures employed in developing the proposals? Were the proposals partly consensual or entirely adversarial?

Let us look first at the National Curriculum. The two most salient features of this proposal are the specification of what subjects must be taught and the notion of an eleven-year continuous programme of teaching across a selected group of subjects. Not only is the so-called National Curriculum a grand inconsistency in Thatcherite doctrines in so far as it drastically curtails choice on the part of the consumer (that is, the pupil), but also it is in no sense a new idea. 'The course should provide for instruction in English Language and Literature, at least one Language other than English, Geography, History, Mathematics, Science ... not less than four and a half hours per week must be allotted to English, Geography and History, not less than three and a half hours to the Language ... and not less than seven and half hours to Mathematics, of which at least three must be for science [which] must be both theoretical and practical.' Although very similar to the 1988 Act, this is in fact an extract from the 1904 Secondary School Regulations which arose out of the Balfour Act of 1902.

In respect of the continuity of the curriculum, what the Baker planning has brought to the surface is the need to think about the 5- to 16-year-old curriculum as a whole, a consideration which was not only apparent to the DES in the 1970s (and which was inquired about officially in Circular 14/77), but which has for even longer been the subject of professional and academic attention. This can therefore be seen as a long-standing DES strategy rather than a Secretary-of-State initiative. Indeed, the LEAs were beginning to come to terms with the curriculum continuity problem in the early 1980s, when most English authorities had set up working parties to investigate the structural relationships between the primary and the secondary curriculum. Progress in these discussions were, however, impeded in two significant ways. In the first place, many teachers and local advisers became immersed in the problem of *transfer*, rather than in curriculum structure, with the result that only cosmetic changes were made to what was actually taught. In the second place, the deterioration of relations with the DES during Joseph's period in office led to a widespread breakdown in voluntary activities on the part of teachers, and, unfortunately, liaison between schools was on the voluntary agenda.[8]

The only really ideological, as opposed to pragmatic, element of the National Curriculum is the emphasis which it places upon science education. There was already an overwhelming body of professional and lay opinion that science must be more effectively taught in British schools. Unfortunately, the Reform Bill did not come up with a solution to the problem of the almost complete failure of the country since 1945 to produce sufficient science teachers. Many of the remaining outcomes of the 1988 initiatives were concerned with assessment, and although there were understandable professional anxieties about assessment-led curricula, teachers have faced and overcome such problems before. In the event, as Baker was succeeded by MacGregor, and MacGregor by Clarke, the whole assessment package bundle unwound yet again.

A second element of the Act - the powers which it gave, or, as many have argued, restored to the Secretary of State - was similarly predictable, certainly from Shirley Williams's time (and the Callaghan speech of 1976) and possibly even from the days of Sir David Eccles. The question about how far the powers stretched was clearly put by at least one group of observers:

> [One] interpretation is that control is being exercised by the centre partly to break the vested interests of . . . the 'corporate' educational groups (LEAs and teacher unions) that resisted the curricular changes necessary to modernize the system. But we must be clear about means and ends in this respect. Breaking the power of corporate interest groups is not an end in itself; if it is 'broken' in order that power may be devolved to other non-governmental groups, such as parents, governing bodies, or community groups, the exercise may be supportable. But if it is broken with the intention or with the consequence that power flows back to the central government it becomes dangerous, and in conflict with the market approach.
>
> (Campbell *et al.*, 1987, p. 376)

But Baker insisted that the 1988 Act simply elaborated the powers which were already his by virtue of the 1944 Act. Many observers expressed serious doubts about such reassurances, and when in 1991 Kenneth Clarke began to tear up proposals for examination procedures which had taken consultative groups three years to develop, it was generally felt that such fears had been well-founded.

DES powers in respect of the curriculum were, however, not the main thrust of the redistribution of power. The power conflicts of the mid-1980s between central and local governments were much wider and deeper than those which surfaced in education policy - and they were conflicts which central government was bound to win. The DES was simply dragged into the much bigger antagonisms created by the Department of the Environment. Nevertheless, parts of the Act such as open enrollment in schools, local management, grant-maintained status, the separation from LEAs of higher and further education, the abolition of the Inner London Education Authority, and the enhanced powers of schools' governing bodies all provided the Secretary of State with more duties and the DES with more powers.

Not only had the manifestos already argued for such developments, but phrases such as 'national standards' had already been introduced into party conferences by the mid-1970s. What took many by surprise was that Baker stayed long enough in the department to oversee their delivery. The 1980s had seen a gradual move away from the idea of approval of teacher (professional) control of the curriculum to state control of the curriculum, but it was a control masquerading under the banner of consumer protection and the market economy. Since the private sector was not subject to such assessment regulations and curriculum specifications, would the public sector be the only area where consumerism prevailed?

* * *

Away from the sound of the battle that was raging over the Reform Bill, other events took place during 1988 which in their own way reveal a great deal more about the nature of the DES and its influence on the education system. In January the Treasury White Paper appeared as usual for this time of the year. As had been the habit during the 1980s, the ESAC scrutinized the education elements of the White Paper and produced its own report in April. In turn the DES responded to the ESAC's report by September. It goes without saying that, of course, once the new Parliamentary year had got going, the issues raised in these exchanges had somewhat lost their political immediacy. But to look back at them now provides evidence about the processes of government (as they relate to education) which is of fundamental importance.

In the Treasury White Paper (January 1988, p. 215) the government's 'principal aims for education' were set out as follows:

> to raise standards at all levels of ability;
> to increase parental choice;
> to secure the best possible return from the resources that are invested in the education service;
> to widen access to further and higher education and to make them more responsive to the needs of the economy;
> to enhance the strength and quality of the science base, and of learning and scholarship.

As if to reinforce the general aims for education, it amplified the aims for schools and higher education thus:

> to improve the standards of achievement of all pupils across the curriculum, to widen the choice available to parents for the education of their children and to enable schools to respond effectively to what parents and the community require of them, *thus securing the best possible return from the substantial investment of resources.* [my italics]

> to provide a high quality, cost effective Higher Education system which both plays its part in meeting the nation's economic and social needs and provides the necessary opportunities for the advancement of knowledge and the pursuit of scholarship.

Like that of most statements of aims that dwell in the world of generalities, the significance of these ideas cannot be tested without further investigation. It depends, after all, on what is meant by standards, choice, return from resources, service, access, needs and quality. The assumption that 'parents' and 'the community' speak with one voice is equally uncertain. At one level, therefore, the aims are all broadly acceptable notions. But in the arena of educational politics, they also all possess several layers of meaning. It was to the process of unpacking these meanings that the Select Committee addressed itself during the months of January, February and March 1988.

The chairman of the committee of eleven MPs was Timothy Raison, the former junior Minister at the DES during the Heath government, and the witnesses included Kenneth Baker, Sir David Hancock, the Permanent Secretary, and two of his Deputies, Nicholas Stuart, and Eric Bolton, the Senior Chief Inspector (SCI). It soon became apparent to the committee that DES expenditure was erratic. For example, during the period 1982-88 the spending on schools varied between a high of 6.5 per cent of total public expenditure and a low 5.7 per cent, a considerable variation. 'Thus there is no consistent relation,' the committee reported (ESAC, 1987-88, par. 7), 'between changes in pupil numbers and the share of public spending devoted to the DES programme. The number of pupils may go up while school spending as a proportion of public spending may go down, *and vice versa*.' In pursuing the reason for this aberrant, if not capricious, course of events, the committee focused on the actual workload of the department. Hancock argued that whereas between 1979 and 1984 the DES had been 'contributing to the reduction in civil service manpower . . . the demands were fairly static, but since 1984 there has been a revival of interest in education policy at all ends of the spectrum, and the burden of work in the Department has risen steadily.' Asked if this had meant an increase in productivity, the Permanent Secretary simply observed (ESAC, 1987-88, minutes, p. 3) that 'productivity is almost impossible to measure in a policy department like the DES . . . but the Department has told me that they are working very much harder.'

SCI Bolton made the same point in respect of HMI: 'Government interest over the last decade has actually increased in education, as has the amount of policy . . . in areas which have traditionally been left to the professional expertise of HMI and Office on curricula and standards.' But the massive increase in HMI publications (120 in circulation in 1988) was perhaps at the expense of routine inspections. When asked if schools could expect to have a visit from HMI within a five-year period, he answered, 'No, I am sorry, I cannot say that. Some schools may not have had a visit *for a much longer period than that* [my italics] . . . some schools have not been visited for a very long time . . . however, in every authority there are local authority inspectorates . . . who are fulfilling that sort of regular monitoring function . . . Our function is to try to get a national picture' (ESAC, 1987-88, minutes, pp. 3-5).

The committee also raised the question of its own role in relation to DES policy-making. One member pointed to the unhappy situation that had arisen in respect of its previous year's reports in which the response time was one month (one very short report), seven months (three reports), twelve months (one report) and fifteen months (one report). 'Can we be assured' it was asked, 'that, given the sort of matters we will be discussing later regarding the extra work . . . arising out of the Reform Bill, you will do your very best to see that the guidelines laid down by government [normally two months] will be adhered to?' To which Sir David blandly responded, 'I will certainly bear that in mind' (ESAC, 1987-88, minutes, p. 7).

Nicholas Stuart's turn came when the committee moved on to the impact on the DES of the 1988 Act itself. His role had been to organize the processes leading to the national curriculum and to financial delegation to schools. He had used some 50 staff full-time on the Bill, as well as all the DES lawyers. It was his view that 'within that organizational framework we have been able . . . to deal with the consultation process and the follow up . . . which is the examination of the responses, their analysis, and subsequent advice to Ministers, and that has been reflected in continuing discussion which go on . . . with different interests, local authority associations, teachers' unions, the Society of Education Officers, and so on' (ESAC, 1987-88, minutes, p. 8). But many others (though outside the committee) had an entirely different perspective on these processes, feeling that such consultations as there were slanted heavily towards the superficial, the inadequate and the specious.[9]

The committee also drew attention to some of the possible changes that would be caused by an increase in grant-maintained schools. Members wondered if the department saw a likely increase in its work (especially over admissions appeals) resulting from the shift of responsibility from LEAs to the DES. 'I hope not', responded Sir David, 'because the proposal is not to shift the responsibilities of the LEAs onto the DES, but to shift them to the governing body of the schools.' 'But,' as a committee member was quick to point out, 'LEAs have a system set up with staff to be able to deal with this, how are governing bodies going to be able to do this?' The answers given and subsequent exchanges reinforced the view that this was yet another example of what happens when a bill is rushed through Parliament without sufficient consultation (ESAC, 1988, pp. 11-13).

When Sir David was asked if he thought there had been a major shift of power to the centre, his answer turned again to the curriculum: 'There will be a very significant change, but that is because for the very first time the country will have a national curriculum . . . In some LEAs which had very clearly defined curricula, that will be seen as a shift to the centre . . . In the case of other LEAs who have not been very active in these matters it will be the creation of a new enterprise.' A strange response indeed, raising all sorts of questions about the nature of the curriculum and the relation between LEAs, schools and examination boards. But the committee were not thinking only of the curriculum. 'Do you accept,' it was pressed, 'that you will actually have to create some kind of department within the DES to regulate and advise, keep an eye on and monitor and generally watch and match the progress of the new grant-maintained schools?' To which the somewhat evasive answer was that DES officers, HMI (without increases in staffing) and internal auditors would be expected to take over these former LEA responsibilities (ESAC, 1988, pp. 12-14). Kenneth Baker was also challenged on centralism, including the idea that teachers should be paid directly from Whitehall, an idea which at the time he rejected (ESAC, 1988, pp. 82-3). It emerged again in the poll-tax emergencies of 1990-91 as a classic example of conflicts between departments and between local and central government. An earlier plan to cushion the impact of the poll tax by transferring the £15b a year cost of funding the education service from the local authorities to the Treasury was considered for a while by Chris Patten when he became the new Environment Secretary in 1989. It could cut poll-tax bills by 40 per cent, it was claimed, but also, instead of a hoped-for tax reduction, add 2p to income tax, an increase which could be absorbed. Such were the state of rumours, promises and interdepartmental rivalries.

The main thrust of Kenneth Baker's examination was the perceived reluctance of the government to provide sufficient funds for improving the physical condition of many ageing schools and for the updating of their equipment and books. His response was characteristically robust, returning again and again to the government's increased educational budgets, but skirting round the figures (provided to the committee), which revealed a decline in educational spending, as a proportion of the national output, from 4.5 per cent to 3.8 per cent.[10] It was the chairman, however, who went a long way towards identifying the real problem when he wondered if we were 'running into problems of structure in schools ... Is faulty construction beginning now to produce some very substantial bills for remedying?' To which Baker's response was very frank: 'The big problem is the buildings built in the 1960s, and the late 1950s and early 1970s, the flat-roofed schools ... These are proving very difficult to maintain and repair, and that is a big problem which affects the public estate of the country. When one looks back at the buildings built at that time, council houses or office buildings, it was not really a glorious age for British architecture.' So much for the triumphs of Housing Minister Harold Macmillan's notorious building-boom, and so much for the wholly unjustified, self-congratulatory reputation of the DES's architects' division.[11]

In their answer to questions on the new General Certificate of Secondary Education, both Baker and Bolton acknowledged the importance of good teaching. 'If you have a gifted teacher,' said Baker, 'then you can draw a tremendous amount out of the child *under whatever particular system*' (my italics), and Bolton confirmed this by adding, 'good teaching, no matter what the examination system, goes far beyond what is required' (ESAC, 1988, Appendix 1, p. 89). But on other matters, such as the nature of testing proposed in the Reform Bill, the concept of moral education, the funding of CTCs, the resourcing of higher education, and the production of trained scientists, the exchanges in committee revealed only the continuing uncertainties that surrounded all these issues. In its final report the committee made 21 recommendations, most of which were procedural or presentational. When the DES published its formal response some five months later, it agreed to many of the administrative points, but simply *noted* the controversial ones. As usual, the value of the committee's discussions lay not in the immediate reactions of the DES, but in the potential for long-term improvements to our general understanding of the nature of educational systems.

If we return now to the more public façade of the educational debate, it is possible to trace the progress of the notion of education as the 'big idea' which had gained a lot of mileage in respect of the 16-18 age group, and particularly in the context of the ERM and the closer links with Europe. Despite the fact that the low take-up of courses for this age group had worried many British educationists and some politicians for over 40 years, it at last became only too clear to a large section of the electorate that at least one of the reasons for the UK's economic difficulties lay in the failure to attract school-leavers to pursue further study. The DES statistics[12] published in October revealed that the UK remained at the bottom of the ladder as far as the percentage of 16-18-year-olds on full-time courses was concerned, and was only slightly better placed if part-time study was taken into account.

	Full-time	Part-time	F-t and P-t
Germany	47%	43%	90%
Netherlands	77%	9%	88%
Belgium	77%	4%	81%
Sweden	76%	2%	78%
Denmark	70%	7%	77%
France	66%	8%	74%
UK	35%	34%	69%
Italy	47%	18%	65%
Spain	52%	0%	52%

As usual, a vast range of inferences was made: that British teenagers were put off further study by the depressing experience of schooling that they had already gained; that full-time study was unattractive because it was too academic/intellectual/non-practical; that supported part-time study was available from only a very limited section of industry, and was often extremely makeshift; that there was no guarantee that further study would provide employment; that the pervasive anti-intellectual stance of the DES had denied the proper allocation of resources to this age range for decades; that continued separation of schools from further and adult education should cease; that the relatively high take-up of part-time courses should be developed into a national strength; and that the newly instituted National Curriculum would soon lead either to an amazing improvement or to a further decline in the situation.

The 'big idea' had also been fuelled by a speech in August 1990 by Sir Claus Moser, the former head of government statistics. He had pointed to the same stark fact that the British were now the worst educated people in the industrial world. While the Secretary of State was on holiday, his stand-in, the newly appointed Under-Secretary, Michael Fallon, uttered a banal rejection and claimed that the DES had everything in hand. In fact all three major parties really agreed with Moser's point of view, but, naturally, differed about what to do next. The Conservatives found themselves in the apparently contradictory situation of wanting more choice over schools (in order to encourage competition) but less choice about what was taught in them. The choice for parents, therefore, simply became a matter of delivery, since the commodity, the National Curriculum, would be identical throughout the state system. In practice the only way the strait-jacket of the National Curriculum could be avoided was for parents to pay for their children to be educated privately, thus giving rise to the speculation that the National Curriculum was simply a device to increase the influence of the independent schools. For Labour, Moser merely provided ammunition for the argument that eleven years of Thatcherism had ruined state education; that two-thirds of local authority schools were now in desperate need of repair; that teachers' salaries and status had been systematically undermined to the point where vacancies could no longer be filled; and that most higher-education establishments were now bankrupt. For the Liberal Democrats (and their parent parties), education had always been the big idea in any case, but since they had never held office, they were in the enviable position of not having to take the blame for the failures of the past.

When Margaret Thatcher was replaced in Downing Street by John Major, education struggled to remain the 'big idea.' At least for the voters in by-elections, first the poll tax and then the national health service loomed larger. During his first six months in office, Kenneth Clarke acquiesced in the gradual demolition of crucial elements of the 1988 Act: that hurried legislation experienced all sorts of difficulties when it came to the implementation of the National Curriculum. First, subjects began to disappear; then the Standard Attainment Targets proved too cumbersome. In May 1991 an attempt to revive the 'big idea' was created by the introduction of two White Papers: *Education and Training for the 21st Century* and *Higher Education: A New Framework*. Such portentous titles inevitably attracted a certain level of derision, for most of the ideas contained in the former had been around for half a century already, and the 'framework' language of the latter served only to remind everyone of the failures of the 1972 White Paper, *A Framework for Expansion*. As a DES buzz-word of the 1970s (and still used in *A Framework for the School Curriculum* of 1980), the term 'framework' now seemed to have lost its trail-blazing vitality.

The two sets of proposals were closely related, the first offering strategies for dealing with the problem of 16-19-year-olds, and the second suggesting a long overdue rationalization of the binary system in higher education, providing for the eradication of boundaries between the universities, polytechnics and colleges. It was inevitable, however, that the 16-19 proposals attracted more attention. They fell into two distinct categories: ownership and curriculum. The further erosion of LEA control over institutions was entirely predictable, continuing the trend set by legislation from the Heath government when Margaret Thatcher was at the DES, and continuing throughout the 1980s. The revival of the link between education and training and the specific proposals for the implementation of National Vocational Qualifications (with transferability and equivalence to GCSE and A levels) drew many to the conclusion that someone at the DES had dusted down a copy of the 1944 Act or even reread some of the numerous reports from Royal Commissions dating back to mid- and late-Victorian times. Perhaps it was Tim Eggar, the Minister of State, who had brought with him from his previous post as Employment Minister a level of experience and understanding in this field that commanded respect.

The immediate political problem with these proposals lay in their timing. As we have already seen, proposals in these categories hit the buffers both in the 1969-70 session, when Edward Short was deprived of the opportunity of developing his ideas by the general election, and in 1978-79 when Shirley Williams had to leave on the shelf substantial parts of her programme. Could the two new White Papers pass into an Act before Parliament ran out of time? Would the pressure groups from the LEAs who saw their grip on the whole 16-19 sector suddenly disappearing be sufficiently powerful to defer matters until after the election?

A month later (June 1991) Labour's shadow Education Secretary, Jack Straw, reintroduced the idea of a professional council for teaching which had featured in so many earlier discussions. If not a new concept, it at least had a new name: the Independent Standards Commission. It would have a membership of ten to fifteen, *nominated* by Ministers but *approved* by the House of Commons Select Committee. Crucially, the Commission would absorb the responsibilities and personnel of HMI, and have direct responsibility for inspection and the advisory services at local as well as national levels. Politicians in opposition often see the reduction of ministerial powers as a worthy objective, but the real test comes when they themselves assume office. In any case two factors always appear to distort the picture: in the first place, individual opposition speakers hardly ever go on to become Ministers *in the same department*; in the second place, the DES machinery usually succeeds in restraining the development of any plans which would curtail or diminish its own powers.

By July it was the Prime Minister's turn to capture the headlines again. He chose to use a speech outside Parliament to drive yet another nail in the coffin of the 1988 Act by rubbishing many of the planned assessment procedures. The intervention was remarkable in three ways at least: first, because it was the Prime Minister rather than the Secretary of State who appeared to be making the decisions; second, because three years of consultations had effectively revealed a series of problems that had been brought in vain to Kenneth Baker's attention during his lemming-like rush to the cliffs in 1987-88; and, third, because it left the entire educational community questioning the DES officials' and HMI's apparent failure to warn their masters of the dangers ahead. As if this were not enough, John Major also found himself having to find new solutions to the CTC mirage by asking LEAs to consider using existing schools rather than newly built state-of-the-art shrines to the opting-out dogma. In September the Secretary of State fought to reassert his authority by introducing his Parent's Charter, a half-baked mixture of simplistic consumerism and ill-considered swipes at teachers, which also contained proposals for the privatization of school inspections and a substantial reduction in the numbers of HMI. SCI Bolton's premature departure in August left an unfilled vacancy at the top of an already demoralized Inspectorate. The autumn Queen's Speech signalled the abolition of the CNAA and changes to the structure of initial teacher training. By January 1992 John Wiggins, the Deputy Secretary responsible for teacher training, had been 'removed' from that portfolio, and by March Clarke's legislative programme had disintegrated in the scramble leading to the General Election of 9 April 1992.

NOTES

1 That is, providing open-access courses in addition to the traditional A-level courses.

2 Christopher Price was the chairman of the Select Committee of Education, Science and the Arts from 1979 to 1983.

3 Within weeks of his appointment MacGregor was being greeted by teachers' organizations with a warmth totally absent from the Joseph–Baker days.

4 The Minister of State post was used for the Minister of the Arts.

5 Joint editor of the *Black Papers on Education* (1969–77), editor of *Education: Threatened Standards* (1972) and *The Accountability of Schools* (1973), and author of *Crisis in Education* (1975).

6 See especially Walsh *et al.* (1984) and Bernbaum (1979).

7 The period in which Mrs Thatcher had been Secretary of State for Education had seen the number of HMIs fall from 483 in 1970 to 430 in 1975. Yet while she was Prime Minister, the numbers had risen from 421 in 1980 to 465 in 1986, when extra staff were needed to deal with CATE matters, and to 476 by 1988 with a planned ceiling of 485, representing nearly 20 per cent of the DES workforce.

8 See also J. Castle and I. Lawrence (1985), *Policies for Curriculum Continuity*; J. Castle and I. Lawrence (1987), *Continuity Models in the Curriculum*; R. Derricott (1985), *Curriculum Continuity: Primary to Secondary*; P. Dodds and I. Lawrence (1984), *Curricular Continuity: Fact or Fiction?*; M. Galton and J. Willcocks (1983), *Moving from the Primary Classroom*; A. Stillman and K. Maychell (1984), *School to School*.

9 See especially J. Haviland, ed. (1988), *Take Care, Mr Baker!: a selection from the advice on education which the government collected but decided not to publish*.

10 4.5 per cent in 1982–83 (actual) to 3.8 per cent in 1990–91 (planned) (ESAC Report, Appendix 1, p. 99).

11 Ibid., pp. 84–5. Mr Baker added, 'There are some schools built with a wooden structure in the '60s which are very unsatisfactory. The people who designed and built these led various authorities to believe that they had a very much longer life.' For the further discussion of this matter, and the role taken by the Audit Commission, see Chapter 7.

12 The figures were the best available at the time, but since they ranged from 1982 to 1988, could provide only a rough guide. Germany still meant *West Germany*. Leading industrial nations outside Europe also recorded impressive figures, Japan and the US both registering 80 per cent take-up.

Chapter 7

Delegation, devolution and deregulation

During the last 50 years there has been a very gradual, almost imperceptible, change in our understanding of the purpose of schools, colleges and universities. In the very simplest terms, they have begun to change from quasi-self-governing communities, with their own values, their own rules and their own rulers, to places where it is reasonably convenient and reasonably congenial for the individual to pursue a course of learning. The emphasis has moved away from the institution as a microsociety in which the individual struggles to establish him/herself in the group, and towards the notion of the institution as a provider of coherent courses, compatible both with the pursuit of excellence and also with the needs of the individual. Thus, the salient feature of the 1944 Act was the creation of secondary schools for all, while the crucial feature of the 1988 Act was the emergence of the structured, eleven-year curriculum; similarly, in higher education the dominant characteristic of the 1940s was exclusiveness, and in the 1990s it is accessibility.

As one would expect, schools, colleges and universities have perceived the need for, and organized their embrace of, such transformations with varying degrees of tolerance, speed and success. But inasmuch as nearly every secondary school, college, polytechnic and university now actively seeks *clients*, the transformation would appear to be irreversible. In higher education the Open University model helped to map out the new direction, a path increasingly followed by polytechnics and colleges through the validation procedures of the CNAA, and one which many universities have developed independently. During the early 1980s a substantial number of secondary schools were also evolving their own modular structures, and actively encouraging their students to take an active personal role in the growth of individualized learning programmes.

In Open University courses the concept of common-aged cohorts never had any reality. Gradually courses in the polytechnics and colleges also began to attract people of all ages, even though the 18-21 age group remained preponderant. Among the 16-19-year-olds a significant minority began to find tertiary and further education institutions more user-friendly than the conventional school provision. It will, therefore, surely be only a matter of time before secondary schools generally adapt to the course-providing model rather than the single-age-cohort model within the self-contained institutionalized community. The DES has gradually moved from its *Better Schools* position of 1985 through the 1988 National Curriculum proposals to the potential realization that there will be better schools only if there are better courses.

At present, however, such changes remain potential rather than actual. The civil servants at the DES have largely been drawn from a culture strong in traditional school concepts and values, as have most of their Ministers. Indeed, the notion of the school as the provider of social and welfare services is ingrained as much in the fabric of independent boarding schools as it is in the local authority school. It will be recalled that the three notable achievements of the Beveridge-Keynes epoch of the 1940s were National Insurance, National Health and, in effect, National Education. They were all instruments of national policy, but since schooling was administered on a local basis, it was often seen by the public as belonging to a different category of provision. And, emphatically, the 'national' education service required local authorities not only to provide schools, but also to operate in and around them several welfare services, including medical, dental, psychological, catering, transport and, sometimes, clothing. The education service was thus, unequivocally, a key element of the social services as a whole, just as the boarding house within an independent school was explicitly the creator of social behaviour patterns and the resource centre for all these same needs.

State insurance, state health and state education schemes supplemented, but did not replace, opportunities for the individual to make his or her own arrangements in these matters. Through national insurance contributions and increasingly through payments for medical prescriptions, most people recognized that they were paying for these services. However, because of the complex relationships between Treasury revenue and local authority revenue in the funding of schools and further and higher education, there has always been a widespread tendency to speak of the education service as 'free'. Linking the costs of schools, colleges and universities to inputs in taxation whether direct or indirect, national or local, is not susceptible to easy explanations or simple formulae. Most Conservative Party supporters have traditionally emphasized the need to preserve the right of the individual to select alternatives to state provision without, however, the right to opt out of taxation and national insurance contributions. Most Labour Party supporters have traditionally emphasized the need to inject into the social services sufficiently high levels of funding to ensure and enhance the quality of such services. A powerful consensus has existed among the majority of members of both parties, together with other middle-ground parties, on the need to maintain and improve services. As far as education is concerned, only minorities within the parties have developed policies against this consensus, whether it be a few far-Right Conservatives who wish to take education out of the public sector entirely, or a few far-Left Labour supporters who wish to make any form of private education illegal.

In this consensual context, however, the appraisal of educational resourcing is often made more difficult by the apparent obscurity of the issues and problems surrounding it. The recognition that the changes in society which have taken place in the UK since 1945 might be reflected in the education system is a task that politicians tend to avoid. This is particularly true in what is provided for children and adolescents between the ages of 5 and 16. Simple incremental gains make good rhetoric. Elect us and you will have more of everything.

Just to demand more schooling and higher standards, as successive manifestos from all parties have done, election after election, ignores matters that should not be disregarded. It is only too easy to argue that better schools will lead to better education, bringing to individuals and communities alike the benefits of progress and prosperity. But few politicians, and apparently few civil servants, have been prepared to grapple with the notion that *schooling* is not just a synonym for *educating*, and that, in particular, the education of adolescents and adults may, in the late twentieth century, require forms of provision in which the old concept of the school is no longer valid.

If the concept of the school is changing, then so is its role as a provider of social services. The Beveridge amenities can now be more effectively delivered by agencies outside the school, allowing the school to concentrate entirely on the delivery of the curriculum. However appropriate and urgent it was in the postwar UK to use the school as a diagnostic clinic for the inherited social and medical problems of the family, it is now clearly not the most efficient or effective way to tackle such problems. In Whitehall terms, the DES may need to concentrate on educational objectives, and the departments of the Environment, of Employment, and of Health and Social Security may need to focus on other social aims. This is not to suggest that such matters are not interrelated. But administrative confusion is bound to result from the conceptual disorder that has surrounded the development of schooling in the UK for half a century.

Brian Simon (1985a, p. 19) has correctly pointed to the fact that 'interpretations of the relations between education and society are themselves subject to change, and ... the degree of optimism or pessimism expressed ... appears to vary with the economic situation: an expansionist phase appears sympathetic to concepts stressing the importance of the role of education, a recessionary phase the opposite.' If this were true, then the current pessimistic interpretation of the role of schooling in our society would simply be the product of economic stagnation and recession. 'But if we extend our analysis historically,' Simon goes on to assert, 'other strands in the argument may be elucidated or defined, extending the complexity of the situation beyond the simplistic conclusion just presented.' Of these strands, perhaps the two most important are the 'unintended outcomes' of educational processes and the 'human subjective experience', which includes 'people's capacity for movement, for acting on the environment, transforming it, and so for self-change. It is this process which is educative, and profoundly so' (p. 30). In so far as governments can neither plan the unintended outcomes (they have sufficient difficulty with the intended outcomes) nor take account of the enormous scope of subjective experiences, it can be argued that the role of government is intrinsically limited.

But political parties do have the ability to observe and learn from people's capacities for movement, transformation and self-change. If they did not, they would never be in government. In the field of educational policy the transformations, which can sometimes be detected more easily in countries outside the UK, are consistent with other social changes. The reality of increased freedom of choice in most forms of adult activity is not replicated in the notion that freedom of choice in education means the spurious freedom of choosing *between* schools, each of which sells the same product, in only slightly differing packaging.

If we compare schooling in the 1940s with schooling in the 1990s, the similarities outmatch the differences. Schooling is still compulsory; the school day still ends in the middle of the afternoon; schools organize their teaching in classes comprising pupils of the same age in numbers only slightly smaller; schools still work in fixed terms with fixed holidays; and the school year is still an entrenched structural device as well as the mere measurement of time. Why should schools throughout this long and in other ways dramatically changing period have been bound by standard opening hours, term times, academic years and other residual inheritances from a previous epoch? In so far as we know anything worth knowing about the learning habits of children and adolescents, we know that learning speeds and learning strategies are extremely variable and idiosyncratic. And yet, especially in secondary schools, the theory of synchronic anthesis, the simultaneous flowering or coming into bloom of pupils at certain times of the year (particularly in the summer), is ingrained into society's thinking. So too are opening times. When the question of European Standard Time is raised every year and an end proposed to the crazy system of different British and European times, people still complain that children would have to go to school in the dark. Why should anyone now think that standard hours should be maintained in both summer and winter, let alone in both Inverness and Cornwall? And why should rural schools be like urban schools? Are we not aware that many children spend up to three hours a day just to get to and from a school that provides perhaps only four and half hours of formal tuition?

The artificial standardization of courses creates educational nonsense. Why do we still behave as if good educational planning must always start with quantitative factors, and then force the qualitative experience into predetermined moulds? The traditions in secondary schools which have led to subjects such as mathematics, English and science each occupying about 18 per cent of the timetable, and subjects such as history, geography and French each about 9 per cent, have now been reinforced by the National Curriculum. But so also has the assumption that everything must be taught every week, in spite of our growing awareness that there are many other patterns of learning, and that young adults may have more in common with the learning styles of adults than children. For some subjects and some learners two hours per week over 36 weeks is not an effective substitute for the same 72-hour course delivered in, say, six weeks, or even two weeks, as it would be in industry.

If it is possible to think of schools providing variable programmes of learning that are not impeded by school terms and school years, then it is also possible to enter into the analysis of the variable structures of courses. We know already that different programmes of study may require different types of resources. Some subjects, such as drama or music, for example, thrive upon group activities, and thus can benefit hugely from the circumstances that a school can provide. But in many other subjects the individual learner does not necessarily gain from group interaction. If young adults are to become self-educating mature adults, then, clearly, it is the duty of a school curriculum to foster some feeling for self-directed learning. Essentially, society needs to provide real learning opportunities, some of which will still lie within the school while others may not.

Schooling surrounds itself with myths, and in particular continues to demonstrate a sentimental nostalgia for two of the greatest myths of British education: that of the Educational Partnership, and that of the Teaching Profession. For most people, the term 'partnership' has the connotation of equality, in which individual partners, even senior partners, seek to reach agreement on the conduct of their affairs. The notion of partnership in education always introduces a need to define the participants: the State and the Church? Central and local government? Teachers? Their unions? Parents (on behalf of their children)? Students? Clients? Does anyone who has read the 1944 Act carefully, let alone the 1988 Act, believe that central government has not always had the power to *control* the education system?

Again, for most people, the term 'profession' implies self-governance, and in practice is principally associated with self-employment, as is the case with medicine and the law. Teachers and lecturers are not self-employed, and they do not have a self-regulating body to supervise their 'professional' standards. If, however, both partnership and profession are myths, that does not make them untrue or valueless. These myths are the traditional narratives we tell about teaching, and they incorporate the popular concepts of what most people would like to believe. On the whole they provide an element of self-respect for teachers and administrators alike, and in so far as they encourage well-meaning aspirations, they can do little harm.

What, then, are the equally powerful myths about the nature of political involvement in education? That politicians create, rather than react to, changes in schooling and higher education? That Secretaries of State at the DES can influence the Treasury's quotas? That Ministers can learn their jobs quickly enough to exercise real authority and leadership before rapidly passing on to another portfolio? That civil servants merely advise while politicians decide? That manifestos lead to specific government actions? That Parliamentary committees have a hold on departmental decision-making? That the reports of commissions of inquiry, chaired by the great and the good, receive the attention they deserve?

Let us spend a little time thinking about the last two examples - Parliamentary committees and official reports. The House of Commons completely revised its committee structure in 1979. The Education, Science and Arts Committee (ESAC)[1] soon established itself as one of the most industrious of the Select Committees:

Session	Report	Area of investigation
1979-80	1	Funding and organization of higher education
1979-80	5	Funding and organization of higher education
1979-80	Special	The provision of information by government departments to select committees
1981-82	1	Expenditure cuts in higher education
1981-82	2	Secondary school curriculum and examinations
1981-82	7	School meals
1981-82	9	Further and higher education in Northern Ireland

1982-83	1	Prison education
1982-83	2	Further and higher education in Northern Ireland
1983-84	2	Prison education
1985-86	2	DES expenditure plans 86/87-88/89
1985-86	3	Achievements in primary schools
1986-87	1	Student awards
1986-78	2	Prison education
1986-87	3	Special educational needs
1986-87	4	DES expenditure plans 87/88-89/90
1987-88	1	DES expenditure plans 88/89-90/91
1988-89	1	Educational provision for under 5-year-olds
1988-89	2	DES expenditure plans 89/90-91/92
1989-90	2	Supply of teachers for the 1990s
1989-90	3	Prison education
1989-90	4	DES expenditure plans 90/91-92/93
1989-90	5	Staffing for SEN pupils
1990-91	2	Prison education
1990-91	3	Standards of reading in primary schools
1990-91	4	Sport in schools

This list does not include reports on the arts or civil science, nor does it indicate the many scrutiny sessions which also took place, but did not present reports. It can be seen, therefore, that the committee's activities during this period were very wide-ranging and, in practice, very demanding on the membership. MPs estimated that they spent some 13 hours per week on average on work connected with the committee, and the chairmen as many as 30 (Rush in Drewry, 1989, p. 94). Members frequently visited institutions in various parts of the country, and received evidence from many sources. The chairmen included two former junior Ministers at the DES (van Straubenzee and Raison) and a former PPS to the Secretary of State (Price), while the committee itself bristled with former teachers. Up to five academic advisers were regularly used by the committee, together with a permanent secretariat.

Its impact on the DES must, however, be described as less than satisfactory. While roughly a quarter of its recommendations (including those on the arts and civil science) were accepted by the DES, a quarter were rejected outright, and a half were 'kept under review', a civil service euphemism for inaction. Only reports connected with the annual round of Treasury estimates normally reached the floor of the Commons, and the committee uncovered no scandals that captured the headlines. Nevertheless, ESAC continues to exercise influence in the educational world:

> The Education Committee played a role in the wider policy process by making information publicly available through its hearing of oral evidence and the publication of much written evidence which, in many cases, would not otherwise have been available or would be more difficult to obtain. Furthermore the interest shown in the committee by professional organizations and pressure groups was considerable, and the Committee provided them with an additional means of making their views known ... [it] played a part in opening up the policy process [and] had a considerable impact outside Parliament.
>
> (Rush, in Drewry, 1989, p. 101)

However, the *Special Report* of the 1979-80 session did reveal a closing-up rather than an opening-up of the policy process. The Secretary of State (Carlisle) and his senior officials refused the committee's requests to hear more about the department's decision to increase the fees paid by overseas students, and the report clearly identified the committee's disquiet about such secrecy. Later a similar situation occurred in respect of an HMI report (Rush, in Drewry, 1989, pp. 97-8). That such a climate of secrecy existed was also confirmed by a Deputy Secretary: 'In the government of education where so many parties have legitimate interests, much of the business consists in the striking of balances and bargains ... Experience shows that the best, and most enduring, bargains are those reached by responsible representatives ... free from the distractions of playing to various galleries. In other words, in privacy' (Simpson, in Ransom and Tomlinson, 1986, p. 30).

In the case of the official reports, the range of inquiries has also been impressive:

Adult and further education	Russell 1973; Alexander 1975; Mansell 1979
Higher education	Robbins 1963; James 1972; Oakes 1978; Lindop 1985
Independent schools	Newsom 1968; Donnison 1970
Primary schools	Plowden 1967; Gittings 1967; Halsey 1972; Bullock 1975; Rampton 1981; Cockcroft 1982; Swann 1985; Kingman 1988; Alexander 1992
Schools/community	Clarke 1947; Clarke 1948; Albermarle 1960; Taylor 1977; Thompson 1982
16-19-year-olds	Gurney-Dixon 1954; Crowther 1959
Secondary schools	Newsom 1963; Bullock 1975; Waddell 1978; Keohane 1979; Rampton 1981; Cockcroft 1982; Swann 1985; Kingman 1988; Elton 1989

Science and technology ed.	Percy 1945; Barlow 1946; Oldfield-Davies 1961; Dainton 1968; Haslegrave 1969; Swann 1974; Swinnerton-Dyer 1982
Special educational needs	Underwood 1955; Warnock 1978

But when the search is made for answers to two particular questions, the reports' overall value seems limited. The questions are: Did the government of the time act upon the advice of the reports? and Did the reports reveal anything that the DES (with its massive HMI team) did not know already? As we have seen in the earlier chapters, the reports usually took two years to produce. The government which commissioned them was not necessarily the government which received them. The acceptability of the reports therefore depended more on the political climate of the publication date than the originating date. And if the information was (or should have been) already available to Whitehall, was the rationale for most of these investigations deferment rather than discovery?

Royal commissions and committees of inquiry have been particularly prone to erupt at the start of a new Prime Minister's regime: 25 new investigations (in government as a whole) for Macmillan in 1957, 21 for Douglas-Home in 1963, 19 for Wilson in 1965, 24 for Heath in 1971, and 16 for Callaghan in 1977. Possibly they were used as a mechanism to establish a new Prime Minister's identity, although they were not at all characteristic of the Thatcher governments. In many ways they may be more popular than productive, sharing with the Select Committees in Parliament a function not directly connected with government. In education certain reports - Robbins, Newsom (1963), Plowden and Taylor - have undoubtedly had an impact on educational thinking in a general way, but it is very difficult to pin down cause-and-effect relationships between their recommendations and DES actions. Hennessy's admirable study (1989, p. 586) of this problem asks if the official reports still have a place in government, and suggests that they can continue to serve as 'aids to high-quality and timely policy making', but only in a 'repaired, strengthened and modernized form'. There is also another obstacle: 'The ministries become bogged down in detail when their energies and resources should be concentrated more on overall policy and the *ad hoc* commissions grow disillusioned and frustrated because they are not allowed to get on with their job' (Mackintosh, 1988, p. 179).

If there are legitimate doubts, anxieties and reservations that we may experience, not only about the use made of the work of Select Committees and of Commissions, but also, more broadly, about those government mechanisms which are themselves concerned with the development and implementation of education policy, then we may need to look more closely at the possible answers to four broad groups of questions:

1. those concerned with the relationship between the DES and Parliament;
2. those concerned with the relationship within the DES between politicians and administrators;

3. those concerned with the relationship between central government and local governments;
4. those concerned with the relationship between teachers or lecturers and their employers.

THE RELATIONSHIP BETWEEN THE DES AND PARLIAMENT

When Churchill offered R. A. Butler the post of President of the Board of Education in 1941, he is said to have expressed some surprise at Butler's acceptance, and it has remained the case that 'education is important to individual people but lacks political glamour in central government' (Kogan, 1978, p. 148). Of course some politicians have attempted to create an element of glamour for education (or for themselves), and this was particularly true of the elaborate fanfaronade which attended the 1988 Education Reform Act. But in real terms, Education Ministers continue to find themselves trapped in the past:

> Ministerial appointments and careers in Britain today follow a pattern first discernible in the Victorian era: a backbench apprenticeship in the House of Commons, leading to one or more junior posts on the ministerial hierarchy before promotion to the Cabinet or (more likely) a return to the backbenches or retirement from politics. Today, as in the nineteenth century, MPs continue to win office primarily for political reasons and because of their skills as parliamentarians, and not because of their specialist subject expertise or extraparliamentary executive experience. Similarly, successful ministers continue to be generalists, typically serving in a number of quite different departments and posts over the course of their careers in government. Despite sharp criticisms of this traditional model since the 1960s, it is almost certain that the ministers who will carry responsibility for the conduct of government as Britain enters the twenty-first century will have been selected and trained for office in a way familiar to Sir Robert Peel or Gladstone.
>
> (Theakston, 1987, p. 41)

It is not only the transient role of the Secretaries of State that is the cause of grave concern, but also the failure to establish the concept of promotion *within* a department that has made worse an already precarious situation. Since the Second World War only three Ministers occupying second-level posts in education have been promoted to the top level: Sir Edward Boyle, Reg Prentice and Shirley Williams, and even in these cases they 'returned' to education after holding posts in other ministries.

The potential for 'training' a junior Minister in a department's portfolio is cruelly squandered, for, as one former Secretary of State has put it, 'a junior Minister is a political eunuch. He has lost the power to speak out boldly and to influence events, to be creative in the broad political arena' (Rogers, 1980, p. 11). Junior Ministers, though given plenty of department tasks to oversee, are still *junior* Ministers, and it is the Secretary of State who takes the final responsibility; thus, 'the political and administrative work of junior ministers cannot be fully understood without reference to their constitutional position as it has been defined since the nineteenth century. But constitutional doctrine alone is an inadequate basis for assessing the nature of junior ministers' jobs' (Theakston, 1987, p. 76). Seen from another point of view, we can also understand that the political stepladder (Parliamentary Under-Secretary, Minister of State, Secretary of State) is no longer an adequate training scheme for work at cabinet level: 'The job of a junior minister was *not* designed as a training ground for Cabinet ministers. The fact that service in such a post is today virtually *sine qua non* for Cabinet office does not ensure that the time spent in these qualifying posts necessarily imparts skills useful in higher offices' (Rose, in Harman and Alt, p. 16).

Not that one would want Ministers to become managers:

> It would be a serious mistake if in some way Ministers were given new and extensive responsibilities for the day-to-day management of their departments, including the scale and efficiency of their executive operations. I do not believe that their talents and training suit them for this task or that they could accommodate the extra burden. It would certainly be quite indefensible if any such change took Ministers away from the House of Commons. Many of them spend too little time there already.
>
> (Rogers, 1980, p. 12)

In order to understand the nature of the politician's role at the DES, we may need to come to terms with the following proposition, namely that 'education as a rule does not initiate social change but rather reflects or reinforces a process that has already begun. However, once radical changes in the educational system have been made, the working out of the logic of such changes does produce important modifications in society at large' (Harrison, 1990, p. 199). It is surely the politician's task first to identify the social process, and then to watch over the 'logic of change'.

Similarly, if we can agree with the idea that 'whatever the other functions of the increasingly large and complex system of education, its history can be written in terms of social policy - the attempt to use education to solve social problems, to influence social structures, to improve one or more aspects of the social condition, to anticipate crisis' (Silver, 1980, p. 17), then today's education policy clearly lacks coordination. Firstly, the DES informs Parliament only on schooling in England, leaving the Welsh Office, the Scottish Office and the Northern Ireland Office to act separately. Secondly, several other Whitehall departments are responsible to Parliament for various aspects of educational provision: In 1991 the Employment Department Group (i.e. the former Department of Employment) had a Training, Enterprise and Education Directorate, including separate directors for youth and adult training, and for education in general (including higher education, further education, TVEI, the careers service and strategic planning). The Department of the Environment, in addition to its dominating control of local authority funding, also possessed its own Sports and

Recreation Directorate working in areas that overlapped with LEA interests. Similarly, the Department of Health shared common interests within the school health service, and, additionally, was answerable to Parliament for certain aspects of health education and 'for all matters relating to nurse training and education', even though the DES also had an interest in this area as a part of its responsibility for higher education. The Home Office's education branch has responsibility for prison education, but ESAC has also produced no fewer than five recent reports on this topic. The Department of Trade and Industry is responsible, quite properly, for policy developments in science and technology research, even though the DES has similar science research interests.

The case for a single education department that is responsible to Parliament for all aspects of education is surely overwhelming. It has featured from time to time in earlier political discussions (including the 1983 Alliance manifesto), but usually gets lost in the tangle of interdepartmental power struggles and the uncharismatic nature of the solutions. When such a rationalization does arrive, however, it would mean that the DES would lose its science element, which more naturally fits into the DTI portfolio. The further matter of Parliament's responsibility for schooling in Scotland, Wales and Northern Ireland will be tackled later in this chapter.

To summarize: the relationship between the DES and Parliament could be improved by

1. ministerial continuity at the DES;
2. a clear separation between making policies and managing resources;
3. a more powerful role for Parliamentary Select Committees;
4. the establishment of *one* Department of Education.

THE RELATIONSHIP WITHIN THE DES BETWEEN POLITICIANS AND ADMINISTRATORS

In Chapters 3 and 5 there was some discussion of the Fulton Committee's recommendations and Crowther-Hunt's reaction to the DES's failure to implement them. Four of the recommendations are still in urgent need of further consideration by the DES: a new recruitment programme looking for specialists with 'relevant degrees'; career specialization; increased exchange between civil servants and the teaching profession; and the establishment of departmental planning units involving specialist advisers.

If it is in the nature of things that only a few Ministers are likely to be drawn from the ranks of teachers, lecturers or educational administrators, then it is all the more important that they be advised by civil servants with specialist knowledge of schools, colleges, universities and local authorities. The 'relevant degrees' need to range over the whole width of the curriculum, and we can surely not afford to repeat the Part experience - 'This was completely strange territory to me, and deplorably, to most of the Ministry's administrators' - referred to in Chapter 2. Since the 1960s, arguments about the merits of specialists and generalists have continued, but have not been resolved. The DES has experienced the results of appointing an ex-headmaster (Halsey) and two men with both teaching and local authority experience (Embling and Weaver) at Deputy level; indeed, it has brought in people from the business and industrial fields, but we still await the appointment of experienced educationists in significant numbers, or the appointment of, say, a university vice-chancellor as Permanent Secretary. Exchange programmes between civil servants and those working in senior posts in schools, higher education and local authority administration remain an urgent priority for a civil service staff development programme. William Rogers (1980, p. 17) took the view that junior civil servants should be seconded for six months at a time to work as personal assistants to MPs in order to familiarize themselves with work in the House of Commons, in the constituencies, in the party machine and in the sphere of activity with which their department is concerned. In the case of the DES this would mean that the civil servants as well as HMI actually came into contact with children and teachers in schools, and students and lecturers in higher education.

The DES was quick to develop Fulton-type planning units but has singularly failed to recruit the specialists that Crowther-Hunt identified in the mid-1970s. As long ago as 1974, the concept of 'validating' the work of the DES was in circulation (Pratt and Burgess, 1974). Participatory evaluation is, of course, a quite different process from investigation by a Parliamentary Select Committee, where the element of adversarial confrontation still lingers. Of the many accounts which have pointed to the nature of the problems which face the DES, this 1981 analysis is still a useful springboard:

> The sheer volume of work which a new, inadequately prepared and short-lived Secretary for Education has to face may leave him bogged down in the detail of cases and the incessant flow of meetings at the expense of involvement in policy formation. The Ministers are often faced with recommendations that are difficult to dispute in the limited time they have to master a brief that will have taken many highly skilled man-hours to prepare. Again, civil servants are situated at every nexus of decision-making and have the advantage of observing the fate of policies across the life-span of governments and Parliaments . . . It seems unwise to rely entirely on the personal characteristics of successive Ministers to shore up a constitutional relationship . . . that is, arguably, increasingly ill-suited to present-day administration and political realities.
>
> (Fenwick and McBride, 1981, p. 30)

Let us separate out the six principal elements of the problem, which are as much in evidence today as they were a decade ago:

1. the sheer volume of work that confronts ministerial decision making;
2. the time needed by new, inadequately prepared Ministers to adjust to the work;

3. the short life of Ministers;
4. the tendency for Ministers to become bogged down in the detail of cases;
5. the incessant flow of meetings at the expense of involvement in policy formation;
6. a constitutional relationship between politicians and civil servants that is increasingly ill-suited to present-day administration and political realities.

Of these items it would seem to many that nos 1., 2., 4. and 5. are susceptible to improved management strategies and to the benefits that would flow from a fundamental rethink of no. 6. The remaining problem, no. 3., can be resolved only by a Prime Minister determined to restructure the politician's role in the machinery of government.

It is not at all surprising that Ministers feel themselves to be overtaken by the sheer volume of activity at the DES, as Shirley Williams (1981) later admitted (see Chapter 5). Let us consider this analysis of a typical DES Minister's tasks:

1. Parliamentary duties, e.g.:
   answers to written and oral questions in the House;
   answers to MPs' letters;
   House of Commons Standing Committees;
   cabinet and cabinet committees;
   departmental bills.
2. departmental public relations, e.g.:
   visits to LEAs, schools, colleges, polytechnics and universities;
   media events;
   international delegations.
3. policy development, e.g.:
   planning strategies via departmental committees;
   consultation with HMI;
   research and development;
   liaison with other government departments;
   liaison with teachers' organizations;
   liaison with LEAs, universities, etc.

MPs also have their normal load of constituency and party business. It has been argued (Headey, 1974; Drewry and Butcher, 1988) that as much as *two-thirds* of a Minister's time is spent on non-departmental matters. Ministers in the House of Lords may also have to present bills and answer questions for other departments.

If it can be argued that Ministers at all levels are prevented from carrying out their duties in respect of policy-making by factors which include the time-consuming activities in categories 1. and 2. above, then a solution needs to be found which effectively separates at least some part of ministerial responsibilities from Parliamentary and representative duties. The fact that we already employ such a system in various departments at various levels and at various times often seems to be ignored by many commentators. In practical terms, the alternative system is called the House of Lords.

Now let it be clear that I am not making a case for increasing the power of the House of Lords, or even for its retention. I simply point to the fact that in the DES, as in many other government departments, Secretaries of State, Ministers of State and Under-Secretaries have not always been MPs, have not always had constituencies to represent, and have not always been directly involved in the constant jockeying for position that characterizes the careers of MPs. In other words, suitably qualified persons have been appointed from outside the limited world of MPs to carry out high-level political activity. The argument that they are answerable to Parliament via the House of Lords is really only a fiction, just as the notion of the 'sovereignty of Parliament' is similarly a fiction. If we wish to have Ministers who are expert in their subject fields, then the injection of politicians who are not simply generalists seeking to creep up the hierarchical ladder to cabinet rank, armed only with ambition, is long overdue.

But if the politicians at the DES have their career goals set for them by political traditions, so also the DES officials have theirs set by the mores of the civil service. What Shirley Williams had to say in 1980 may seem less true today (after a decade of Thatcherite restructuring), but it is only marginally less true in the case of the DES, which has remained separate from the mainstream of Whitehall reforms:

> Hierarchical, large, well-disciplined, inbred management structures are excellent for the carrying out of orders, and for the execution of policy ... They are much less effective as innovators and inventors. And that is indeed my impression of the British civil service. It is a beautifully designed and effective breaking mechanism. It produces a hundred well-argued answers against initiative and change ... The imbalance between the negative forces in Britain and the positive ones lies at the centre of our problems, and the civil service is the most effective of the negative ones.
>
> (1980, p. 81)

If innovation, originality and remodelling are indeed urgently needed in the British education system, then we may have to look elsewhere than the 'negative forces' of the civil service and the career-opportunism of politicians for viable solutions. These two powers have traditionally combined together to operate against fundamental restructuring, and have continued to do so even in the so-called Reform Act of 1988, which promised so much and achieved so little. Such a search requires us to move outside the immediate framework of the DES as it now stands, and this process leads us towards our third set of considerations.

THE RELATIONSHIP BETWEEN CENTRAL GOVERNMENT AND LOCAL GOVERNMENTS

When McPherson and Raab (1988, p. 487) came to draw some conclusions from their powerful study of the Scottish educational system since 1945, they pointed to three major changes in schooling: first, that the scope of schooling had increased substantially; second, that the emphasis on managerial efficiency had gradually become more dominant; and, third, that the Scottish Education Department had 'moved from a regulatory to a promotional stance'. In England the DES's long-standing view of itself, at least until the 1988 Act, was that it had few executive functions (although these did include the supply and training of teachers), but carried out broad allocations of resources and *influenced* the other parties in the education service.[2] The traditional role of the British monarchy 'to comment, advise and warn' was also carried out by the DES in relation to its LEA subjects. But, as we have already seen, from the mid-1970s its management role and its promotional stance changed.

By the early 1990s the vocabulary of the DES had become saturated with aims, objectives, priorities, and targets; with efficiency, effectiveness, inputs, and outputs; and especially with performance measurements and performance indicators. Armed with its Trident Top Management System, the DES attempted to assume the characteristics of 'proactive management', employing 'state-of-the-art' communications systems, and providing a 'competitive edge' and 'know-how' for all those who wished 'to enter the fast track'. Or so it would have us believe. Unfortunately, the DES had been claiming for some time that it was mainly concerned with policy development. The question of whether this was a spurious claim we shall set aside for a moment. If it were true, however, it would be recognized that 'there are of course difficulties in measuring performance within policy formation and associated activities',[3] such as, it might be suggested, the processes of educating, most of which usually take a generation at least to evaluate. Let us, nevertheless, pursue the measuring idea further:

> The progress made by departments in the development and use of performance measurement systems depends on a number of factors, including departmental complexity and structure, the nature of the department's work and the availability of resources. And there are often inherent difficulties in devising performance measures and indicators, for example, measuring the impact of policies; allowing for the effects of factors outside the control of the department; assessing the quality of the services provided; and quantifying the results of basic research.[4]

Thus, very neatly, the DES hid behind the 'inherent difficulties' of being a 'policy department'. If only it were. Unfortunately, the DES, in becoming more directly responsible for the day-to-day running of schools and higher education, has become even more burdened with what Sir Edward Boyle called 'lowish-level administrative work', and which Crosland, Williams and Crowther-Hunt all encountered with some bitterness.

In respect of this management role, the relationship between the DES and the LEAs is well illustrated by reference to the present school-buildings crisis. In Chapter 6 we saw how ESAC drew from Kenneth Baker an admission that 'the big problem is the buildings built in the 1960s, and the late 1950s and early 1970s, the flat-roofed schools.' No doubt he had already seen the draft of an absolutely damning report for the Audit Commission, published also in 1988:

> The deteriorating condition of much local authority property is causing concern. An analysis of the school building profile since the War suggests that there is a worse problem round the corner. In many authorities a maintenance 'time-bomb' is ticking away and on present plans they will not have the resources to defuse it ... as the components of the buildings erected in the 1950s, 1960s and early 1970s begin to wear out ... Even in the absence of an existing backlog, the maintenance bill for schools will rise inexorably for years to come ... Children are being educated in substandard accommodation, and in some authorities it is only a matter of time before it becomes necessary to close schools for safety reasons.[5]

The principle here must surely be that 'he who takes the credit must also take the blame'. It was central government, both Conservative and Labour, that took the credit for the building booms of the three postwar decades. When things were going well, it was central government that was responsible, with the DES loud in self-applause for its architects' department, but when things started to go badly, it was local government's fault. In 1991 the Audit Commission repeated its warning - the time bomb was ticking away and nothing had been done to defuse it. Local government was blamed for not allocating its resources to essential maintenance, and central government was blamed for starving local government of the necessary funds.

Whose managerial efficiency are we talking about, and whose influence? If central government *influenced* LEAs to put up schools that would fall down within 30 years, it was surely now central government's responsibility to rebuild or replace them. But local government also played its part in the predicament:

> In many local authorities property is considered to be 'owned' by the individual service committee occupying it. This means that property which is unused or under-used by the service area cannot readily be exploited by another because there is no mechanism to encourage their joint occupancy. This *fundamental weakness* arises because authorities have failed to recognize the corporate aspects of property portfolio management.[6]

Thus, with declining school rolls throughout the 1980s, local authorities have sold off redundant schools via their education departments, while searching for properties for their social services:

> The demands on authorities' services are now changing very rapidly, so property must be regarded as a dynamic rather than a static resource. Demographic changes are often shifting the balance of need from services for children and young people to those for retired people.[7]

By the summer of 1991 the Audit Commission estimated that there were some 2 million surplus places in schools, and yet the highly stratified and departmentalized education service was unable or unwilling to derive from these circumstances the strategic advantages that would accrue from a radical review of educational provision, and in particular from a reappraisal of the learning requirements of young adults. Inexplicably, village schools in some rural communities were being closed while the demands for adult education remained unsatisfied, and when joint-use programmes by the education, health, social, and recreational services would not only have provided more viable local services, but also have ensured the survival of local schools until the gradual growth in demand estimated for the first quarter of the twenty-first century materializes.

If the underlying strategies of the 1988 Act were relentlessly pursued, no doubt all the opting-out schools with leaking roofs could have them immediately repaired with DES funds. But since the global funds for education provided either by 'a national system locally administered' or for a national system nationally administered would still be insufficient to 'defuse the time bomb', the crisis remains. What, then, is the future for central versus local management and regulatory versus promotional attitudes for the DES?

How this question is answered depends of course on how other prior questions are dealt with. Let us, for example, consider the following line of questioning. If there were regional governments, would we still need the DES? Regional *governments*, not assemblies, incorporating the nations and regions of the UK (Wales, Scotland, Northern Ireland, together with Northern England, the North-West, the Midlands, Eastern England, the Metropolitan area, Southern and South-West England[8]) might take over the major responsibilities for Education, Health and Social Security, Employment, Energy, Transport, Agriculture, and Fisheries and Food, leaving central government still with the Treasury, the Foreign and Commonwealth Office, the Ministry of Defence, the Home Office and Lord Chancellor's Department, the Department of the Environment, and much of the Department of Trade and Industry.[9]

With such arrangements the potential for improvements in education might be created simply by the increased range of perspectives that regional governments could offer. If at least one of the regions or nations were to succeed in reversing the decline in schooling, the others would at least have something to follow. Regional and national governments need not lead to increased layers of bureaucracy: their introduction might coincide with the abolition of the Upper House (which, in the context of the European Parliament, already seems redundant) and with the merging of overlapping local and district councils. A reformed Department of Education (not *and Science*) might need to retain certain regulatory functions and might need to maintain the conduit between the Treasury and the regional governments, but would no longer be responsible for the *promotion* of education, nor for its general management. It would no longer need to get involved with teachers' salaries and approvals for school closures nor with any of the relatively low-level administrative tasks that have traditionally got in the way of its true function - to comment, advise and warn.

It would not be unreasonable, I suppose, to foresee the arrival of some aspects of regionalism before the end of the century - a Scottish Assembly at least. But if regional governments are in reality still a long way off, then it may be necessary to pursue other strategies in order to adjust the relationship between schooling and the DES. In the past it was often argued that 'it cannot be overemphasized that the governmental process in education, as in any other sphere, involves a complex interplay of forces operating in a constantly changing environment' (Fenwick and McBride, 1981, p. 225). This view of the political process was only too common a decade ago. And it was, surely, the unravelling of such complexities, and their replacement by new purpose-built systems, that needed to be explored. A decade ago the dilemma was self-evident: 'in a *national system locally administered* . . . it is inevitably difficult to harmonize fully or to plan coherently. Greater local autonomy could rationalize planning within local authority boundaries but might well increase disparities of provision. On the other hand, more precise long-term planning by central government could well erode all genuine discretion exercised by the other partners in education . . . any fundamental restructuring of national planning for education may well be incompatible with the genuinely decentralized direction of the education service' (Fenwick and McBride, 1981, pp. 41-2). But the solutions offered in the 1980s did almost nothing to find a way out of this labyrinth, and, indeed, may have blinded many to the principal underlying problem: that of the inappropriateness of the DES mechanisms themselves. A new relationship between the DES and local and regional authorities depends therefore on the implementation of the solutions already outlined in this chapter; depends, perhaps crucially, on a better approach to the appointment and career structures of cabinet and other Ministers, and on the generation of civil service specialization and in-service training that involves 'hands-on' experience of schooling and higher education.

THE RELATIONSHIP BETWEEN TEACHERS OR LECTURERS AND THEIR EMPLOYERS

During the Parliamentary year 1989-90, the Education, Science and Arts Select Committee considered the thorny question of the supply of teachers in the 1990s, and after prolonged and careful thought, presented the government with a valuable set of recommendations. But it recognized that the supply of teachers depended not only on the numbers entering teaching, but also on the numbers leaving, which were now reaching alarmingly high levels. It therefore included two recommendations that attempted to stem the flow; that

> an advisory body, on which teachers are represented, should be established. Projections and action on teacher supply should be among the major topics for discussion by such a body. A General Teaching Council would be a suitable body to undertake this task.

> The Government should create a General Teaching Council to work for the enhancement of the profession.[10]

Now the idea of a General Teaching Council (GTC) was not new - Edward Short had proposed the establishment of such a body in July 1968, and the 1970 Weaver report had investigated *A Teaching Council for England and Wales*, while long before that it had been the subject of intermittent discussion by teachers. Indeed, the Select Committee could not have been unaware of the conclusions of no fewer than seventeen educational associations that had been published in 1989 and which identified ten agreed functions for such a council:

> supply of teachers;
> initial training;
> registration;
> professional discipline;
> entry to teaching;
> initial service;
> in-service education;
> retraining and re-entry;
> research and enquiry;
> external relations.[11]

Clearly, many of these functions which are at present carried out by the DES could be handled more effectively by the profession itself.

In its response the DES said: 'With such a considerable number of new bodies recently created and new initiatives being undertaken, the Government does not consider that the creation of a General Teaching Council would in the near future contribute to the success of its education reforms or to an improvement in teacher supply.'[12] This attitude may have been expected, but was disappointing nevertheless. What the committee sensed, I believe, was that the teaching workforce had, during the 1980s, lost confidence in itself, had been marginalized in society, and had grown to meet each setback with resignation. In order to restore confidence, regain its self-esteem and re-establish its poise, teaching needed at last to become a profession, and the profession needed to have a focal point. A real GTC would of course bring challenges as well as benefits to teaching. It would need to challenge many of the conspicuous vested interests of the DES, of HMI, of the LEAs, of initial and in-service teacher training, and of teachers' and lecturers' unions, and it would certainly have to avoid the weaknesses of the old Schools' Council. But within the context of ESAC's recommendation it would surely mean that a robust, dynamic and energetic profession would attract *and retain* a workforce of potent strength. The relationship between teachers, lecturers and their employers may soon encompass a range of options: self-employment, employment by the governing bodies of institutions (e.g. universities, colleges, schools), employment as civil servants or by regional or national governments, or by combinations and variations of all of these. An essential prerequisite, however, would be the establishment of a GTC.

There have always been four separate agendas which have monopolized the affairs of the DES (and the ministry before it), and which, for the sake of brevity, we shall call the external, the internal, the deferred and the hidden agendas. The external (or imperative) agenda is one created by what Harold Macmillan identified as the most difficult aspect of a Prime Minister's life, simply coping with events. The internal (or adopted) agenda is one created by the DES politicians and civil servants and their interactions. The deferred agenda is an endless list of deprioritizations awaiting a change in policy or politicians or administrators, or a return of the circumstances that first originated the proposals. The hidden agenda is filled by the unwritten assumptions of tradition, of style, of attitude, of social preference, and of custom and practice.

The 1945-51 period was governed by the external agenda, on which appeared the following items: the replacement of war-damaged buildings, the geographical redistribution of population; the shortage of teachers; the expansion of pupil numbers towards the end of the period; and, not least, a fragile economy. These were all external factors created by the circumstances and consequences of war and which imposed on the Ministry of Education a command agenda of huge proportions, casting its shadow over the internal agenda to an extent that may explain the latter's almost complete disappearance. It is true, of course, that the internal agenda did add to the problems of the external by raising the school-leaving age to 15 in 1947 and thus exacerbating the overall school population difficulty. Undoubtedly the government did increase its own reconstruction problems, both in terms of the provision of schools and in respect of the supply of industrial manpower, but this was justified by the transfer from the deferred agenda of the agreed 1939 starting date. The main item on the internal agenda was, not surprisingly, the implementation of the 1944 Act. But this also supplied new items for the deferred agenda, particularly in the context of technical education and in the education and support of the 15-18 age group. The hidden agenda revolved round the relationships caused by the appointment of two well-meaning but less-than-visionary Ministers to a department that was led by a civil servant of conspicuously above-average ability and supported by a staff of able but entrenched traditionalists.

During the 1951-64 era the external agenda gradually became less demanding, but there were still significant numbers of postwar headaches to be cleared up, especially those attached to the replacement of school buildings and the now massive increase in the school population. New expenditure restraints were caused by new conflicts such as those of Malaya, Korea, Suez, Cyprus and the 'Cold War', while the pattern of educational provision in the UK remained distorted by the retention of National Service for all 18-20-year-olds until 1960. While the internal agenda remained preoccupied with the implementation of tripartite secondary schooling, the new item was higher education and especially the need to expand it. The deferred agenda retained its items on technical education (since, in reality, the tripartite system had remained obstinately bipartite - grammar schools and 'modern' schools) and on the financial support of the 15-18-year-olds. It also added to this agenda by creating the illusion of solving the school-building programme when the reality was the creation of 'time-bomb' architecture. The hidden agenda was determined by the consequences attributable to the existence of an Eton-and-Oxford cabinet sponsoring an Eton-and-Oxford ministry supported by an independent-school-and-Oxbridge civil service, all vainly trying to understand why those in receipt of public education were less than satisfied. Also hidden was the reaction of the civil servants to the high turnover rate of Ministers: the five averaged only two years and seven months, but this figure conceals the fact that two of them had two separate periods in office, thus creating no fewer than seven start-ups for the system.

The external agenda for the 1964-70 governments was dominated by the population explosion. Vastly increased resources could hardly keep abreast of demand. In an era of relatively high full-employment, a shortage of teachers led to the recruitment of some substandard personnel. From 1968 onwards, economic restraint again become a factor. On the internal agenda the rationalization of secondary schooling became the prime issue, while the deferred agenda still set aside the whole expensive business of an improved technical and scientific curriculum and the education of 15-18-year-olds. On the hidden agenda were the conflicts aroused by Fulton and the reduction of the average duration in office for Secretaries of State to one year and five months.

By contrast the 1970-74 department was marked by stability - one Secretary of State and one Permanent Secretary. But the external agenda reasserted itself with a vengeance in the form of the oil crisis and the resultant inflation in the British economy. Whether the fall in the birth rate should have been perceived as an external agenda problem rather than a bonus is still a matter of contention. The internal agenda meanwhile had to deal with the conflict between the politicians' desire to reverse the trend towards comprehensive secondary schools, and the rolling programme of the LEAs which doubled their number during these same four years. The deferred agenda at last dealt with the problem of the 15-18-year-olds, but only by replacing it with that of the 16-18-year-olds after the raising of the school-leaving age to 16. The UK continued to sink inexorably towards its destiny of becoming bottom of the European league in this age range. The hidden agenda centred on Sir William Pile's advocacy of 'the continuity of things' and Margaret Thatcher's deep-rooted mistrust of the whole of the civil service as it then was.

For education, the 1974-79 period meant reduced public expenditure in an attempt to introduce counterinflationary measures. But the external agenda also included the continued decline in the birth rate, the effects of which were now reaching secondary schools. The internal agenda continued to grapple with secondary reorganization, but even this gradually become overshadowed by worries (real or imagined) about the curriculum - the what and the when of education overtaking the who and the where. The deferred agenda gave long-service medals to post-compulsory provision and technical and scientific education, and established a teachers' council as its latest acquisition. The hidden agenda witnessed the paradox of a Secretary of State failing to push through any major educational reforms while the department itself became increasingly more powerful in the so-called partnership with the LEAs.

The external agenda for the 1979-92 education programme revolved round the government's economic strategies, the policy of curbing local authority expenditure and the substantial increase in unemployment having the most

direct influence on educational services. The internal agenda was dictated by the process of shifting power away from LEAs and higher-education institutions and towards the DES, a process in which the 1988 Act was the clearest example. The deferred agenda grew even larger; the older and apparently permanent elements were now joined by the accumulated good advice of Parliamentary Select Committees and official reports, while the further decline in building maintenance threatened to force its way on to the imperative agenda at any moment. The hidden agenda now presented the enigma of the DES in the hands of transient lawyer-politicians trying to maintain a public service in an enterprise culture and advised by civil servants with less and less experience of educational administration.

Education will flourish once more in the UK only if politicians and those who advise them can become more expert in dealing with the external agenda and better informed and more decisive in activating the internal agenda. In order to achieve either of these goals, they will need to have solved the four relationship puzzles which have formed the core of this chapter and the theme of this book.

NOTES

1 ESAC chairmen: 1979–83, Christopher Price; 1983–87, Sir William van Straubenzee; 1987–89, Timothy Raison; 1989–92, Malcolm Thorton.
2 See, for example, DES (1985), *The Education System of England and Wales*, p. 6.
3 National Audit Office (1991), *Performance Management in the Civil Service – Experience in the FCO, HM Customs and DES* (HC399, HMSO), p. 25.
4 Ibid., p. 4.
5 Audit Commission (1988), *Local Authority Property – A Management Overview*, pp. 3–5, 14, 18. The 'existing backlog' also includes the increased impact of noise levels from aircraft and road transport.
6 Ibid., p. 7.
7 Ibid., p. 7.
8 Defining regions is not agreed by different government departments – some have six; others eight, for example.
9 See especially Raison (1975), Hogwood and Keating, eds (1982), Garside and Herbert (1989).
10 ESAC (89–90), 2nd report, final recommendations 4 and 5.
11 Sayer (1989): see also Sayer (1991).
12 Cmnd 1148, p. 8, July 1990.

Chronology of Ministers and Civil Servants since 1944

MINISTRY OF EDUCATION

	Minister	Parliamentary Secretary	Permanent Secretary	Deputy Permanent Secretaries	Senior Chief Inspector
1944	R.A. Butler	J. Chuter Ede	Sir Maurice Holmes	Sir Robert Wood W.C. Cleary	M.P. Roseveare
1945	R.K. Law *from 23 May to 26 June*				
LABOUR GOVERNMENT July					
1945	Ellen Wilkinson	D.R. Hardman	J.P.R. Maud *from Nov.*	Sir Robert Wood W.C. Cleary	M.P. Roseveare
1946	Ellen Wilkinson	D.R. Hardman	Sir John Maud	Sir Robert Wood W.C. Cleary G.G. Williams	Sir Martin Roseveare
1947	Ellen Wilkinson George Tomlinson *from Feb.*	D.R. Hardman	Sir John Maud	Sir William Cleary G.G. Williams	Sir Martin Roseveare
1948	George Tomlinson	D.R. Hardman	Sir John Maud	Sir William Cleary G.G. Williams	Sir Martin Roseveare
1949	George Tomlinson	D.R. Hardman	Sir John Maud	Sir Willian Cleary Sir Griffith Williams	Sir Martin Roseveare
1950	George Tomlinson	D.R. Hardman	Sir John Maud	Sir William Cleary Sir Griffith Williams	Sir Martin Roseveare
1951	George Tomlinson	D.R. Hardman	Sir John Maud	Sir Griffith Williams G.N. Flemming	Sir Martin Roseveare

	Minister	Parliamentary Secretary	Permanent Secretary	Deputy Permanent Secretaries	Senior Chief Inspector
CONSERVATIVE GOVERNMENT					
Nov 1951	Florence Horsburgh *not in cabinet*	K.W. Pickthorn	Sir John Maud	Sir Griffith Williams G.N. Flemming	Sir Martin Roseveare
1952	Florence Horsburgh	K.W. Pickthorn	Sir John Maud G.N. Flemming *from Oct.*	Sir Griffith Williams G.N. Flemming	Sir Martin Roseveare
1953	Florence Horsburgh *in cabinet from Sept.*	K.W. Pickthorn	Sir Gilbert Flemming	Sir Griffith Williams	Sir Martin Roseveare
1954	Florence Horsburgh Sir David Eccles *from Oct.*	K.W. Pickthorn	Sir Gilbert Flemming	R.N. Heaton	Sir Martin Roseveare
1955	Sir David Eccles	D.F. Vosper	Sir Gilbert Flemming	R.N. Heaton	Sir Martin Roseveare
1956	Sir David Eccles	D.F. Vosper	Sir Gilbert Flemming	R.N. Heaton	Sir Martin Roseveare
1957	Lord Hailsham *from Jan. to Sept.* Geoffrey Lloyd *from Sept.*	D.F. Vosper Sir E. Boyle *from Jan.*	Sir Gilbert Flemming	R.N. Heaton	Sir Martin Roseveare
1958	Geoffrey Lloyd	Sir E. Boyle	Sir Gilbert Flemming	R.N. Heaton	P. Wilson
1959	Geoffrey Lloyd Sir David Eccles *from Oct.*	Sir E. Boyle K.P. Thompson *from Oct.*	Sir Gilbert Flemming Dame Mary Smieton *from Oct.*	R.N. Heaton	P. Wilson
1960	Sir David Eccles	K.P. Thompson	Dame Mary Smieton	R.N. Heaton A.A. Part	P. Wilson
1961	Sir David Eccles	K.P. Thompson	Dame Mary Smieton	R.N. Heaton A.A. Part	P. Wilson
1962	Sir David Eccles Sir Edward Boyle *from July*	C.J. Chataway *from July*	Dame Mary Smieton	R.N. Heaton A.A. Part	P. Wilson
1963	Sir Edward Boyle *until March 1964*	C.J. Chataway	Dame Mary Smieton	A.A. Part T.R. Weaver G.H. Andrew *from July*	P. Wilson

DEPARTMENT OF EDUCATION AND SCIENCE

	Secretary of State for Education and Science	Ministers of State	Parliamentary Under-Secretaries	Permanent Secretary	Deputy Permanent Secretary	Senior Chief Inspector
April 1964	Quintin Hogg	Sir E. Boyle *in cabinet* Lord Newton	C.J. Chataway Lord Bessborough	Sir Herbert Andrew	H.F. Rossetti T.R. Weaver Sir Frank Turnbull	P. Wilson
LABOUR GOVERNMENT Oct 1964	Michael Stewart	Lord Bowden R. Prentice	H.J. Boyden D. Howell*	Sir Herbert Andrew	H.F. Rossetti T.R. Weaver	P. Wilson
1965	Anthony Crosland	Lord Bowden *until Oct.* E.C. Redhead *from Oct.* R. Prentice	H.J. Boyden *until Feb.* D. Howell*	Sir Herbert Andrew	H.F. Rossetti T.R. Weaver	P. Wilson
1966	Anthony Crosland	E.C. Redhead R. Prentice *until Apr.* G.O. Roberts *from Apr.*	D. Howell*	Sir Herbert Andrew	H.F. Rossetti T.R. Weaver	C.R. English
1967	Anthony Crosland Patrick Gordon- Walker *from Aug.*	S. Williams G.O. Roberts A. Bacon *from Aug.*	D. Howell*	Sir Herbert Andrew	H.F. Rossetti T.R. Weaver J.F. Embling	C.R. English
1968	Patrick Gordon- Walker Edward Short *from Apr.*	S. Williams A. Bacon	D. Howell*	Sir Herbert Andrew	H.F. Rossetti T.R. Weaver J.F. Embling	W.R. Elliott
1969	Edward Short *until June 1970*	S. Williams *until Oct.* G. Fowler *from Oct.* A. Bacon	D. Howell* Joan Lestor *from Oct.*	Sir Herbert Andrew	H.F. Rossetti T.R. Weaver J.F. Embling	W.R. Elliott

* Post of Parliamentary Under-Secretary, Sport *and* Schools. After 1969 the Sports Minister was located in another department

	Secretary of State for Education and Science	Ministers of State	Parliamentary Under-Secretaries	Permanent Secretary	Deputy Permanent Secretary	Senior Chief Inspector
CONSERVATIVE GOVERNMENT June						
1970	Margaret Thatcher		Lord Belstead W. van Straubenzee	W. D. Pile *from Aug.*	T. R. Weaver J. F. Embling J. A. Hudson	W. R. Elliott
1971	Margaret Thatcher		Lord Belstead W. van Straubenzee	W. D. Pile	T. R. Weaver J. F. Embling J. A. Hudson	W. R. Elliott
1972	Margaret Thatcher		Lord Belstead W. van Straubenzee	Sir William Pile	T. R. Weaver R. R. Odgers J. A. Hudson C. W. Wright	W. R. Elliott
1973	Margaret Thatcher		Lord Sandford N. St John-Stevas T. Raison *from Dec.*	Sir William Pile	T. R. Weaver R. R. Odgers J. A. Hudson C. W. Wright	H. W. French
1974	Margaret Thatcher		Lord Sandford T. Raison	Sir William Pile	J. A. Hudson R. R. Odgers E. H. Simpson C. W. Wright	H. W. French
LABOUR GOVERNMENT March						
1974	Reg Prentice	G. Fowler Lord Crowther-Hunt *from Oct.*	E. Armstrong	Sir William Pile	J. A. Hudson R. R. Odgers E. H. Simpson C. W. Wright	S. J. Browne
1975	Reg Prentice Fred Mulley *from June*	Lord Crowther-Hunt	E. Armstrong J. Lestor *from June*	Sir William Pile	J. A. Hudson R. R. Odgers E. H. Simpson C. W. Wright	S. J. Browne
1976	Fred Mulley Shirley Williams *from Sept.*	G. Fowler G. Oaks *from Sept.*	J. Lestor M. Jackson *from Mar.*	Sir William Pile J. A. Hamilton *from June*	J. A. Hudson A. Thompson E. H. Simpson C. W. Wright	S. J. Browne
1977	Shirley Williams	G. Oaks	M. Jackson	J. A. Hamilton	J. A. Hudson A. Thompson E. H. Simpson W. O Ulrich	S. J. Browne

	Secretary of State for Education and Science	Ministers of State	Parliamentary Under-Secretaries	Permanent Secretary	Deputy Permanent Secretary	Senior Chief Inspector
1978	Shirley Williams	G. Oaks	M. Jackson	Sir James Hamilton	J. A. Hudson A. Thompson E. H. Simpson W. O. Ulrich	S. J. Browne
1979	Shirley Williams *until May*	G. Oaks	M. Jackson	Sir James Hamilton	J. A. Hudson A. Thompson E. H. Simpson W. O. Ulrich	S. J. Browne
CONSERVATIVE GOVERNMENT May						
1979	Mark Carlisle	Lady Young	R. Boyson	Sir James Hamilton	J. A. Hudson E. H. Simpson W. O. Ulrich A. Thompson	S. J. Browne
1980	Mark Carlisle	Lady Young	R. Boyson	Sir James Hamilton	R. H. Bird E. H. Simpson A. Thompson W. O. Ulrich	S. J. Browne
1981	Mark Carlisle Sir Keith Joseph *from Sept.*	Lady Young	R. Boyson W. Shelton W. Waldegrave	Sir James Hamilton	R. H. Bird E. H. Simpson W. O. Ulrich	S. J. Browne
1982	Sir Keith Joseph		R. Boyson W. Shelton W. Waldegrave	Sir James Hamilton	R. H. Bird E. H. Simpson W. O. Ulrich	S. J. Browne
1983	Sir Keith Joseph		W. Waldegrave *until June* R. Dunn P. Brooke	D. J. S. Hancock *from May*	R. H. Bird W. O. Ulrich P. H. Halsey	E. J. Bolton
1984	Sir Keith Joseph		R. Dunn P. Brooke	D. J. S. Hancock	R. H. Bird W. O. Ulrich P. H. Halsey	E. J. Bolton
1985	Sir Keith Joseph	C. Patten *from Sept.*	R. Dunn G. Walden	Sir David Hancock	R. H. Bird W. O. Ulrich P. H. Halsey	E. J. Bolton
1986	Kenneth Baker *from May*	C. Patten	R. Dunn G. Walden	Sir David Hancock	P. H. Bird W. O. Ulrich P. H. Halsey	E. J. Bolton

	Secretary of State for Education and Science	Ministers of State	Parliamentary Under-Secretaries	Permanent Secretary	Deputy Permanent Secretary	Senior Chief Inspector
1987	Kenneth Baker	A. Rumbold *from June*	R. Dunn R. Jackson Lady Hooper	Sir David Hancock	R.H. Bird W.O. Ulrich	E.J. Bolton
1988	Kenneth Baker	A. Rumbold	R. Jackson J. Butcher	Sir David Hancock	R.H. Bird N.W. Stuart J.M.M. Vereker A.J. Wiggins	E.J. Bolton
1989	Kenneth Baker John MacGregor *from July*	A. Rumbold	R. Jackson J. Butcher/ A. Howarth	Sir David Hancock/ J. Caines	R.H. Bird N.W. Stuart J.M.M. Vereker A.J. Wiggins	E.J. Bolton
1990	John MacGregor Kenneth Clarke *from Nov.*	A. Rumbold T. Eggar *from July*	M. Fallon A. Howarth	J. Caines	R.H. Bird N.W. Stuart J.M.M. Vereker A.J. Wiggins	E.J. Bolton
1991	Kenneth Clarke	T. Eggar	M. Fallon A. Howarth	Sir John Caines	N.W. Stuart J.M.M. Vereker A.J. Wiggins	E.J. Bolton *(until Aug.)*
1992	Kenneth Clarke	T. Eggar	M. Fallon A. Howarth	Sir John Caines	N.W. Stuart J.M.M. Vereker A.J. Wiggins	

MINISTERIAL CAREERS AT DES SINCE 1964*

(not including Sports or Arts Ministers)

Secretary of State	*1st time SS*	*Previous MS*	*Later posts*
Baker	No (Environment)	DTI and DoE	Party Chairman, Home Secretary
Carlisle	Yes	Home Office	No
Clarke	No (Health, PMG)	Health	No
Crosland	Yes	Economic Affairs	SS Environment, Foreign Minister
Gordon-Walker	No (Foreign Min.)	Yes, various	No
Hogg (Hailsham)	No (Science)	Yes, various	Lord Chancellor
Joseph	No (Industry)	Yes, various	No
MacGregor	No (Agriculture)	Agriculture	Leader, Commons

Chronology of ministers and civil servants since 1944

Secretary of State	*1st time SS*	*Previous MS*	*Later posts*
Mulley	No (Transport)	Defence, FCO	No
Prentice	Yes	Yes, various	DHSS
Short	Yes	PMG.	Leader, Commons
Stewart	Yes	No (PUS War Office and Min. Supply)	Foreign Minister and SS Economic Affairs
Thatcher	Yes	No (PUS Pensions)	Prime Minister
Williams	No (Consumer Affairs)	DES, HO	No

Ministers of State	*1st time MS*	*Previous*	*Later posts*
Bacon	No (HO)	No	No
Bowden	Yes	No	No
Boyle	(in cabinet)	No	No
Crowther-Hunt	Yes	No	Cabinet Office
Eggar	No (Employment)	FCO	–
Fowler	Yes	Technology	Returned to DES twice
Oaks	Yes	DoE and Energy	No
Patten	Yes	NI office	MS (FCO), SS (Environment)
Prentice	Yes	No	SS, DES (MS Social Security)
Redhead	No (Bd of Trade)	No	No
Roberts	No (Welsh Office)	No	MS (FCO), Deputy Leader Lords
Rumbold	Yes	Environment	MS Home Office
Williams	Yes	Min. Labour	MS (HO), SS (Prices and Consumer Protection) SS (DES)
Young	Yes	Environment	MS (FCO), Lord Privy Seal

Under-Secretary	*1st time PUS*	*Later posts*
Armstrong	Yes	Environment
Belstead	Yes	MS (FCO, HO, Ag), Lord Privy Seal
Bessborough	No	MS (Technology)
Boyden	Yes	PUS (MOD)
Boyson	Yes	MS (DHSS, NI, DoE)
Brooke	Yes	MS (Treasury) SS (N. Ireland)
Butcher	No (DoI, DTI)	No
Chataway	Yes	MS (DTI)
Dunn	Yes	No

Under-Secretary	*1st time PUS*	*Later posts*
Fallon	Yes	–
Hooper	Yes	PUS Energy, Health
Howarth	Yes	–
Howell	Yes	Minister of Sport
Jackson [Beckett]	Yes	(Shadow Treasury)
Jackson, Robert	Yes	PUS Employment
Lestor	Yes	PUS (FCO)
Raison	Yes	MS (FCO, HO)
Sanford	No (DoE)	No
Shelton	Yes	No
Stevas	Yes	Leader, Commons
van Straubenzee	Yes	MS (NI)
Waldegrave	Yes	MS (FCO), SS (Health) Party Chairman

* Abbreviations used: SS, Secretary of State; MS, Minister of State; PUS, Parliamentary Under-Secretary; DoE, Department of the Environment; DTI, Department of Trade and Industry; FCO, Foreign and Commonwealth Office; HO, Home Office; NI, Northern Ireland; PMG, Postmaster-General.

Bibliography

Addison, P. (1975) *The Road to 1945: British Politics and the Second World War*. London: Cape.

Ahier, J. and Flude, M. (eds) (1983) *Contemporary Educational Policy*. London: Croom Helm.

Alexander, R. *et al.* (eds) (1984) *Change in Teacher Education: Context and Provision since Robbins*. Holt, Rinehart and Winston.

Andrew, H. (1964) 'Education - the responsibility of the state'. British Association Education Conference, DES.

Association of County Councils *et al.* (1979) *Review of Central Government Controls over Local Authorities*. ACC.

Attlee, C. (1954) *As It Happened*. London: Heinemann.

Ball, S. (1990) *Politics and Policy-making in Education*. London: Routledge.

Baker, K. (1989) 'Change is our ally'. *Education and Training* **31**(6), 12-17.

Barker, B. (1986) 'The politics of education'. *Forum* **28**(3), 82-3.

Barker, R. (1972) *Education and Politics 1900-1951*. Oxford: Oxford University Press.

Barnett, C. (1986) *The Audit of War*. London: Macmillan.

Bash, L. and Coulby, D. (1989) *The Education Reform Act*. London: Cassell.

Batho, G. (1989) *Political Issues in Education*. London: Cassell.

Becher, T. and Maclure, S. (1978) *The Politics of Curriculum Change*. London: Hutchinson.

Becher, T. and Maclure, S. (eds) (1978) *Accountability in Education*. Windsor: NFER.

Becher, T., Eraut, M. and Knight, J. (1981) *Policies for Educational Accountability*. London: Heinemann.

Beer, S.H. (1982) *Modern British Politics: Parties and Pressure Groups in the Collectivist Age*. London: Faber.

Benn, C. (1980) 'Comprehensive school reform and 1945 Labour government'. *History Workshop* 10, 197-204.

Benn, T. (1980) 'Manifestos and mandarins'. In *Royal Institute of Public Administration* (1980).

Benn, T. (1989) *Diaries*. London: Hutchinson.

Bernbaum, G. (ed.) (1979) *Schooling in Decline*. London: Macmillan.

Blackburn, F. (1954) *George Tomlinson: A Biography*. London: Heinemann.

Blackstone, T. and Crispin, A. (1982) *How Many Teachers? Issues of Policy, Planning and Demography*. London: University of London Institute of Education.

Bolton, E. (1985) 'Curriculum 5-16'. *Education Review* **37**(3), 199-205.

Bolton, E. (1986) 'Quality issues arising from expanding access'. *Journal of Access Studies* **1**(1), 3-10.

Bolton, E. (1987a) 'The debate on a national agreement on the curriculum and its implication for standards'. *NUT Education Review* **1**(1).

Bolton, E. (1987b) *The Control of the Curriculum*. Durham University School of Education.

Booth, C. (1987) 'Central government and higher education planning 1965-1986'. *History of Education Quarterly* **4**(1), 57-72.

Boyle, Lord [Sir Edward] (1960) 'Teaching race relations in school'. *Common Ground* **14**(1), 13-16.

Boyle, Lord [Sir Edward] (1961) 'Students and universities'. *Accent on Youth.*

Boyle, Lord [Sir Edward] (1963) *This Is Conservative Party Policy for Education.* Conservative Party.

Boyle, Lord [Sir Edward] (1965) 'Minister or civil servant?'. *Public Administration* **43**(Autumn), 251-87.

Boyle, Lord [Sir Edward] (1966) *Education for International Understanding.* David Davies Memorial Lecture.

Boyle, Lord [Sir Edward] (1967a) 'Minister, civil servants and policies'. Acton Society paper.

Boyle, Lord [Sir Edward] (1967b) 'Thoughts on educational advance'. Sidney Ball Lecture, University of Oxford.

Boyle, Lord [Sir Edward] (1968) 'Teacher training and the state'. The Colston Papers, vol. 20.

Boyle, Lord [Sir Edward] (1969) 'Student revolt'. Lecture in Canterbury Cathedral (5 November 1969).

Boyle, Lord [Sir Edward] (1970) 'Race relations and education'. Eleanor Rathbone Memorial Lecture. Liverpool University Press.

Boyle, Lord [Sir Edward] (1970) 'Education in the 70s'. *Education in the Seventies: Goals and Techniques.* Report of seminar held in the Royal Festival Hall, London.

Boyle, Lord [Sir Edward] (1970) 'The politics of secondary school reorganisation: some reflections'. *Journal of Educational Administration and History* **4**(2), 28-38.

Boyle, Lord [Sir Edward] (1971) 'The future of adult education'. William F. Harvey Memorial Lecture.

Boyle, Lord [Sir Edward] (1973) 'A Classical education re-visited'. *Proceedings of the Classical Association* **70**.

Boyle, Lord [Sir Edward] (1976) *Parliament's Views on Responsibility for Education Policy since 1944.* Alfred G. Mays Memorial Lecture, Institute of Local Government Studies, Birmingham.

Boyle, Lord [Sir Edward] (1979) 'Government, Parliament and the Robbins report'. Joseph Payne Memorial Lecture.

Boyle, Lord [Sir Edward] (1979) 'Ministers and the administrative process'. *Public Administration* **58**(1), 1-12.

Boyle, Edward and Crosland, Anthony [in conversation with Maurice Kogan] (1971) *The Politics of Education.* Harmondsworth: Penguin.

Brighouse, T. (1984) 'The influence of Her Majesty's Inspectors'. In Harling (1984), pp. 89-104.

Brighouse, T. and Moon, B. (eds) (1990) *Managing the National Curriculum.* Harlow: Longman.

Broadfoot, P. (1986) 'Power relations and English education: the changing role of central government'. *Journal of Education Policy* **1**(1), 53-62.

Broadfoot, P. *et al.* (eds) (1981) *Politics and Educational Change.* London: Croom Helm.

Browne, S. (1977) 'Curriculum: an HMI view'. *Trends in Education,* **3**. London: HMSO.

Browne, S. (1979) 'The accountability of HM Inspectorate'. In Lello (1979), pp. 35-46.

Butler, [R.A.] Lord (1965) *The Education Act of 1944 and After.* University of Essex Noel Buxton Lecture. London: Longman.

Butler, [R.A.] Lord (1971) *The Art of the Possible.* London: Hamish Hamilton.

Butler, [R.A.] Lord (1982) *The Art of Memory*. London: Hodder & Stoughton.

Campbell, J. *et al.* (1987) 'Multiplying the divisions? intimations of educational policy post-1987'. *Journal of Education Policy* **2**(4), 369-78.

Carswell, J. (1986) *Government and the Universities in Britain: Programme and Performance 1960-1980*. Cambridge: Cambridge University Press.

Centre for Contemporary Cultural Studies (1981) *Unpopular Education: Schooling and Social Democracy in England since 1944*. London: Hutchinson.

Chapman, R. (1991) 'The civil service: changes since Fulton'. *Contemporary Record* **17**(4), 28-32.

Chitty, C. (1988) 'Central control of the school curriculum 1944-87'. *History of Education* **17**(4), 321-34.

Chitty, C. (1989) *Towards a New Education System: The Victory of the New Right?* Brighton: Falmer.

Cleary, W. (1941) 'Post-war social development and its effect on schools'. Paper now in the Lord Boyle archive, University of Leeds.

Corbett, A. (1968) *Much to Do about Education: A Critical Survey of the Fate of the Major Education Reports*. 4th edn, 1978. London: Macmillan.

CPRS (1977) *Relationships between Central Government and Local Authorities*. London: HMSO.

Craig, F.W.S. (ed.) (1970) *British General Election Manifestos 1918-1966*. Political Reference Publications.

Craig, F.W.S. (ed.) (1975) *British General Election Manifestos 1900-1974*. London: Macmillan.

Craig, F.W.S. (ed.) (1982) *Conservative and Labour Party Conference decisions 1945-1981*. Parliamentary Research Services [Chichester].

Crick, B. (1977) 'Education and the polity'. *Higher Education Review* **9**(2), 7-22.

Crosland, A. (1956) *The Future of Socialism*. London: Cape.

Crosland, A. (1975) *Socialism Now*. London: Cape.

Crosland, S. (1982) *Tony Crosland*. London: Cape.

Crouch, C. and Marquand, D. (1989) *The New Centralism: Britain Out of Step with Europe?* Oxford: Blackwell.

Crowther-Hunt, Lord [Norman] (1964) *Whitehall and Beyond*. London: BBC Publications.

Crowther-Hunt, Lord [Norman] (1975) 'The future of the universities'. MS in Leeds University Library.

Crowther-Hunt, Lord [Norman] and Taylor, G. (eds) (1970) *Personality and Power*. London: BBC Publications.

Cuthbert, R. (1981) 'The *neutrality* of the DES'. *Higher Education Review* **13**(2), 8-21.

Dean, D.W. (1986) 'Planning for a postwar generation: Ellen Wilkinson and George Tomlinson at the Ministry of Education, 1945-51'. *History of Education* **15**(2), 95-117.

Deem, R. (1988) 'The great Education Reform Bill 1988: some issues and implications'. *Journal of Education Policy* **3**(2), 181-9.

Dobinson, C.H. (ed.) (1951) *Education in a Changing World*. Oxford: Oxford University Press.

Donoughue, B. (1987) *Prime Minister: The Conduct of Policy under Harold Wilson and James Callaghan*. London: Cape.

Drewry, G. (1989) *The New Select Committees: A Study of the 1979 Reforms*. 2nd edn. Oxford: Oxford University Press.

Drewry, G. and Butcher, T. (1988) *The Civil Services Today*. Oxford: Blackwell.

Dunford, J.R. (1988) *Central/Local Government Relations 1977-1987 with Special Reference to Education: A Review of the Literature*. Stoke-on-Trent: Trentham Books.
Dunford, J.R. (1988) 'The curriculum private eye: what effect the Education Bill will have on the role of HMI'. *Education* (15 April) p. 315.
Eccles, Viscount [David] (1967) *Life and Politics: A Moral Diagnosis*.
Eccles, Viscount [David] (1966) *Halfway to Faith*.
Eccles, Viscount [David] (1971) Address to the Arts and Education Conference, Newcastle upon Tyne.
Elmore, R. (1987) 'Choice in public education'. *Journal of Education Policy* **2**(5), 79-98.
Embling, J. [J.F.] (1974) *A Fresh Look at Higher Education*. London: University of London.
Englefield, D. (ed.) (1986) *Whitehall and Westminster: Government Informs Parliament: The Changing Scene*. London: Longman.
Eraut, M. (ed.) (1991) *Education and the Information Society*. London: Cassell.
Ermisch, J. (1983) *The Political Economy of Demographic Change*. London: Heinemann.
European Communities (1988) *European Education Policy Statements*. London: HMSO.
Fenwick, K. [I.G.K.] (1976) *The Comprehensive School 1944-70*. London: Methuen.
Fenwick, K. [I.G.K.] (1985) 'Changing roles in the government of education'. *British Journal of Educational Studies* **33**(2), 135-47.
Fenwick, K. [I.G.K.] and McBride, P. (1981) *The Government of Education*. Martin Robinson.
Finch, J. (1984) *Education as Social Policy*. Harlow: Longman.
Fletcher, L. (1986) 'Education administration sharpened by the eyes of Janus: a historical approach to educational decision-making'. *Journal of Education Administration and History* **18**(2), 66-77.
Fowler, G. (1971) *Diverse System of Higher Education: The Ideal and the Achievement*. Association of Colleges for Further and Higher Education.
Fowler, G. (1971) *Mass Higher Education in Britain*. University College Swansea.
Fowler, G. (1974) *Central Government of Education*. Open University Course E221, Unit 2. Milton Keynes: Open University Press.
Fowler, G. (1975) 'DES, ministers and curriculum'. In Bell, R. and Prescott, W. (eds) *The Schools Council*. London: Ward Lock Educational.
Fowler, G. (1979) 'The accountability of Ministers'. In Lello (1979), pp. 13-34.
Fowler, G. (1979) 'The politics of education'. In Bernbaum (1979), pp. 47-90.
Fowler, G. (1981) 'The changing nature of educational politics in the 1970s'. In Broadfoot (1981), pp. 13-28.
Fowler, G. *et al.* (1973) *Decision-Making in British Education*. London: Heinemann.
Fowler, G. *et al.* (1976) *Education Service: Management Problems and Perspectives*. Manchester: Manchester Polytechnic.
Garside, P. and Hebbert, M. (1989) *British Regionalism 1900-2000*. London: Mansell.
Gewirtz, S. and Ozga, J. (1990) 'Partnership, pluralism and education policy: a reassessment'. *Journal of Education Policy* **5**(1), 37-48.
Gipps, R. (1988) 'The debate over standards and the use of testing'. *British Journal of Educational Studies* **36**(1), 21-36.
Gordon, P. (ed.) (1985) *Is Teaching a Profession?* London: University of London Institute of Education.
Gordon, P., Aldrich, R. and Dean, D. (1991) *Education and Policy in England in the Twentieth Century*. London: Woburn Press.
Gosden, P. (1972) *The Evolution of a Profession*. Oxford: Blackwell.
Gosden, P. (1974) *Education in the Second World War*. London: Methuen.
Gosden, P. (1983) *The Education System since 1944*. Martin Robertson.

Gosden, P. (1985) 'Educational policy'. In Bell, D. (ed.) *The Conservative Government 1979-84*. London: Croom Helm.

Gosden, P. (1988) 'From board to ministry: the impact of the war on the education department'. *History of Education* 18(3), 183-93.

Grace, G. (1989) 'Education: commodity or public good?'. *British Journal of Educational Studies* 37(3), 207-21.

Guthrie, J. and Koppich, J. (1987) 'Exploring the political economy of national education reform'. *Journal of Education Policy* 2(5), 25-47.

Hamilton, Sir James (1976) Speech at Association of Education Committees (25 June 1976).

Hargreaves, D. (1990) 'Accountability and school improvement in the work of LEA inspectors: the rhetoric and beyond'. *Journal of Education Policy* 5(3), 230-41.

Harling, P. (ed.) (1984) *New Directions in Educational Leadership*. Brighton: Falmer Press.

Harris, K. (1982) *Attlee*. London: Weidenfeld & Nicolson.

Harris, K. (1988) *Thatcher*. London: Weidenfeld & Nicolson.

Harrison, J.F.C. (1990) *Late Victorian Britain 1875-1901*. London: Fontana Press.

Hartnett, A. (ed.) (1982) *The Social Sciences in Education*. London: Heinemann.

Hartnett, A. and Naish, M. (eds) (1986) *Education and Society Today*. Brighton: Falmer.

Hartnett, A. and Naish, M. (1990) 'The sleep of reason breeds monsters: the birth of a statutory curriculum in England and Wales'. *Journal of Curriculum Studies* 22(1), 1-16.

Haviland, J. (1988) *Take Care, Mr Baker!: A Selection from the Advice on Education Which the Government Collected but Decided Not to Publish*. London: Fourth Estate.

Headey, B. (1974) *British Cabinet Ministers: The Roles of Politicians in Executive Office*. International Publishing Services.

Hellawell, D. (1987) 'Education under attack: the response of European politicians'. *European Journal of Teacher Education* 10(3), 245-58.

Hennessy, P. (1988) *Whitehall*. London: Secker & Warburg.

Hennessy, P. (1990) *The Attlee Government*. Oxford: Blackwell.

Hennessy, P. and Seldon, A. (eds) (1987) *Ruling Performance: British Governments from Attlee to Thatcher*. Oxford: Blackwell.

Herman, V. and Alt, J. (1975) *Cabinet Studies: A Reader*. St Martin.

Holt, M. (1987) *Judgement, Planning and Education Change*. Harper & Row.

Hogwood, B.W. and Keating, M. (eds) (1982) *Regional Government in England*. Oxford: Oxford University Press.

Hughes, B. [H.D.] (1979) 'In defence of Ellen Wilkinson'. *History Workshop* 7 157-9.

Hughes, R., Robbins, P. and Thomas, H. (eds) (1987) *Managing Education*. London: Cassell.

Husen, T. (1979) *The School in Question: A Comparative Study of the School and Its Future in Western Societies*. Oxford: Oxford University Press.

Husen, T. (1988) 'From consensus to confrontation in education policy'. *Oxford Review of Education* 14(3), 363-9.

Husen, T. and Kogan, M. (eds) (1984) *Educational Research and Policy: How Do They Relate?* Oxford: Pergamon Press.

Jeffreys, K. (1984) 'R.A. Butler, The Board of Education and the 1944 Education Act'. *History* 69(227), 415-31.

Johnson, R. (1989) 'Thatcherism and English education: breaking the mould, or confirming the pattern?'. *History of Education* 18(2), 91-121.

Jonathan, R. (1990) 'State education service or prisoner's dilemma: the *hidden hand* as source of education policy'. *British Journal of Educational Studies* **38**(2), 116-32.

Jones, T. (1987) 'Politics against choice: school finance and school reform in the 1980s'. *Journal of Education Policy* **2**(5), 183-97.

Joseph, Sir Keith (1984) Speech at North of England Education Conference, January 1984. *Oxford Review of Education* **10**(2), 137-48.

Judges, A.V. (ed.) (1952) *The Pioneers of English Education*. London: Faber.

Kallen, D. (1985) 'Education systems and preparation for work'. *Education Today* **35**(3), 24-31.

Karmel, P. (1988) 'The role of central government in higher education'. *Higher Education Quarterly* **42**(2), 119-33.

Kavanagh, D. and Morris, P. (1989) *Consensus Politics from Attlee to Thatcher*. Oxford: Blackwell.

Kellner, P. and Crowther-Hunt, Lord (1980) *The Civil Servants: An Inquiry into Britain's Ruling Class*. Macdonald & Janes.

Kingdom, J. (ed.) (1989) *The Civil Service in Liberal Democracies: An Introductory Survey*. London: Routledge.

Knight, C. (1990) *The Making of Tory Education Policy in Post-war Britain 1950-86*. Brighton: Falmer Press.

Kogan, M. (1975) *Education Policy-Making: A Study of Interest Groups and Parliament*. London: Allen & Unwin.

Kogan, M. (1978) *The Politics of Educational Change*. London: Fontana.

Kogan, M. (1980) 'Policies for the school curriculum in their political context'. *Cambridge Journal of Education* **10**(3), 122-33.

Kogan, M. (1983) 'The case of education'. In K. Young (1983).

Kogan, M. (1984) 'Curriculum innovation: the impact of central government initiatives'. *Secondary Educational Journal*, Oct.

Kogan, M. (1986) *Educational Accountability: An Analytic Overview*. London: Hutchinson.

Kogan, M. and Packwood, T. (1974) *Advisory Councils and Committees in Education*. London: Routledge & Kegan Paul.

Lapping, B. (1970) *The Labour Government 1964-70*. Harmondsworth: Penguin.

Lauglo, J. and McLean, M. (eds) (1985) *The Control of Education*. London: Heinemann.

Lawton, D. (1979) *The End of the Secret Garden?* London: University of London Institute of Education.

Lawton, D. (1980) *The Politics of the School Curriculum*. London: Routledge & Kegan Paul.

Lawton, D. (1984) *The Tightening Grip: Growth of Central Control of the School Curriculum*. London: University of London Institute of Education.

Lawton, D. (1986) 'The DES: policy making at the centre'. In Hartnett and Naish (1986), pp. 19-36.

Lawton, D. (1988) 'The contemporary role of HMI in England'. *Journal of Education Policy* **3**(2), 191-6.

Lawton, D. (1989) *Education, Culture and the National Curriculum*. Sevenoaks: Hodder & Stoughton.

Lawton, D. and Chitty, C. (eds) (1990) *The National Curriculum*. London: Kogan Page.

Lawton, D. and Gordon, P. (1987) *HMI*. London: Routledge & Kegan Paul.

Lello, J. (1979) *Accountability in Education*. London: Ward Lock Educational.

Locke, M. (1974) *Power and Politics in the School System: A Guidebook*. London: Routledge & Kegan Paul.

Lowe, R. (1988) *Education in the Post-War Years: A Social History*. London: Routledge.

Lukes, J.R. (1975) 'Power and policy at the DES: a case study'. *Universities Quarterly* **29**(2), 133-65.

Mackintosh, J.P. rev. Peter Richards (1988) *The Government and Politics of Britain*. London: Hutchinson.

Maclure, S. (1965) *Educational Documents*. 5th edn, 1986. London: Methuen.

Maclure, S. (1985) 'Forty years on'. *British Journal of Educational Studies* **33**(2), 117-34.

Maclure, S. (1987) 'The emperor's old clothes'. *Journal of Education Policy* **2**(4), 335-9.

Maclure, S. (1988) *Education Re-formed: A Guide to the Education Reform Act 1988*. Sevenoaks: Hodder & Stoughton.

McCormick, R. (ed.) (1982) *Calling Education to Account*. London: Heinemann.

McCulloch, G. (1986) 'Policy, politics and education: TVEI'. *Journal of Education Policy* **1**(1), 35-52.

McLean, M. (1988) 'The Conservative education policy in comparative perspective'. *British Journal of Educational Studies* **36**(3), 200-17.

McLean, M. (1990) *Britain and a Single Market Europe: Prospects for a Common School Curriculum*. London: Kogan Page.

McNay, I. and Ozga, J. (eds) (1985) *Policy Making in Education*. Oxford: Pergamon Press.

McPherson, A. and Raab, C. (1988) *Governing Education*. Edinburgh: Edinburgh University Press.

Manning, L. (1970) *A Life for Education: An Autobiography*.

Manzer, R.A. (1970) *Teachers and Politics*. Manchester: Manchester University Press.

Margrave, P. (1989) 'Labour's education policy for the 1990s'. *Education Today* **39**(3), 4-15.

Marland, M. (1982) 'The politics of improvement in schools'. *Educational Management and Administration* **10**(2), 119-34.

Marquand, D. (1988) *The Unprincipled Society*. London: Cape.

Marwick, A. (1982) *British Society since 1945*. Harmondsworth: Penguin.

Mathieson, M. and Bernbaum, G. (1988) 'The British disease: a British tradition?'. *British Journal of Educational Studies* **36**(2), 126-74.

Maud, Lord Redcliffe-[John P.R.] (1946) 'The prospect for education'. *NUT Conference Papers* (Easter 1946).

Maud, Lord Redcliffe-[John P.R.] (1948) 'Presidential address'. 31st Annual Report of the Conference of Educational Associations, King's College London.

Maud, Lord Redcliffe-[John P.R.] (1950) *Adult Education: Current Trends and Practices: The Significance of Adult Education*. UNESCO.

Maud, Lord Redcliffe-[John P.R.] (1951) '1851-1951: a century of British education'. *Journal of the Royal Society of Arts* (June 1951).

Maud, Lord Redcliffe-[John P.R.] (1951) 'The international aspect of education'. In Dobinson (1951), pp. 62-83.

Maud, Lord Redcliffe-[John P.R.] (1952) 'The twentieth century administrator'. In Judges (1952), pp. 227-48.

Maud, Lord Redcliffe-[John P.R.] (1962) 'Expanding horizons in a contracting world: the challenge of education'. In Macmillan, R.G., Hey, P.D. and Macquarrie, J. (eds) *Education and Our Expanding Horizons*. Proceedings of the National Conference in Education, Durban, University of Natal, 1960.

Maud, Lord Redcliffe-[John P.R.] (1981) *Experiences of an Optimist*. London: Hamish Hamilton.

Maud, Lord Redcliffe-[John P.R.] (1981) 'The framework of progress'. P.D. Leake Lecture.

Meny, I. (trans. J. Lloyd) (1990) *Government and Politics in Western Europe*. Oxford: Oxford University Press.

Mitchell, D. and Goertz, M. (eds) (1990) *Education Politics for the New Century*. Brighton: Falmer.

Morgan, K.O. (1984) *Labour in Power*. Oxford: Oxford University Press.

Morrell, F. (1988) 'The management of education: a political perspective'. *Educational Management and Administration* **16**(2), 103-14.

Morris, B. (ed.) (1990) *Central and Local Government Control of Education after the Education Reform Act 1988*. Harlow: Longman.

Morris, M. and Griggs, C. (eds) (1988) *Education - The Wasted Years: 1973-1986*. Brighton: Falmer Press.

Musgrave, P. (ed.) (1970) *Sociology, History and Education*. London: Methuen. [see esp. 'Constant factors in the demand for technical education 1860-1960'].

Nugent, N. (1989) *Government and Politics of the European Community*. London: Macmillan.

Oakes, G. (1978) *The Management of Higher Education in the Maintained Sector*.

Oakes, G. (1977) 'The function of regional management centres'. *Education and Training* **19**, 195-201.

Oakes, G. (1977) 'Hot line to the DES'. *Education and Training* **19**, 10-12.

Oakes, G. (1976) 'Polytechnics: a decade of development'. *Times Educational Supplement* (29 October 1976).

Organisation for Economic Co-operation and Development (1975) *Educational Development Strategy in England and Wales*. OECD.

Organisation for Economic Co-operation and Development (1989) *Schools and Quality*. OECD.

Parkinson, M. (1970) *The Labour Party and the Organization of Secondary Education 1918-1965*. London: Routledge & Kegan Paul.

Parkinson, M. (1982) 'Politics and policy-making in education'. In Hartnett (1982), pp. 114-26.

Part, A. (1990) *The Making of a Mandarin*. London: André Deutsch.

Pelling, H. (1984) *The Labour Governments 1945-51*. London: Macmillan.

Pile, W. (1974) 'Corporate planning for education in the DES'. *Public Administration* **52** (Spring), 13-25.

Pile, W. (1979) *The Department of Education and Science*. London: Allen & Unwin.

Pile, W. (1984) 'National policies for education'. In Harling (1984), pp. 79-88.

Plaskow, M. (ed.) (1985) *Life and Death of the Schools Council*. Brighton: Falmer Press.

Postlethwaite, N. (1986) 'Policy-orientated research in education'. *Oxford Review of Education* **12**(2), 135-51.

Pratt, J. and Burgess, T. (1974) *Polytechnics: A Report*. London: Pitman.

Pring, R. (1987) 'Privatization in education'. *Journal of Education Policy* **2**(4), 289-99.

Pring, R. (1989) *The New Curriculum*. London: Cassell.

Radice, G. (1984) 'Comments on Sir Keith Joseph's (1984) speech'. *Oxford Review of Education* **10**(2), 149-58.

Raggatt, P. and Weiner, G. (1985) *Curriculum and Assessment: Some Policy Issues*. Oxford: Pergamon Press.

Raison, T. (1975) *Regional Devolution and Social Policy*. London: Macmillan.

Raison, T. (1976) *The Act and the Partnership: An Essay on Educational Administration in England*. Centre for Studies in Social Policy.

Raison, T. (1979) *Power and Parliament*. Oxford: Blackwell.

Ransom, S. and Tomlinson, J. (1986) *The Changing Government of Education*. London: Allen & Unwin.

Ratcliffe, R. (1988) 'A Baker's dozen, 13 ways to slice up education'. *School Organization* **8**(1), 91-7.

Richardson, J. (ed.) (1987) *Education and Research 1928-86: Government Information.* London: Greenwood Press.

Roessner, D. (1987) *Government Innovation Policy*. London: Macmillan.

Rogers, R. (1980) *Crowther to Warnock: How Fourteen Reports Tried to Change Children's Lives*. London: Heinemann.

Rogers, W. (1980) 'Westminster and Whitehall: adapting to change'. In Royal Institute of Public Administration (1980).

Rose, R. (1975) 'The making of Cabinet Ministers'. In Herman and Alt (1975).

Rose, R. (1984) *Do Parties Make a Difference?* 2nd edn. London: Macmillan.

Roseveare, M. (1950) 'Age, ability and aptitude'. *Education* (14 April) [speech made at NUT conference].

Royal Institute of Public Administration (1980) *Policy and Practice, the Experience of Government*. London: Royal Institute of Public Administration.

Rubinstein, D. (1979) 'Ellen Wilkinson reconsidered'. *History Workshop* **7**, 161-9.

Rubinstein, D. and Simon, B. (1973) *The Evolution of the Comprehensive School 1926-72*. London: Routledge & Kegan Paul.

Rush, M. (1985) 'The Education, Science and Arts Committee'. In Drewry (1989).

Salter, B. and Tapper, T. (1981) *Education, Politics and the State: The Theory and Practice of Educational Change*. Grant McIntyre.

Salter, B. and Tapper, T. (1985) *Power and Policy in Education*. Brighton: Falmer Press.

Salter, B. and Tapper, T. (1988) 'The politics of reversing the ratchet in secondary education, 1969-86'. *Journal of Educational Administration and History* **20**(2), 57-70.

Saran, R. (1973) *Policy-Making in Secondary Education*. Oxford: Oxford University Press.

Sayer, J. (1989) *Towards the General Teaching Council*. London: London University Institute of Education.

Sayer, J. (1992) *The Future Governance of Education*. London: Cassell.

Scott, P. (1988) 'Blueprint or blue remembered hills? The relevance of the Robbins report to the present reforms of higher education'. *Oxford Review of Education* **14**(1), 33-48.

Shaw, K.E. (1986) 'The politics of higher education'. *Teaching Politics* **15**(1), 129-38.

Shattock, M. (1984) 'British higher education under pressure: politics, budgets, and demography and the acceleration of ideas for change'. *European Journal of Education* **19**(2), 201-16.

Short, E. (1971) *Education in a Changing World*. London: Pitman.

Short, E. (1983) *I Knew My Place*. London: Macdonald.

Silver, H. (1980) *Education and the Social Condition*. London: Methuen.

Silver, H. (1981) 'Policy as history and as theory'. *British Journal of Sociology of Education* **2**(3), 293-9.

Silver, H. (1983) *Education as History: Interpreting Nineteenth and Twentieth Century Education*. London: Methuen.

Silver, H. (1990) *Education, Change and the Policy Process*. Brighton: Falmer Press.

Simon, B. (1955) *The Comprehensive Secondary School*. London: Lawrence & Wishart.

Simon, B. (1974) *The Politics of Educational Reform 1920-1940*. London: Lawrence & Wishart.

Simon, B. (1985a) *Does Education Matter?* London: Lawrence & Wishart.

Simon, B. (1985b) 'The Tory government and education, 1951-1960; background to breakout'. *History of Education* **14**(4), 283-97.

Simon, B. (1986) 'The 1944 Education Act: a conservative measure?' *History of Education* **15**(1), 45-57.

Simon, B. (1988) *Bending the Rules*. London: Lawrence & Wishart.

Simon, B. (1991) *Education and the Social Order 1940-1990*. London: Lawrence & Wishart.

Simpson, E. (1986) 'The Department of Education and Science'. In Ransom and Tomlinson (1986), pp. 22-30.

Smith, D.M. (1986) 'Central government agencies and the management of vocational education and training'. *Educational Studies* 12(2), 213-22.

Stacy, F. (1975) *British Government 1966-75*. Oxford: Oxford University Press.

Statham, J. and Mackinnon, D. (1989) *The Education Fact File*. Sevenoaks: Hodder & Stoughton.

St John-Stevas, N. and Brittan, L. (1975) *How to Save Your Schools*. Conservative Political Centre.

Straw, J. (1987) 'Backlash: a threat to stability'. *British Journal of Special Education* 14(4), 166.

Tapper, T. and Salter, B. (1978) *Education and the Political Order*. London: Macmillan.

Tapper, T. and Salter, B. (1986) 'The politics of secondary education'. *Teaching Politics* 15(2), 204-18.

Tawney, R.H. (ed.) (1922) *Secondary Education for All: A Policy for Labour*. London: Allen & Unwin.

Theakeston, K. (1987) *Junior Ministers in British Government*. Oxford: Blackwell.

Theakeston, K. (1991) 'The civil service'. *Contemporary Record* 4, 24-5.

Thompson, K. (1986) 'Education, capability and action'. *British Journal of Educational Studies* 34(1), 203-12.

Thompson, K. [K.P.] (1966) *Member's Lobby*.

Thompson, K. [K.P.] (1967) *Pattern of Conquest*.

Tomlinson, G. (1949) 'Education for living'. *W.F. Harvey Memorial Lecture*.

Tomlinson, G. and Maud, J. (1951) *Education 1900-1950*. London: HMSO.

Tomlinson, J. (1989a) 'The Education Reform Bill - 44 years of progress?'. *Journal of Education Policy* 4(3), 275-9.

Tomlinson, J. (1989b) *Assessing the Impact on Local Education Authorities of Current Reforms*. Sheffield: Sheffield City Polytechnic.

Vernon, B.D. (1982) *Ellen Wilkinson*. London: Duckworth/Croom Helm.

Vincent, B. (1983) 'The influence of pressure groups on the policy-making process in further education; with special reference to provision for sixteen to nineteen year olds'. *Journal of Further and Higher Education* 7(1), 62-72.

Walsh, K. *et al.* (1984) *Falling School Rolls and the Management of the Teaching Profession*. Windsor: NFER-Nelson.

Walker, S. and Barton, L. (1987) *Changing Policies, Changing Teachers*. Milton Keynes: Open University Press.

Wallace, R.G. (1981) 'The origins and authorship of the 1944 Education Act'. *History of Education* 10(4), 238-90.

Wann, P. (1971) 'The collapse of Parliamentary bi-partisanship in education 1945-52'. *Journal of Educational Administration and History* 3(2), 24-34.

Warnock, M. (1988) *A Common Policy for Education*. Oxford: Oxford University Press.

Weaver, T. (1957) *Report of the Working Party on Educational Maintenance Grants*. London: Ministry of Education/HMSO.

Weaver, T. (1966) *Report of the Study Group on the Government of Colleges of Education*. London: Ministry of Education/HMSO.

Weaver, T. (1967) 'The educational campaign: survey and reconnaissance'. Spring Lecture, University of Manchester.

Weaver, T. (1970) 'Unity and Diversity in Education'. Address at Goldsmiths' College, London. DES/HMSO.

Weaver, T. (1973) 'Higher education and the polytechnics'. Payne Memorial Lecture, City University, London.

Weaver, T. (1976) 'What is the good of higher education?'. *Higher Education Review* **8**(3), 3-14.

Weaver, T. (1979) 'DES: central control of education?'. Open University course E222 - *The Control of Education*. Milton Keynes: Open University Press.

Weaver, T. (1981) 'Can institutions learn? The survival of higher education'. Conference paper, Higher Education Group.

White, J. (1987) 'The comprehensive ideal and the rejection of theory'. *British Journal of Educational Studies* **35**(3), 196-210.

White, J. (1988) 'Two national curricula - Baker's and Stalin's: towards a liberal alternative'. *British Journal of Educational Studies* **36**(3), 218-31.

Williams, G. (1955) 'The first ten years of the Ministry of Education'. *British Journal of Educational Studies* **3**(2), 101-14.

Williams, S. (1977) 'Robbins plus 20'. Birkbeck College Lecture.

Williams, S. (1980) 'The decision makers'. In Royal Institute of Public Administration (1980).

Williams, S. (1981) *Politics Is for the People*. Harmondsworth: Penguin.

Williams, S. (1981) 'The broader economic and social questions relating to youth employment'. *Policy Studies* **1**(4), 200-12.

Williams, S. (1981) *Education: The Divisions Widen*. University College Swansea.

Wilson, H. (1974) *The Labour Government 1964-70*. London: Weidenfeld and Nicolson/Michael Joseph.

Wilson, P. (1961) *Views and Prospects from Curzon Street: Seven Essays and Addresses on the Future of Education*. Oxford: Blackwell.

Wilson, P. (1964) 'Inspecting the Inspectorate'. *Twentieth Century* (Spring).

Wood, R. (1955) 'Liberal education in a technical age'. Speech made at conference on Adult Education and Working Life. Published by National Institute of Adult Education.

Wragg, T. and Partington, J. (1989) *Schools and Parents*. London: Cassell.

Young, H. and Sloman, A. (1986) *The Thatcher Phenomenon*. London: BBC Publications.

Young, K. (ed.) (1983) *National Interests and Local Government*. London: Heinemann.

Index